EXPORT PROMOTION MEASURES IN INDIA
Role of Institutional Support

EXPORT PROMOTION MEASURES IN INDIA

Role of Institutional Support

MONIKA KOTHARI
Faculty Member
ICFAI National College, Udaipur, Rajasthan

DEEP & DEEP PUBLICATIONS PVT. LTD.
F-159, Rajouri Garden, New Delhi - 110 027

EXPORT PROMOTION MEASURES IN INDIA
Role of Institutional Support

ISBN 978-81-8450-012-7

Typeset by RAHUL COMPOSERS
358, Sector 16-B, Phase-II, Pocket-B, Dwarka, New Delhi - 110 075

Printed in India at MAYUR ENTERPRISES
WZ Plot No. 3, Gujjar Market, Tihar Village, New Delhi - 110 018

Published by DEEP & DEEP PUBLICATIONS PVT. LTD.
F-159, Rajouri Garden, New Delhi - 110 027 • Phone : 25435369, 25440916
E-mail : deep98@del3.vsnl.net.in • ddpbooks@yahoo.co.in
Showroom :
2/13, Ansari Road, Daryaganj, New Delhi - 110 002 • Telefax : 23245122

Contents

Preface xvii

Acknowledgements xxi

1. EXPORTS AND ECONOMIC DEVELOPMENT 1

1.1 Introduction 1

1.2 Export as an Engine of Growth : Export or Perish 2

1.2.1 What is Export ? *4*

1.2.1.1 Classification of Exports *4*

1.3 Impact of Exports in the Development Process 5

1.4 Exports and Indian Economy 7

1.5 Exports and Imports of Principal Commodities (2001-02 and 2002-03) 13

1.6 FDI and Exports 16

1.7 Foreign Direct Investment (FDI) 16

1.7.1 FDI in India *17*

1.7.1.1 FDI Policy at a Glance (Highlights) *17*

1.7.1.2 FDI—The Trends *19*

1.8 Comparison with Other Developing Nations i.e. India *vis-a-vis* Developing Economies 22

2. INDIAN EXPORTS : A CRITIQUE **35**

2.1 The New Horizon 35

2.2 Export Performance 36

2.2.1 Month-wise Export-Import Performance (2003-04) *36*

2.2.2 Terms of Trade and Index Numbers of Foreign Trade *36*

2.3 Commodity Composition 42

2.3.1 Agricultural and Allied Products *42*

2.3.2 Gems and Jewellery *53*

2.3.3 Textiles (Yarn, Fabrics, Madeups, Readymade Garments) *54*

2.3.4 Engineering Goods *54*

2.3.5 Petroleum and Crude Products *55*

2.3.6 Chemicals and Allied Products *55*

2.4 Project Exports 56

2.5 Service Exports 60

2.5.1 Software Exports *62*

2.6 Exports Expectation of Industry 63

2.7 Indian Exports by Region 64

2.8 Import Intensity of Exports 64

2.9 Export Road Map 72

3. THE EXIM POLICY (2002-07) **79**

3.1 Exim Policy, 2002-07—An Introduction 79

3.2 Main Features of Exim Policy (2002-07) 80

3.2.1 General Provisions Regarding Imports and Exports (As amended upto 15th Dec. 2003) *80*

3.2.2 Promotional Measures *83*

3.2.3 Duty Exemption/Remission Scheme 88

3.2.3.1 Advance Licence *89*

3.2.3.2 Duty Free Replenishment Certificate (DFRC) 89
3.2.3.3 Duty Entitlement Passbook Scheme 90
3.2.4 Export Promotion Capital Goods Scheme 91
3.2.5 Export Oriented Units (EOUs), Units in Export Processing Zones (EPZs), Electronics Hardware Technology Parks (EHTPs) and Software Technology Parks (STPs) 92
3.2.6 Special Economic Zones 93
3.2.7 Deemed Exports 93
3.3 Exim Policy (2003-04) 94
3.4 Mini Exim Policy, 2004 95
3.5 New Foreign Trade Policy (2004-09) 97
3.6 Exim Policy, 2002-07 : A Critical Appraisal 99

4. STUDIES ON EXPORT AND EXPORT PROMOTION INSTITUTIONS 104

5. RESEARCH METHODS ON EXPORT AND EXPORT PROMOTION INSTITUTIONS 120
5.1 Importance 120
5.2 Objectives 122
5.3 Research Process 122
5.3.1 The Research Problem 123
5.3.2 Hypotheses Formulation 123
5.3.3 Research Design 126
5.3.4 Data Collection 126
5.3.5 Sampling Design 128
5.3.6 Data Analysis 129
5.3.6.1 Statistical Techniques Used for Analysis and Interpretations 129

5.4 Profile of the Respondents 132

5.4.1 Breakup of the Respondents According to the Commodities *132*

5.4.2 Break-up of Respondents on the Basis of Status *133*

5.4.3 Nearest Port as Mentioned by the Respondents *133*

5.4.4 Unit-wise Classification of Sample Respondents *133*

5.4.5 Profile of Respondents on the Basis of Type of Exports Involved in *134*

5.4.6 Profile of Respondents on the basis of their export product falling into restricted category or free with terms and conditions etc. *135*

5.4.7 Firms certified by ISO 9000, 14000 etc. *135*

5.4.8 Zone-wise Classification *136*

5.5 Other Related Findings 153

5.5.1 Export Obligation to be Fulfilled with Respect to EPCG Licence *137*

5.5.2 Green Card Facility and Export and Import of Free Trade Sample *137*

5.5.3 Advance Licence and DEPB *138*

5.5.3.1 Chi-square Test *138*

5.5.4 Letter of Permission/Letter of Intent *138*

5.5.4.1 Validity period of Letter of Permission/Letter of Intent *138*

5.5.4.2 Chi-Square Test *139*

5.5.5 Research Findings Regarding Export Documentation *140*

5.5.5.1 Average Score *140*

6. INSTITUTIONS ENGAGED IN EXPORT PROMOTION 144

6.1 Introduction 144

6.1.1 The Top Tier *145*

6.2 Export Credit Guarantee Corporation (ECGC) (You Focus on Exports. We Cover the Risks) 146

6.2.1 Introduction *146*

6.2.2 Objectives of ECGC *147*

6.2.3 Covers Issued by ECGC *149*

6.2.4 Underwriting Policy *151*

6.2.5 ECGC's Performance *152*

6.2.5.1 Business Highlights (1999-04) *152*

6.2.5.2 India's Exports and ECGC Coverage *153*

6.2.5.3 Performance of ECGC from 1994-95 to 2003-04 *154*

6.2.6 Research Findings Regarding ECGC *159*

6.2.6.1 Awareness Regarding the Policies Issued by ECGC *159*

6.2.6.2 Rating of the Various Policy Schemes Issued by ECGC on the Basis of Risk Covered and Premium *159*

6.2.6.3 Payment of Claims *160*

6.2.6.4 Risk which should be Covered by ECGC which it is not Covering *160*

6.2.6.5 Chi-Square Test *160*

6.2.6.6 Average Score *161*

6.3 Export-import Bank of India (Exim Bank) 161

6.3.1 Exim Bank's Operation *162*

6.3.2 Exim Bank : Other Developments *166*

6.3.3 Research Findings Regarding Exim Bank *167*

6.3.3.1 Rating of Working of Exim Bank in Terms of Financial and Other Assistances *168*

6.3.3.2 Access to Exim Bank Finance *168*

6.3.3.3 Average Score *168*

6.3.3.4 Kolmogorov-Smirnov One Sample Test *169*

6.4 Bureau of Indian Standards 169

6.4.1 Introduction *169*

6.4.2 Organisation *170*

6.4.3 Functions *170*

6.5 Export Inspection Council (EIC) 171

6.5.1 About Export Inspection Agencies *171*

6.5.2 EIA on Quality Complaints *172*

6.5.3 Grievances Committee in EIA *173*

6.5.4 Notification for Extension of Term Period *173*

6.6 Indian Institute of Packaging 173

6.6.1 Quality Policy *173*

6.6.2 Objectives *173*

6.6.3 Research Findings Regarding Indian Institute of Packaging (IIP) *175*

6.6.3.1 Rating of Working of IIP *175*

6.6.3.2 Average Score *175*

6.6.3.3 Chi-Square Test *176*

6.7 Indian Council of Arbitration 177

6.7.1 An Introduction *177*

6.7.2 Services of ICA *177*

6.7.3 Rules of Arbitration of ICA *178*

7. EXPORT PROMOTION INSTITUTIONS 188

7.1 Export Promotion Councils (EPCs) 188

7.1.1 Historical Perspective *188*

7.1.2 Objectives and Functions of Export Promotion Councils *190*

7.1.3 List of Export Promotion Councils in India 191
7.1.4 CAPEXIL 192
7.1.4.1 The Vision 192
7.1.4.2 About CAPEXIL 192
7.1.4.3 Product Spectrum 192
7.1.4.4 CAPEXIL's Services to its Members 194
7.1.4.5 Export Performance 195
7.1.5 Research Findings Regarding Export Promotion Councils (EPCs) 195
7.1.5.1 Process of Registration with EPCs 195
7.1.5.2 Rating the Working of Export Promotion Councils in Discharging its Functions 195
7.1.5.3 Average Score 197
7.1.5.4 Chi-Square Test 197
7.2 Commodity Boards 198
7.2.1 Spices Board 199
7.3 MPEDA and APEDA 201
7.3.1 Marine Products Export Development Authority (MPEDA) 201
7.3.2 APEDA 202
7.4 Niryat Bandhu (Nodal Officers) 202
7.5 State Liaison Officer 202
7.5.1 Research Findings Regarding State Liaisoning Officer 203
7.6 Federation of Indian Export Organisation (FIEO) 203
7.6.1 An Introduction 203
7.6.2 Membership 204
7.6.3 Organisation 204
7.6.4 Federation's Activities 205

7.7 Federation of Indian Chambers of Commerce and Industry (FICCI) 206
7.7.1 Research Findings Regarding FIEO and Chambers of Commerce and Industry *207*
7.7.1.1 Working of FIEO and Chambers of Commerce and Industry *207*
7.7.1.2 Average Score *207*
7.7.1.3 Kolmogorov-Smirnov one-sample Test *207*
7.8 India Trade Promotion Organisation (ITPO) 208
7.8.1 About ITPO *208*
7.8.2 Fairs in India and Abroad *209*
7.8.3 Trade Development Activities *209*
7.8.4 Financial Highlights *210*
7.9 Indian Institute of Foreign Trade (IIFT) 210
7.10 Marketing Development Assistance (MDA) Scheme 212
7.10.1 MDA : Its Objectives *212*
7.10.2 Administration of the Scheme *213*
7.10.3 Important Assistances under MDA *213*
7.10.3.1 Assistance to Individual Exporters for Export Promotion Activities Abroad—Participation in EPC etc. Led Trade Delegations/BSMs/Trade Fairs/Exhibitions *212*
7.10.3.2 Publicity through Printed Material *215*
7.10.3.3 Sales-*cum*-Study Tour *216*
7.10.4 Reimbursement of Assistance to Exporters *216*
7.10.5 Consortium Marketing Approach Abroad *217*
7.10.6 Assistance to EPCs, Other Institutions and SSIs *217*
7.10.7 MDA, 2004-05 *218*

7.11 Market Access Initiative (MAI) 218
7.11.1 Objectives of MAI 218
7.11.2 MAI—2004-05 218
7.12 Research Findings with Respect of Marketing Development Assistance (MDA) and Marketing Access Initiative (MAI) 219
7.12.1 Ratings of the Various Assistances Offered by MDA and MAI 219
7.12.2 Availing any of the above Mentioned Assistances Provided by MDA 220
7.12.3 Release of Approved MDA Grant 220
7.12.4 Average Score 220
7.12.5 Chi-square Test 221
7.12.6 'F' Test 222
7.13 Findings on Support of Local Authorities and Promotional Agencies 223
7.13.1 Support of Local Authorities 224
7.13.1.1 Average Score 224
7.13.1.2 Kolmogorov Smirnov one Sample Test 225
7.13.2 Findings on Support of Local Promotional Agencies 225
7.13.2.1 Average Score 225

8. SUPPORTING INSTITUTIONS 234
8.1 Introduction 234
8.2 Export Oriented Units (EOUs), Units in Export Processing Zones (EPZs), Electronics Hardware Technology Parks (EHTPs) and Software Technology Parks (STPs) 235
8.2.1 Eligibility, Export and Import 235
8.2.2 Net Foreign Exchange Earning as a Percentage of Exports, Letter of Intent and Legal Undertaking 235

8.2.3 Application and Approvals 236

8.2.4 Entitlements 236

8.2.5 Bonding and Debonding 238

8.3 Confederation of 100 Per Cent Export Units (CEUs) and EPCES 238

8.3.1 CEU 238

8.3.2 EPCES 238

8.4 Special Economic Zones 239

8.4.1 An Introduction 239

8.4.1.1 Origin 239

8.4.1.2 Objectives 240

8.4.2 Functional and Approved SEZs So Far 240

8.4.3 SEZs : International Experiences 241

8.4.4 Important Incentives for SEZ Units 244

8.4.5 Key Reforms Needed to Change Indian SEZs' Face; Generating New Success Stories 245

8.5 Institutions Supporting Small Exporters 247

8.5.1 Good Things in Life begin Small 247

8.5.2 Institutional Framework 248

8.5.2.1 Small Scale Industries Board 248

8.5.2.2 National Small Scale Industries Corporation (NSIC) 249

8.5.2.3 Office of the Development Commissioner for SSIs and the Small Industries Development Organisations (SIDOs) 250

8.5.2.4 Small Industries Development Bank 250

8.5.2.5 Small Industries Service Institutes (SISIs) 251

8.5.2.6 Other Institutions for Small Exporter's Assistance 252

8.5.3 Credit Institutions and Small Exporters : An International Experience 252
8.5.4 Challenges of a Global Market 253
8.6 Infrastructural Support : A Comprehensive Note 254
8.6.1 Introduction 254
8.6.2 Infrastructure Bottlenecks 255
8.6.3 Steps to Overcome Obstacles 256
8.6.4 Research Findings Regarding Infrastructure 258
8.6.4.1 Average Score 259
8.6.5 What Lies Ahead .... ? 260

9. CONCLUSIONS AND SUGGESTIONS 271

BIBLIOGRAPHY 292

INDEX 298

Preface

Today's global trade and economic environment had undergone change at the speed never before experienced. Three trends in particular are creating an important impact. First, values are changing as to what constitutes competitiveness. Second, the importance of regional blocks is growing with the spread of global economic standards. Third, the digital revolution has changed the speed at which information is disseminated, thrusting trade into a world of information, knowledge and spawning borderless competition. Thus, the rules of the trade games are being redefined, markets are liberalizing and globalizing, international business practices are changing and competition is becoming much more intense. So the question which comes in front of nations is—'Can countries create and sustain export strategies that will foster growth and development as well as exploit commercial opportunity in such turbulent times'?

A National Export Strategy, keeping in view all relevant players including institutions need to be redesigned. As 'staying relevant' would be the important key words for export promotion institutions in turbulent business times.

Export promotion organizations need to refocus and adopt a "total competitiveness approach" to help their exporters to succeed in difficult and challenging trade environment. Export promotion organization must evaluate where they are, what are their core strengths, how their performance is perceived by exporters, what lies ahead in future and how to create capacity to adapt to changing trade opportunities. This work intends to focus on all such concerns. The basic objective of this work is to evaluate the performance of network of institutional support to Indian exporters. This study becomes important and significant as today's export promotion strategies must reflect the changing nature of the international trade environment, if they are to have an impact, and for this the assessment of 'present' situation is necessary, which this study does.

Exhaustive literature review was done to have secondary data and to collect primary data, survey of 70 exporters was done. A structured questionnaire was used for this purpose to get general and specific information from exporters as how they rate the services of various institutions engaged in export promotion.

The present book has been divided into nine chapters.

The first chapter titled 'Exports and Economic Development' throws light on introductory aspects of exports and impact of exports in the development process.

This chapter also discusses foreign direct investment and exports, FDI policy in India, its trends and exports of selected east Asian countries, i.e. comparison of India's export trade with other developing nations.

The second chapter, 'Indian Exports: A Critique' gives necessary data on trade of principal commodities, direction and trends of Indian exports, including import intensity of exports.

Chapter third 'Export-Import Policy, 2002-07' throws light on main features of Exim Policy, 2002-07, Exim Policy, 2003, Mini-Exim Policy, 2004 and New Foreign Trade Policy, (2004-09) followed by critical appraisal of Exim Policy, 2002-07.

The fourth chapter 'Studies on Export and Export Promotion Institutions' reviews the earlier research work conducted on export promotion and on institutions boosting the exports.

The fifth chapter 'Research Methods on Export and Export Promotion Institutions' discusses the research methodology in detail including the significance of the research work and its objectives. It also includes the profile of respondents and highlights on other research findings.

The sixth chapter 'Institutions Engaged in Export Promotion' discusses institutions like Export Credit Guarantee Corporation (ECGC), Exim Bank, Indian Institute of Packaging, Bureau of Indian Standards (BIS), Export Inspection Council

(EIC) and Indian Council of Arbitration (ICA) with research findings.

Chapter seventh 'Export Promotion Institutions' covers Export Promotion Councils, Commodity Boards, FICCI, IIFT, FIEO and ITPO. It also throws light on Marketing Development Assistance (MDA) and Marketing Access Initiative (MAI).

The eighth chapter 'Supporting Institutions' focuses on SEZs, EOUs , EPZs and institutions promoting small exporters. This chapter also includes a special note on infrastructural support.

The last chapter 'Conclusions and Suggestions' includes summary of findings, conclusions, suggestions and further researches which can be taken in the concerned area.

This book will be helpful for academic purpose and can serve as a good base for further researches to be taken in future. It is wished that the conclusions drawn in the study and suggestion made will act as vital input to increase export competitiveness. This book can also be helpful to least developing countries trying to develop institutional framework and enhancing their exports.

MONIKA KOTHARI

Acknowledgements

To get reward without work and to get assistance and guidance without saying a word of gratitude is as impossible as it is to live without being born. Uptill, this point, it has been a long journey, full of bumps and blows, trials and tribulations, hopes and sorrows, but with constant inspiration from all the persons who stood my me; I have been able to give proper shape to this research work successfully.

It would be difficult for me to adequately acknowledge my indebtedness to all such peoples, but with all my true feelings, deep from my heart, I would like to make an effort.

First and foremost I would like to thank the Almighty God whose blessings have made this work reality.

I feel a profound sense of gratitude to my teacher, mentor and revered guru Prof. P.K. Jain, Professor and Director, Faculty of Management Studies, MLSU.

Udaipur for suggesting the topic judiciously, helping me in laying my hands on relevant literature, graciously giving his time and clarifying the concepts. He stood by me like a lighthouse with his critical inputs and constant source of motivation. This whole research work is dedicated to him. I am also highly grateful to Dr. (Smt.) Maina Jain for her continuous encouragement.

I feel profound sense of regards for Dr. Ashok Singh, Associate Professor, F.M.S., Dr. Anil Kothari, Assistant Professor, F.M.S. and all the faculty members and staff of F.M.S. for their help, guidance and support.

I would like to put on record my sincere thanks to key officials of institutions like Exim Bank, ECGC, Export Promotion

Councils, etc. for giving their valuable time and providing their ideas. I am specially thankful to Mr. G.M. Ganapathy, General Manager, ECGC, Mumbai for his critical inputs.

I extend my sincere thanks to Dr. Mohd. Ilyas, Principal, ICF AI National College (INC), Udaipur and all the faculty members at INC for their kind cooperation.

The cooperation from INC headquarters and Regional office was also praiseworthy.

I owe special thanks to Col. Rajiv Sisaudia, ICF AI Hyderabad for his kind support. I am also thankful to Mr. Keshav Maloo, C.A. and Mr. Jugal Lohiya, C.A. who guided me in the research work.

I am thankful to library officials of FMS, MLSU, Udaipur and that of Indian Institute of Foreign Trade, New Delhi who helped and cooperated me. I am also thankful to all the respondents who spare time in filling the questionnaires and who gave valuable suggestions.

Without the encouragement of my parent and their love and sacrifice, this dream of mine would not have been a reality. I owe sincere thanks to my father Shri R.S. Kothari and mother Smt. Tara Kothari. I can hardly thank enough my brother Mukesh, my sister Neelam, my niece 'Lovi' and my cousins for their moral support.

I am also thankful to my friends, students and all my relatives who have directly and indirectly inspired me in completing the book.

I am also highly thankful to Mr. Jinendra Jain and Mr. Bhupendra Jain for computerized laser printing to this manuscript so nicely in a short period.

Last but not the least I would like to express my gratitude to Deep & Deep Publications Pvt. Ltd., New Delhi for publishing this book and towards all those who helped me in this endeavor.

Monika

MONIKA KOTHARI

1

Exports and Economic Development

1.1 INTRODUCTION

Need for International Business

International business has been conducted ever since national borders were formed and has played a major role in shaping world history. International business consists of transactions that are devised and carried out across national borders to satisfy the objectives of individuals and organisations. In its many forms international business ranges from export-import trade to licensing, joint ventures, wholly owned subsidiaries, Turnkey operations, and management contracts.

World Trade and investment have assumed a here to fore unknown importance to the global community. International trade is vital to economic growth because it expands a nation's consumption possibilities.[1] By specializing in its area of greatest relative productivity, each nation can consume more than it could produce alone. This is simple yet elusive assence of foreign trade.[2]

International business is important and necessary because economic isolationism has become impossible. Failure to become a part of the global market answers a nation of declining economic influence and a detoriating standard of living for its citizens.[3] Since the 1950s, growth of international trade and investment has been substantially larger than the growth of domestic economies. In the past centuries trade was conducted internationally, but not at the level or with the impact on nations, firms and individuals that it has recently achieved. In the past 30 years alone, the volume of international trade has expanded from US$ 200 Billion to more than US $ 8 Trillion. Countries that have never been thought of as major participants have emerged as major economic powers. Thus, both as an opportunity and a challenge, international business is important to countries, companies and individuals.

Akamatsu's "Wild Geese" theory of economic development, which was propounded in the early 1960s, to a large extent, explains the growth experience of Japan, South Korea and the other far East Asian miracle economies and also the basic evolution of economies.[4] The theory in brief divides economic development into three phases. Stage one is defined as the period in which domestic production equals domestic consumption. Over time domestic costs tends to decline through economies of scale as well as import of technology within the framework of a protected market. Stage two is marked by a commencement of exports with the domestic cost structure reaching international levels. Thus, domestic production becomes larger than domestic consumption. Stage three envisages a slow down in export expansion with a rise in the cost of the domestic factors of production like labour as well as the operation of the 'catching up cycles' in other developing countries. India is rapidly entering stage two of Akamatsu's theory.

1.2 EXPORT AS AN ENGINE OF GROWTH : EXPORT OR PERISH

Countries have achieved rapid economic development through export-led growth strategy. Export growth not only contributes directly to economic growth but, more importantly, also permits more imports, and a rapid modernization of production.

The result is efficient domestic industry that meets the market test of international competition. According to World Development Report, 1989 :

"Global development experience of the past few decades show that a policy regime with fewer barriers to trade, both tariff and non-tariff and which provides equal incentives for exports as well as production for the domestic market enables countries to achieve not only impressive export growth but also rapid and sustainable economic growth".

The fact that high growth rates can be achieved via export route has been brought out by the experiences of great many countries across the world. The experiences of Japan and South Korea provides interesting examples. Historically speaking, Japan could not have been described as a developing country prior to World War II. After the war, however, its economy was in shambles and the development process had to commence afresh. The national goal, which reflected the aspirations of most Japanese, was to become an economic superpower. Japan proceeded to do this not on the strength of domestic consumption, which was low on account of paucity of incomes but on the basis of accessing international markets. Their ingenuity and innovativeness helped them to produce cheaper and better. Their burgeoning export surpluses helped in creating an increasingly prosperous middle class, which also maintained a significantly high saving rate. Clearly its economic development was vigorously export-driven.[5]

Same is the case with Korea—Korea, like Japan was war shattered in 1950 with the difference that it was a poorly developed country before the war. It commenced its recovery by addressing the export market in consumer goods like shoes, garments and sportwear. Soon it began an aggressive drive to develop more complex industries like ship building, steel and electronics. Development impulses along these lines created the 'Asian Tigers', which aside from Japan and South Korea, included Hongkong, Taiwan, Singapore, Indonesia, Malaysia and Thailand. Despite the many differences in their political philosophies they shared a similar approach to economic development, high domestic savings and an accent on exports. In the history of world many examples can be cited which shows export led economic growth. Even the slogan of Hitler's Germany was 'export or perish'. It is also said that exports must be encouraged in order to fortify the Balance of Payments (BOP) for this in turn will hoist the exchange rate and a strong currency is esteemed as a touchstone of political and economic virility.

It is a cause for optimism that exports are finally responding to economic reforms. Apart from the increase in unit value realisation what is also encouraging is the diversification in the export basket (covered in subsequent chapters).

1.2.1 What is Export ?

The foreign trade (Development and Regulation) Act, 1992 defines export as taking out of India any goods by land, sea or air.

"Export" with its grammatical variations and cognate expressions, means taking out of India to a place outside India, as per section 2(18) or the Customs Act, 1962. The Customs Act further defines "export goods" as "any goods which are to be taken out of India to a place outside India". As such exports mean physical exports of any goods. However, "exports" scope has been widened to include "Services" exports.[6]

1.2.1.1 Classification of Exports

The Exports can be classified into the following categories :

(a) Merchandise Exports
(b) Service Exports
(c) Project Exports
(d) Deemed Exports

(a) *Merchandise Exports* : It refers to the export of physical goods, for example, ready made garments, engineering goods, furniture, work of art, etc.
(b) *Service Exports* : According to the Exim Policy, 2002-07, "Services" include all the 161 tradable services covered under the General Agreement on Trade in Services where payment for such services is received in free foreign exchange. The business firms engaged in export of services are known as "service provider."[7]

As stated in the Exim Policy, 2002-07, "Service Provider" means a person providing :

(i) Supply of a 'service' from India to any other country;
(ii) Supply of a 'service' from India to the service consumer of any other country in India;
(iii) Supply of a 'service' from India through commercial or physical presence in the territory of any other country; and
(iv) Supply of a 'service' in India relating to exports paid in free foreign exchange.

(c) *Project Exports* : Export of Engineering goods as deferred payment terms and execution of turnkey projects and civil construction contracts abroad are collectively referred to as "project exports".

(d) *Deemed exports* : "Deemed exports" means "those transactions in which the goods supplied do not leave the country and the payment for the goods is received by the supplier in India". For example, supply of goods by the main/sub-contractors to Export Oriented Units (EOUs) or EPZs, SEZs, STPs or EHTPs, shall be regarded as "Deemed Exports".

1.3 IMPACT OF EXPORTS IN THE DEVELOPMENT PROCESS

Export led growth is an appealing strategy for developing nations. In the early stages of development, a country needs to import real capital (machines), which often entails borrowing in a foreign currency. Exports allow the borrowing nation to earn the foreign currency required to service its external debt. This strategy is often successful—the USA is perhaps the best example that followed such a strategy in its early stages of development—at least over the short-run.[8]

An important consideration for policy-makers when promoting development is to improve "Export Competitiveness". While export competitiveness starts with increasing international market shares, it goes far beyond that it involves diversifying the export basket, sustaining higher rates of export growth over time, upgrading the technological and skill content of export activity, and expanding the base of domestic firms able to compete internationally so that competitiveness becomes sustainable and is accompanied by rising incomes. *Competitive exports allow countries to earn more foreign exchange, and so to import the products, services and technologies they need to raise productivity and living standards.* Greater competitiveness also allows countries to diversify away from dependence on a few primary commodity exports and move up the skills and technology ladder, which is essential for increasing local value-added and sustaining rising wages. It permits a greater realisation of economies of scale and scope by offering larger and more diverse markets. Exporting feeds-back into the capacities; it exposes enterprises to higher standards, provides them with opportunities for easier access to information and subjects them to greater competitive pressures, thereby encouraging domestic enterprises to make more vigorous efforts to acquire new skills and capabilities.

However, these developmental impacts from improved export competitiveness cannot be taken for granted. For same product at the same time, most of them may well become worse off. Similarly, in the absence of adequate national policies to strengthen national capabilities and increase local value-added, an expansion in market shares may not produce the expected benefits. Export competitiveness is important and challenging, but it needs to be seen as a means to an end—namely development.[9]

The above discussion focuses on the broader outlook of the overall impact of exports in development process. To have specific (company specific) outlook, it would be noteworthy to mention the benefits and risks associated with exporting.

Export Benefits

Some of the export benefits are as follows which may vary by company and product/service.

1. There is the potential for greatly increased company turnover.
2. Economies of scale are achieved.
3. Potential levels of profitability are much increased.
4. The product or service offered is more competitive. It reflects overseas market needs and conforms to a wider legal environment.

5. Companies become much more integrated with the market they serve and this encourages higher standards and the use of more high technology.
6. Diversification of risk. Company risk and business is not confined to one market.
7. The company becomes more competitive in all areas of the business.

Export Risks

1. Repatriation of profits from the target country may be constrained or forbidden.
2. Fluctuation in exchange rate may decrease or eliminate profits, or even result in losses.
3. The export market involves a longer time scale of payment. This may be 90 or 180 days or even some years.
4. Product launch in an overseas market is more costly and complex in comparison with a domestic launch.
5. Trade barriers are politically and economically manipulated.
6. Economic and political risk is much more.
7. Instability in the target market/country can lead to losses from war or civil strife or nationalization by the foreign government.
8. In cases of non-payment or other contractual problems, there may be questions of jurisdiction, i.e. Indian courts may not be able to enforce contracts between parties in different countries.

1.4 EXPORTS AND INDIAN ECONOMY

For several decades, trade policy in India has been formulated in a system of administrative controls and licences. In connection with exports, India followed the policy of extreme pessimism, and by the late 1960s, the loss of competitiveness in the export sector was apparent (Table 1.1a). Almost all imports were subject to licensing or prohibited, and imports of bulk items were a Government monopsony. In mid-1970s, the policy-makers tried to provide some treatments (by establishing promotional

Table 1.1a
India's Export Trade from 1950 to 1980

Year	*Exports as percentage of imports*	*Exports as percentage of GNP*
1951-52	77.7	11.5
1952-53	86.2	9.2
1953-54	92.8	7.9
1954-55	90.5	9.6
1955-56	78.7	9.3
1956-57	68.7	8.3
1957-58	61.3	8.4
1958-59	63.3	6.8
1959-60	66.5	7.3
1960-61	57.2	6.7
1961-62	60.5	6.5
1962-63	60.6	6.3
1963-64	64.9	6.4
1964-65	60.5	8.6
1965-66	55.2	5.3
1966-67	55.7	4.2
1967-68	59.7	3.7
1968-69	71.7	4.1
1969-70	89.3	3.1
1970-71	94.5	3.9
1971-72	89.8	4.1
1972-73	106.0	4.5
1973-74	83.0	4.7
1974-75	64.5	5.3
1975-76	69.5	6.1
1976-77	101.4	7.2
1977-78	90.6	6.7
1978-79	81.0	6.6
1979-80	71.6	6.8

Source : Compiled from many sources (*Lok Udhyog* (1971), various issues of Govt. of India, *Economic Survey,* Ministry of Foreign Trade and Reserve Bank of India.

agencies, etc.) to exports, and another major attempt at liberalisation was done in mid-1980s. However, by the time it was clear that India's the then prevailing trade regime was no longer sustainable. Indian economy faced difficult balance of payment (BOP) problems very frequently (Annexure 1.1, BOP table). Under these circumstances it became essential for India to design export promoting trade policies for long-run sustainability. The new trade policy of 1991 aimed at cutting down administrative controls and barriers to ensure free flow of exports and imports. The tariff rates of the country have gone down considerably over 1990s. The unweighted average nominal tariff rate came down to 40 per cent by 1999 from the high level of 125 per cent in 1991.[10a] There have been important policy changes and initiatives that helped to reduce India's anti-export bias. It is no coincidence that the reduction in tariff rates in this period was accompanied by rapid export growth.[10b]

The share of India's foreign trade in per cent of GDP has increased gradually since 1974, though in a fluctuating fashion. However, this increasing trend (from 10.21% of GDP in 1974 to 14.05% in 1988) was mainly due to rising share of imports, while the share of exports remained largely stagnant.[11] There were some improvements in the volume of both exports and imports during 1988-91 (probably due to the reduction in tariff level from very high level in 1987); however notable improvements both in the quantity of exports and imports took place only following 1991-92. The volume of total trade in GDP crossed 20 per cent mark by 1993, and the figure touched 30 per cent mark in the year 2000 (Table 1.1b).

The trend line of exports of goods and services as percentage of GDP is given in Graph 1.1.

To have the real growth trend, the estimated results are shown in Table 1.2. Both Exports and import data are deflated by their respective unit value index (1978 = 100). To have comparative Scenarion, a linear trend model [Y = Bo + Bt + U, (Eq. 1)], and Growth model [LnY = Bo + Bt + U (Eq. 2)] has been used, taking data on export and imports of India.

The estimated results of the specifications 1 and 2 clearly reveal that there has been notable increase in the average growth rates of exports and imports in the 1990s both in absolute terms and its percentage. The total export of India has increased at the

TABLE 1.1B
Foreign Trade (Exports and Imports) of India

Year	*Exports of Goods and Services (% of GDP)*	*Imports of Goods and Services (% of GDP)*	*Total Foreign Trade (% of GDP)*
1980	6.04	9.32	15.36
1985	5.51	8.38	13.89
1990	7.14	9.76	16.89
1991	8.56	9.14	17.70
1992	8.94	10.59	19.53
1993	10.00	11.26	21.26
1994	9.98	12.54	22.52
1995	10.90	14.07	24.97
1996	10.48	14.02	24.50
1997	10.72	14.09	24.81
1998	11.03	13.75	24.78
1999	12.00	15.10	27.10
2000	14.00	16.60	30.60

Source : World Bank Indicators database (2001).

GRAPH 1.1
Trend for the Last Decade (1990-2000) of Exports of Goods and Services as Percentage of GDP

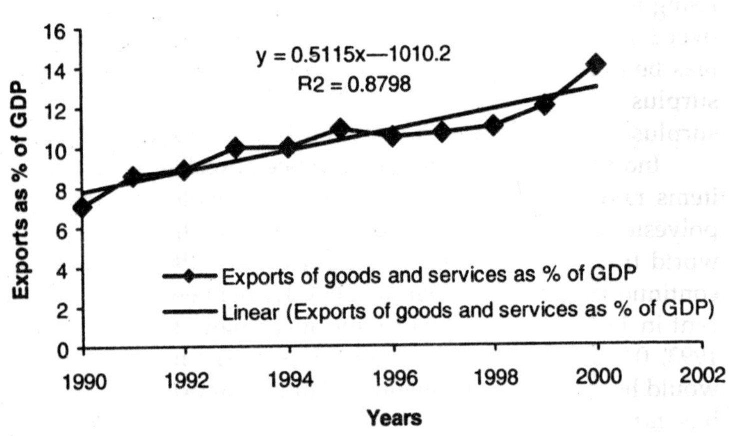

TABLE 1.2
Comparative Growth in India's Exports and Imports (Growth Rates are Annual Averages; and Based on the Values of Slopes of Equation 1 and 2)

	1970-79		*1980-89*		*1990-2000*	
	Absolute (Rs. crore)	*%*	*Absolute (Rs. crore)*	*%*	*Absolute (Rs. crore)*	*%*
Exports	321.50	6.98	357.10	4.64	1975.50	10.42
Imports	265.10	4.28	693.50	5.63	3618.50	12.43
Trade	586.60	5.46	1050.60	5.26	5594.40	11.6

rate of Rs. 1,975 crore (annually) in 1990s, which is six times higher than the annual average figure of 1970s.

India has come a long way, from those gloomy days of 1989-90, when reserves had fallen below $ 1 bn and when the country mortgaged its gold to borrow. However, now it is in the top gear and is an economic giant in the making. The reform process is finally showing results. In the recent past, the country's economy showed exceptional resilience in absorbing external shocks like oil market fluctuations and worldwide recession, in the wake of the collapse of the dotcom bubble. Indian economy is faring better on all fronts. In the current financial year, rail freight sector is buoyant, software exports are up 26 per cent, rupee is appreciating against the US dollar since mid-2002, stock market rising to record levels, forex reserves accumulation has touched over $ 110 bn-mark, soft interest bias and inflation with upward bias being under control.[12] Also current account turned into a surplus in 2001-02, after a gap of 24 years (current account surplus was last recorded in 1977-78) (see Annexure 1.1).

India's export performance has been excellent, supported by items ranging from passenger vehicles, textile machinery and polyester yarn etc.[13] However, the share of India's exports in world trade, which stood at 2.2 per cent in 1948, had declined continuously to 1.3 per cent in 1953, 1.0 per cent in 1963, 0.5 per cent in 1973 and 1983, improving marginally to 0.6 per cent in 1993, 0.7 per cent in 2001 and 0.8 per cent in 2002-03. But it would be noteworthy to mention that Indian export performance has fared better than the world and developing countries averages in both these years (2000-01, 2001-02), resulting in a marginal increase in its world share in 2001.

Exports have done well recently in spite of the appreciating rupee—a growth of 17.3% in 2003-04 on top of 20% in the previous year, according to official trade data.

According to data sourced from CMIE, total export turnover of the top 100 companies, forming part of the BSE's high profile 'A group', increased by 35 per cent to Rs. 55,828 crore in 2003-04, substantially higher than the growth rate of 23 per cent in 2002-03.[14]

The share of exports in their total turnover rose to 18.2 per cent compared to 15.8 per cent. The list is dominated by leading players from petrochemicals. IT, metals, pharmaceutical and automobile sectors, Reliance industries had been the top exporters for past several years.

Encouraged by the current trends the Commerce Ministry has set a target growth rate of 16 per cent for 2004-05 versus 12 per cent for the previous 2 years.[15] The idea is to achieve two goals. In the short-term, the Government wants to cross $ 70 billion mark in exports in 2004-05, after having crossed $ 50 billion and $ 60 billion during the previous two years respectively. Secondly, this growth rate will help in attaining the relatively long-run target of bringing in $ 150 billion worth of exports by 2009-10.

GRAPH 1.2
Quarterly Exports

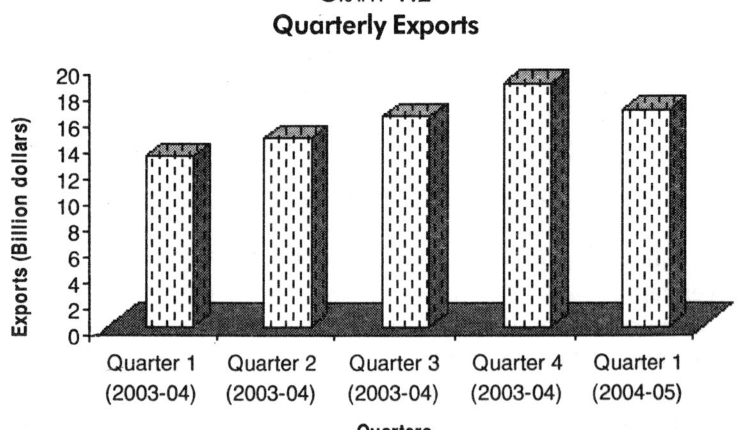

Source : CMIE.

1.5 EXPORTS AND IMPORTS OF PRINCIPAL COMMODITIES (2001-02 AND 2002-03)

(a) The decline in value of exports in 2001-02 was spread across both the agricultural and manufactured commodity groups with decline of 2.2 and 3.9 per cent respectively. However, exports of specified manufactured goods like finished leather, cosmetics and toiletries, non-ferrous metals, machinery and instruments, electronic goods recorded substantial increases in exports during 2001-02.

The buoyancy in exports of petroleum products continued in 2001-02, given the enhanced domestic refining capacity. The continued surge in exports of petroleum products and ores and minerals has further enhanced the share of these exports in total exports to 5.0 and 3.8 per cent respectively in 2002-03.

Next cereals exports have spurted by 33.6 per cent with India emerging as the world's 2nd largest exporter of rice and 6th largest exporter of wheat (Table 1.3).

(b) With respect to imports, imports under the fuel group, fertilizers and paper board, manufactures and newsprint, however, contracted in 2001-02. A significant feature of the performance in 2001-02 was the reversal in trend in imports of capital goods, which increased by 6.3 per cent as against substantial declines in the preceding 2 years. Another highlight was the turnaround in export-related imports that increased by 1.6% in 2001-02 as against a decline of 10.9% in 2000-01.

Import growth in the first seven months of 2002-03 has been high, rising by 13.0% as compared with a modest growth of 1.9% in corresponding previous period. Import of Capital goods have accelerated by 20.9%, that of electronic goods by 35% and of pearls, precious and semi-precious stones by 41.3 per cent. (Table 1.4).

TABLE 1.3
Exports of Principal Commodities

Sl. No.	Commodity	Percentage Share			Percentage Change*		
		2001-02	April-Oct.		2001-02	April-Oct.	
			2001-02	2002-03		2001-02	2002-03
1.	Gems and Jewellery	16.7	15.9	17.3	-1.1	-12.2	28.6
2.	Readymade Garments	11.4	11.6	10.7	-10.2	-12.1	9.0
3.	Textiles, other than RMG	10.7	11.2	10.3	-10.4	-6.0	8.7
4.	Engineering Goods	15.9	16.0	16.0	-0.6	3.1	17.9
5.	Chemical and Related products	13.8	14.0	13.7	1.5	5.9	15.4
6.	Crude and Petroleum products	4.8	4.8	5.0	12.3	40.4	22.0
7.	Leather and Manufactures	4.4	4.7	4.5	-2.1	1.2	11.3
8.	Ores and Minerals	2.9	2.6	3.8	8.9	-1.4	73.7
9.	Marine Products	2.8	3.0	2.8	-11.3	-5.1	7.5
10.	Cereals	2.2	2.1	2.3	30.3	40.3	33.6
11.	Others	14.4	14.1	13.6	0.8	3.4	15.0
	Total Exports	100.0	100.0	100.0	-1.6	-0.9	18.1

* In Dollar Terms.

Source : *Economic Survey*, 2002-03.

Table 1.4

Imports of Principal Commodities

Sl. No.	Commodity	Percentage Share			Percentage Change*		
		2001-02	April-Oct.		2001-02	April-Oct.	
			2001-02	2002-03		2001-02	2002-03
1.	POL	27.2	29.0	29.9	-10.5	-10.2	16.7
2.	Pearls, Precious and Semi-precious stones	9.0	8.3	10.4	-4.4	-15.2	41.3
3.	Capital goods	11.4	9.7	10.4	6.3	6.9	20.9
4.	Electronic goods	7.4	7.1	8.5	6.4	3.9	35.0
5.	Gold and Silver	8.8	9.8	7.4	-2.2	17.4	-14.6
6.	Chemicals (Inorganic + Organic)	5.4	5.4	4.9	13.3	10.8	1.3
7.	Edible oils	2.6	2.8	2.8	1.6	-0.3	10.9
8.	Coal, Coke and briquettes	2.2	2.1	2.0	3.4	2.3	3.0
9.	Metaliferrous ores and metal scrap	2.2	2.3	1.9	44.8	68.4	-7.4
10.	Professional Instruments, Optical goods	2.0	1.9	1.9	18.4	17.1	7.8
11.	Others	21.8	21.6	19.9	14.0	13.4	5.7
	Total Exports	100.0	100.0	100.0	1.7	1.9	13.0

* In Dollar Terms

Source : *Economic Survey*, 2002-03.

1.6 FDI AND EXPORTS

An FDI policy in developing countries would seek to promote exports, technology, or employment. Keeping export promotion as objective, FDI should be encouraged in areas which are presently reserved for the small scale industries (SSIs). India's major exports are garments, gems and jewellery and agricultural products which are largely produced by the SSIs. In order to attract export-oriented FDI and to ensure that such investment translates into development gains, countries need to find the most effective ways to make their locations more conducive to the kind of export activities they aim to foster.

In line with the dynamic changes in corporate strategies affecting key export industries, the rising competition among countries and sub-national entities for export-oriented FDI, care must be taken in policy formulation and implementation to improve the long-term attractiveness of a country as a base for export-oriented production (World Investment Report, 2002).

The next section focusses on FDI policy in India and trends.

1.7 FOREIGN DIRECT INVESTMENT (FDI)

According to International guidelines based on the recommendations by the IMF in its Balance of Payments Manual (Fifth edition, 1993), FDI is defined as international investment that reflects the objective of a resident entity in one economy (foreign direct investor or parent enterprise) obtaining a "lasting interest" (long-term relationship between direct investor and the enterprise) and control in an enterprise resident in an economy other than that of the foreign direct investor. The general rule of thumb presented in the manual is that the direct investor owns (or controls) at least 10 per cent of the ordinary shares, voting power or equivalent. FDI flows are the sum of three basic components, viz. equity capital,[16] reinvested earning,[17] and other capital associated with various inter-company debt transactions.[18]

In case of India, the definition of FDI and computation of FDI statistics used by RBI does not conform to the guidelines of the IMF.[19] For example, India excludes reinvested earning, while estimating actual FDI inflows. Next, India does not include the proceeds of foreign equity listings and foreign subordinated loans to domestic subsidiaries which, according to IMF guidelines should be a part of FDI inflows. India also excludes overseas commercial borrowings. Also in India some foreign institutional investors hold well over 20 per cent of the equity in the form of American Depository Receipts (ADRs) and Global Depository Receipts (GDRs) but these are not a part of FDI.

1.7.1 FDI in India

Compared to most industrialising economies, India followed a fairly restrictive FDI policy until 1991-relying more on bilateral and multilateral loans with long maturities. Inward foreign direct investment was perceived essentially as a means of acquiring industrial technology that was unavailable through licensing agreements and capital goods import. Even for technology licensing agreements, there were restrictions on the rates of royalty payment and technical fees. Foreign Exchange and Regulation Act (FERA), 1974 stipulated foreign firms to have equity holding only up to 40 per cent, exemptions were at government's discretion. Setting up of branch plants was usually disallowed. The law also prohibited the use of foreign brands, but promoted hybrid domestic brands (Hero Honda, for instance).

All this changed since 1991, Foreign investment is now seen as a source of scarce capital, technology and managerial skills that were considered necessary in an open, competitive, world economy. Over the decade, India not only permitted foreign investment in almost all sectors of economy, but also allowed foreign portfolio investment—thus practically divorcing foreign investment from the erstwhile technology acquisition effort. Further, laws were changed to provide foreign firms the same standing as the domestic ones. As part of the ongoing process of liberalizing foreign policies, the planning commission had set-up a Steering Committee on FDI in August 2001, for suggesting measures for enhancing FDI inflows in India (The major recommendations of the committee are given in Annexure 1.2 which presented its report in August 2002).[20]

1.7.1.1 FDI Policy at a Glance (Highlights)

The industrial policy resolution of 1956 and the statement

on industrial policy of 1991 provides the basic framework for the overall industrial policy of the Govt. of India.[20a]

- India welcomes foreign investment in virtually all sectors except defence, railway transport and atomic energy.
- The Foreign Investment Promotion Board (FIPB) considers proposals for foreign participation. This board is a single window institution. Decisions are usually taken within 30 days of application.
- Free repatriation of capital investment and profits thereon is permitted, provided the original investment is in convertible foreign exchange.
- Use of foreign brand names/trade marks for sale of goods in India is allowed.
- Indian capital markets are open to foreign institutional investors.
- Indian companies are permitted to raise funds from international capital markets.
- Special investment and tax incentives for exports and for certain sectors like power, electronics, softwares, data processing, etc.
- Bilateral investment protection agreements with 37 countries.
- 100% FDI may be allowed :

  (a) Where only holding operations is involved and all down-stream investments to be carried out need prior approval.
  (b) Where at least 50% of production is exported.
  (c) In consultancy proposals.
  (d) Where proprietary is sought to be protected or sophisticated technology is proposed to be brought in.
  (e) Projects in power, road, ports and industrial towns and estates, hotels, resorts, city.
  (f) 100% FDI in marketing, oil and gas pipelines exploration.[20b]

FDI has the potential to add a competitive edge, especially

in the industrial sector. In the Union Budget 2004-05, it was declared by Hon'ble finance minister P. Chidambaram that FDI will continue to be encouraged and actively sought, particularly in areas of infrastructure, high technology and exports.[20c] Three sectors of the economy fully meet this discription. They are telecommunications, civil aviation and insurance. There is an urgent need for infusing huge amounts of capital in these sectors.[21] Therefore, he proposed to raise the sectoral cap for FDI in telecommunications from 49% to 74%; in civil aviation from 40% to 49%; and in insurance from 26% to 49%.[22]

1.7.1.2 FDI—The Trends

Approved FDI rose from about Rs. 500 crore in 1992 to about Rs. 55 thousand crore in 1997. Cumulative approved foreign investment during 1991 and 2000, in dollar terms, is about $ 67 bn. at an average exchange rate of Rs. 40 to a dollar (Table 1.5).

In the aftermath of the East Asian crisis in 1997-98, overall net private capital flows to emerging markets, including those in developing Asia, experienced sharp decline. The reduction in FDI inflows in the Indian Economy after 1997-98 therefore, is reflective of the overall depressed trends of private capital flows in emerging market (with the notable exception of China). Against this subdued backdrop, the spurt in FDI inflows in India in 2001-02 inspite of Gujarat earthquake (January 2001) and the terrorist attack on the Indian Parliament (Dec. 2001), September 11 attack on World Trade Centre (Sept. 11, 2001) points to the increasing attractiveness of India's country specific attributes (large pool of human resources, expanding market, strong macro-economic fundamentals, etc.).[23]

As per the revised system of data reporting for FDI inflows adopted recently by the RBI in line with the international best practices, FDI inflows comprise equity inflows, reinvested earnings and other capital. Equity FDI inflows into India recorded a lower volume of $ 3.2 billion in April-Dec. 2003 compared with $3.6 billion in April-Dec. 2002.[24] In 2003-04 (April-Oct.) foreign investment increased to $ 14.5 billion from $ 4.5 billion (Graph 1.3).

Table 1.6 provides the top 10 investing countries in India. US is on the top and Mauritius is the second largest source,

Table 1.5
Foreign Investment Inflows

(in US $ million)

	1991-92	*1992-93*	*1993-94*	*1994-95*	*1995-96*	*1996-97*	*1997-98*	*1998-99*	*1999-2000*	*2000-01*	*2001-02*
(A) Direct Investment	129	315	586	1314	2144	2821	3557	2462	2155	2339	3904
(a) SIA/FIPB	66	222	280	701	1249	1922	2754	1821	1410	1456	2221
(b) RBI	—	42	89	171	169	135	202	179	171	454	767
(c) NRI	63	51	217	442	715	639	241	62	84	67	35
(d) Acquisition of shares*	—	—	—	—	11	125	360	400	490	362	881
(B) Portfolio Investment	4	244	3567	3824	2748	3312	1828	-61	3026	2760	2021
(a) GDRs/ADRs#	—	240	1520	2082	683	1366	645	270	768	831	477
(b) FIIs**	—	1	1665	1503	2009	1926	979	-390	2135	1847	1505
(c) Offshore funds and others	4	3	382	239	56	20	204	59	123	82	39
Total (A+B)	133	559	4153	5138	4892	6133	5385	2401	5181	5099	5925

* Relates to acquisition of shares of Indian companies by non-residents under section 5 of FEMA, 1999. Data on such acquisitions have been included as part of FDI since January 1996.

\# Represents the amount raised by Indian corporates through Global Depository Receipts (GDRs) and American Depository Receipts (ADRs).

** Represents fresh inflow of funds by foreign institutional investors (FIIs).

Source : RBI.

Graph 1.3
Foreign Investment

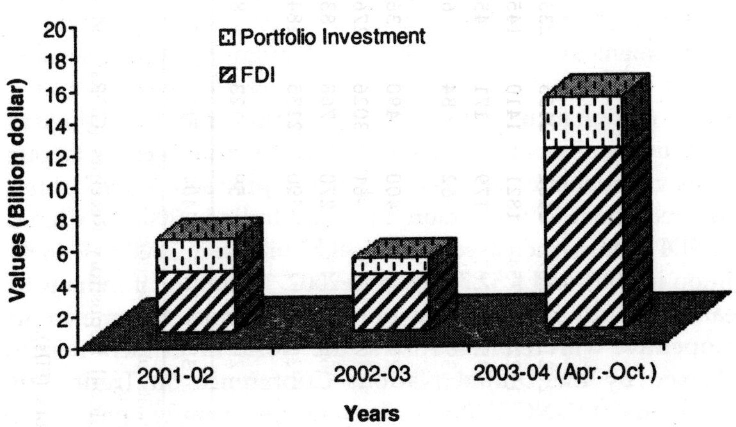

Source : *Economic Survey,* 2003-04.

Table 1.6
Top 10 Investing Countries in India, 1991-2000

Country/Region	*Share (in %)*
US	20.4
Mauritius	11.9
UK	6.4
Japan	4.0
South Korea	3.9
Germany	3.4
Australia	2.7
Malaysia	2.3
France	2.1
Netherlands	1.9

Note : In addition to the countries, external commercial borrowings and non-resident Indian's contributed 17.2% and 3.9% of the FDI approvals.

Source : Handbook of Industrial Policy and Statistics, 2001.

reportedly a conduit for many US-based firms, as India has a tax avoidance treaty with it since 1982.

It is true that, unlike trade in goods and services, FDI is viewed by different countries as a more direct instrument of development and growth. To increase foreign investment, what is needed is to have a strategic view of foreign investment, as a means of enhancing domestic production and technological capability, and as also to access the external market for labour intensive manufactures—as China has precisely done. China attracted about 15 times more FDI than India in 2002. In China, the FDI inflows increased from $ 40.77 billion in 2000 to $ 46.84 billion in 2001 and $ 52.7 billion in 2002. Therefore, if India is to realise its full FDI-drawing potential, it must become more competitive with reforms. Also as the World Investment Report released by the United Nations Conference on Trade and Development (UNCTAD) clearly suggests, "Simply opening up the economy is no longer enough. There is a need to develop attractive configurations of locational advantages". So the gap between reality and rhetoric should be reduced[25] (Annexure 1.3).

1.8 COMPARISON WITH OTHER DEVELOPING NATIONS, i.e. INDIA *VIS-A-VIS* DEVELOPING ECONOMIES

India may have been slow to embark on export-led growth, but its growth rate of exports is among the highest among major Asian countries. Some of the economies like Brazil, Mexico and South Korea sure appeared to be winners if foreign trade in goods and services are taken for 1980, 1990 and 1999 but India was not far behind (Table 1.7).

The performance of exports selected east Asian and developing countries for the year 2000, 2001 and 2002 in the Table 1.8 shows that the world exports declined by 0.4% in 2002. The performance of developing nation was much better (+2.1%). Indian export performance has fared better than the world and developing countries in 2001 and 2002.[26]

The country's average growth rate of exports over the last ten years is well above those of Singapore, Malaysia, Thailand, South Korea and Hongkong and second only to China. In 2003,

Table 1.7

Foreign Trade in Goods and Services in Selected Developing Economies

($ million)

Country	*Exports*			*Imports*			*Total Trade*		
	1980	*1990*	*1999*	*1980*	*1990*	*1999*	*1980*	*1990*	*1999*
(1)	*(2)*	*(3)*	*(4)*	*(5)*	*(6)*	*(7)*	*(8)*	*(9)*	*(10)*
Bangladesh	1,174 (6.7)	8,267 (19.7)	8,088 (17.1)	2,622 (14.9)	4,346 (14.3)	9,142 (19.4)	3,796 (21.5)	7,077 (23.2)	17,230 (36.5)
Brazil	23,331 (10.3)	36,854 (8.1)	60,865 (8.3)	36,250 (15.9)	40,949 (9.1)	86,436 (11.8)	59,581 (26.2)	77,803 (17.2)	147,301 (20.2)
Chile	6,276 (23.6)	10,705 (37.5)	20,509 (30.4)	8,360 (31.5)	11,387 (39.9)	21,041 (31.2)	14,636 (55.1)	22,092 (77.4	41,550 (61.5)
Indonesia	—	29,870 (27.4)	58,800 (44.4)	—	33,110 (30.3)	53,800 (40.6)	—	62,980 (57.7)	121,780 (91.9)
Malaysia	14,836 (61.7)	34,514 (81.9)	97,974 (33.7)	15,100 (62.7)	35,486 (84.2)	83,640 (113)	29,936 (124)	70,000 (1.66)	181.614 (246.9)
Mexico	24,685 (11.4)	54,570 (21.4)	158,924 (33.7)	35,243 (16.2)	63,504 (24.9)	173,495 (36.8)	59,928 (27.6)	118,074 (46.5)	332,419 (70.6)

(Contd.)

TABLE 1.7 (Contd.)

(1)	(2)	(3)	(4)	(5)	(6)	(7)	(8)	(9)	(10)
Pakistan	4,758 (18.2)	8,267 (19.8)	11,631 (18.4)	6,042 (23.6)	10,425 (24.9)	15,273 (24.1)	10,800 (42.2)	18,692 (44.7)	26,904 (42.5)
Philippines	8,206 (25.3)	13,290 (30.4)	47,195 (43.3)	10,348 (31.9)	16,437 (37.3)	39,677 (49.4)	18,550 (57.2)	29,727 (67.4)	86,872 (108.2)
South Korea	22,050 (36.3)	76,679 (30.4)	174,991 (43.5)	27,812 (45.7)	79,343 (31.4)	97,747 (24.3)	49,862 (82.0)	156,022 (61.8)	272,738 (67.8)
Sri Lanka	1,492 (37.3)	2,786 (35.3)	6,789 (43.2)	2,269 (56.9)	3,224 (40.9)	7,137 (45.5)	3,761 (94.1)	6,010 (76.2)	13,926 (88.7)
Thailand	8,575 (26.7)	31,289 (37.1)	74,502 (61.7)	10,861 (33.8)	38,783 (46.0)	62,457 (51.7)	19,436 (60.5)	70,072 (83.2)	136,929 (113.5)
India	15,134 (8.3)	25,064 (8.03)	67,479 (15.2)	17,662 (9.6)	33,610 (10.8)	72,315 (16.3)	32,756 (17.9)	58,674 (18.8)	139,794 (31.4)

Note : Figures in the parentheses are in percentage of GNP.
Source : World Bank, World Development Indicators, 2001.

TABLE 1.8
Exports of Selected East Asian Countries

(in US $ Billion)

Country	*2000*	*2001*	*2002**
China	249 (27.7)	267 (6.9)	171 (15.4)
Malaysia	98 (16.2)	88 (-10.3)	69 (4.7)
Korea	172 (19.9)	150 (-12.7)	133 (5.1)
Singapore	138 (20.2)	122 (-11.6)	92 (0.5)
Thailand	69 (18.2)	65 (-5.7)	57 (4.4)
India	42 (18.8)	43 (2.3)	35 (7.4)
Developing Countries	2347 (23.9)	2255 (-3.9)	1355 (2.1)
World	6340 (12.5)	6121 (-3.5)	3610 (-0.4)

* Data in respect of Thailand and Korea pertain upto October 2002, for Malaysia, India and Singapore upto Sept. 2002 and for China, Developing countries and world upto July 2002.

Figure in the parenthesis shows the percentage change over previous year.

Source : International Financial Statistics, Jan. 2003.

however it seems to be losing some of its edge, with South Korea and Thailand outshipping India in terms of export growth rates.

TABLE 1.9
Average Export Growth Rates (1993-2003) for Major Asian Countries

Country	*Growth Rate*
China	16.6%
India	10.1%
South Korea	9.6%
Malaysia	9.1%
Thailand	9.0%
Singapore	7.7%
Indonesia	6.2%
Hongkong	5.9%

Source : The Economic Times, ET Survey, 5 March, 2004.

AT Kearney's 2003 FDI confidence index upgraded India from rank 15 in 2002 to 6 in 2003. Interestingly manufacturing investors rank India among the top six most preferred destinations in 2003. In the service sector India ranked 4th in 2003 whereas in the previous year it stood at 14th position.

According to the country forecast, the economist's Business not ranking regional rank of India for 2004-08 is 12th as given below in the Table 1.10.

TABLE 1.10
Business Environment Ranking

Value of Index (a)		*Global Rank (b)*		*Regional Rank (c)*	
1999-2003	*2004-08*	*1999-2003*	*2004-08*	*1999-2003*	*2004-08*
5.16	6.20	46	40	13	12

(a) Out of 10

(b) Out of 60 countries

(c) Out of 16 countries—Australia, China, Hongkong, India, Indonesia, Japan, Malaysia, Newzealand, Pakistan, Phillippines, Singapore, South Korea, Srilanka, Taiwan, Thailand and Vietnam.

Source : Country Forecast India, Feb. 2004, The Economist Intelligence Unit, United Kingdom.

According to Goldman Sachs report (October, 2003), China and India would become the first and the third largest economies of the world by 2040, with the US occupying the second slot. The widely circulated report, Dreaming with BRICs : The path to 2050, had analysed the growth prospects for Brazil, Russia, India and China. The estimates of Sachs are in line with estimates by the World Bank which feels that the entire South Asian region is set for a phase of strong growth. While on most counts, there is win-win situation for India, the risk factors include the size of gross fiscal deficit, unemployment and mismatch between the internal reforms and external reforms etc.[27] (The details of selected indicators of external sector from 1990 to 2003-04 is given in Annexure 1.4).

India is on the threshold of becoming an economic superpower. The coming decade is all set to be very exciting for India.[28]

NOTES AND REFERENCES

1. Rubner, Alex, The Export Cult, A Global Display of Economic Distortion, pp. 28-39, 1987.
2. Ohmae, Kenichi Triad Power : The Coming Shape of Global Competition, New York, The Free Press, 1985, p. 9.
3. Czinkota, Ronkainen, Moffett, International Business, The Dryden Press, Third edition, 1994, p. 3.
4. Bhatt, Vinay Ram, 'Wild Geese Chase", *The Times of India*, March 10, 2003, p. 16.
5. Waldmann, Raymond J., Managed Trade : The Competition between Nations, Cambride, Mass : Ballinger, 1986, pp. 12-25.
6. Khurana, P.K., Export Management. Galgotia Publishing Company, Delhi, 2001, pp. 3-4, 23.
7. Exim Policy 2002-07, Government of India.
8. Wray, Randall L., "Export led growth Prospects", *Chartered Financial Analyst*, December 2001, pp. 14-16.
9. Ricupero, Rubens : Transnational Corporations and Export Competitiveness, an Overview, (World Investment Report, 2002, UNCTAD), *Foreign Trade Review*, Vol. 37, No. 3 and 4, Oct. 2002-March, 2003, pp. 105-27.

10a. Habib, Ahsan S.M. and Shah, Pinki, "India's Trade Openness—A Relative Scenario", *Foreign Trade Review*, Vol. 38, Nos. 1 and 2, New Delhi, (2003).

10b. Jain, Bimal, India's Economy Policy—Preparing for the 21st Century, Viking India (1996).

11. Habib, Ahsan S.M. and Shah, Pinki, "India's Trade Openness—A Relative Scenario", *Foreign Trade Review*, Vol. 38, Nos. 1 and 2, New Delhi, (2003).
12. India's Feel Good Factor—A reality check, *Chartered Financial Analyst*, March, 2004.
13. Economic Survey, 2002-03.
14. Vijay Gaurav and Fernandes Daniel, 'India Inc Deepens Export Focus', *The Economic Times*, New Delhi, 1 Aug. 2004. While calculating export turnover, the CMIE considered the total revenue earned from exports of goods and services. It also included income earned in foreign currency in the form of interest, dividend, royalties and consulting fees. Higher export income seems to have helped bottomline growth.
15. Premsingh, Manika, Indian Exports have Arrived to keep going, *The Economic Times*, New Delhi, 4 August, 2004, p. 5.
16. Equity capital constitutes the value of the MNC's investment in shares of an enterprise in a foreign country. An equity capital stake of 10% or more of the ordinary shares or voting power in an incorporated enterprise or its equivalant in an unincorporated enterprise, is normally considered as a threshold for the control of assets.
17. Reinvested earnings consists of the sum of direct investor's share of earnings not distributed as dividends by subsidiaries and earnings of branches not remitted to the direct investor.

18. Other direct investment capital covers the borrowing and lending of funds—including debt securities and supplier's credits—between direct investors and branches, subsidiaries and associates.
19. In case of India, FDI Statistics are Published by two official sources:
    (a) Reserve Bank of India (RBI), and
    (b) Secretariat for Industrial Assistance (SIA).
20. *RBI Bulletin*, Annual Report on the working of the RBI. For the year July, 2001 to June 30, 2002.

20a. 'Fits and starts FDI, More symbol than substance in Govt.'s package'. *The Times of India*, New Delhi, January 17, 2004.

20b. 'Cabinet adds riders to FDI Policy', *The Times of India*, New Delhi, January 16, 2004.

20c. 'India should Push Reforms for FDI', *The Times of India*, New Delhi, Sept. 5, 2003.

21. FDI door wide open, half shut, *The Times of India*, New Delhi, 16 Jan, 2004.

22a. Union Budget 2004-05, The Speech of Finance Minister, GDI—Sh. P. Chidambaram, 8th July, 2004.

22b. FDI in public sector refineries remains limited to 26 per cent. In Private banks FDI limit raised to 74 per cent from 49 per cent, but it actually means a reduction in the cap because till now an additional 49 per cent portfolio investment was allowed.

23. Nagraj, R., Foreign Direct Investment in India in the 1990s: Trends and issues, *Economic and Political Weekly*, April 26, 2003.
24. Srivastava, Sadhna, What is the true level of FDI flow to India?, *Economic and Political Weekly*, February 15, 2003.
25. Padhi, Satya Prasad, 'Attracting Foreign Direct Investment—A Regional Perspective', *Foreign Trade Review*, New Delhi, Vol. 17, Nos. 3 and 4, October 2002-March.
26. S.M. Ahsan Habib, Pinki Shah, 'India's Trade Openness', A Relative Scenario, *Foreign Trade Review*, Vol. XXXVIII, Nos. 1 and 2. April-Sept., 2002, IIFT, New Delhi.
27. Chandran, Bipin, 'Safeguards on FDI in channels mulled' 2/3 August 2003.
28. Indian Economy—Giant in the making?, *Chartered Financial Analyst*, March 2004.

ANNEXURE 1.1
Balance of Payments : Summary

(in US $ million)

Item	1990-91	1995-96	1996-97	1997-98	1998-99	1999-00	2000-01	2001-02	2002-03	2003-04 (Apr.-Dec.)
(1)	(2)	(3)	(4)	(5)	(6)	(7)	(8)	(9)	(10)	(11)
1. Exports	18477	32311	34133	35680	34298	37542	44894	44915	52512	43237
2. Imports	29715	43670	48948	51187	47544	55383	59264	57618	65422	58233
3. Trade blance	-9438	-11359	-14815	-15507	-13246	-17841	-14370	-12703	-12910	-14996
4. Invisibles (net)	-242	5449	10196	10007	9208	13143	11791	14054	17047	18222
Non-factor services	980	-197	726	1319	2165	4064	2478	4199	6765	8814
Investment income	-3752	-3205	-3307	-3521	-3544	-3559	-3821	-2654	-4935	-5195
Pvt. transfers	2069	8506	12367	11830	10280	12256	12798	12125	14807	14494
Official transfers	461	345	410	379	307	382	336	384	410	109
5. Current account balance	-9680	-5910	-4619	-5500	-4038	-4698	-2579	1351	4137	3226
6. External assistance (net)	2210	883	1109	907	820	901	427	1204	-2460	-1814
7. Commercial borrowing (net)@	2248	1275	2848	3999	4362	313	4011	-1147	-2344	-3732

(Contd.)

ANNEXURE 1.1 (Contd.)

(1) (2)	(3)	(4)		(5)	(6)	(7)		(8)	(9)	(10)
8. IMF (net)	1214	-1715	-975	-618	-393	-260	-26	0	0	0
9. NR deposits (net)	1536	1103	3350	1125	960	1540	2317	2754	2976	3502
10. Rupee debt service	-1193	-952	-727	-767	-802	-711	-617	-519	-474	-304
11. Foreign investment (net) of which	103	4615	5963	5353	2312	5117	4588	5286	4555	10135
(i) FDI (net)*	97	1954	2651	3525	2380	2093	3272	4741	3611	2513
(ii) FIIs	0	2009	1926	979	-390	2135	1847	1505	342	7219
(iii) Euro-equities and others	6	652	1386	849	322	889	913	515	602	403
12. Other flows (net)+	2284	-2235	-1131	-606	608	3940	-2291	2828	10590	9776
13. Capital account (total (net))	8402	2974	10437	9393	7867	10840	8409	10406	12843	17563
14. Reserve use (—(increase))	1278	2936	-5818	-3893	-3829	-6142	-5830	-11757	-16980	-20788

@ Figures include receipts on account of India Development Bonds in 1991-92, Resurgent India Bonds in 1998-99 and India Millennium Deposits in 2000-01 and related repayments, if any, in the subsequent years.

\+ Include, among others, delayed export receipts and errors and omissions.

* These figures indicate FDI to India only. FDI to India figures from 2000-01 include reinvested earnings and other capital.

Source : Reserve Bank of India.

ANNEXURE 1.2
Major Recommendations of the Steering Committee on Foreign Direct Investment Set-up by the Planning Commission

The Steering Committee on FDI set-up by the Planning Commission in August 2001 has submitted its report, which is currently being considered by the Government. The main recommendations of the Committee are:

- Enactment of a Foreign Investment Promotion Law incorporating and integrating relevant aspects for promoting FDI.
- Urge States to enact a special investment law relating to infrastructure for expediting investment in infrastructure and removing hurdles to production in infrastructure.
- Empower the Foreign Investment Promotion Board (FIPB) for granting initial central-level registrations and approvals wherever possible, for speeding up the implementation process.
- Empower Foreign Investment Implementation Authority (FIIA) for expediting administrative and policy approvals.
- Disaggregating FDI targets for the length plan in terms of sectors, and relevant administrative ministries/ departments, for increasing accountability.
- Reduction of sectoral FDI caps to the minimum and elimination of entry barriers. Caps can be taken off for all manufacturing and mining activities (except defence), eliminated in advertising, private banks, and real estate, and hiked in telecom, civil aviation, broadcasting, insurance and plantations (other than tea).
- Overhauling the existing FDI strategy by shifting from a broader macro-emphasis to a targeted sector-specific approach.
- Informational aspects of the FDI strategy require refinement in the light of India's strengths and weaknesses as an investment destination and should

use information technology and modern marketing techniques.

- The Special Economic Zones (SEZs) should be developed as internationally competitive destinations for export-oriented FDI, by simplifying laws, rules, and procedurres, and reducing bureaucratic rigmarole on the lines of China.
- Domestic policy reforms in power, urban infrastructure, and real estate, and de-control/de-licensing should be expedited for attracting more FDI.

ANNEXURE 1.3
FDI Inflows in Selected Asian Economies

(in US $ million)

	1996	*1997*	*1998*	*1999*	*2000*	*2001*
World	386140	478082	694457	1088263	1491934	735146
Developed Economies	219905	267947	484239	837761	1227476	503144
Asia	93331	105825	96109	102779	133707	102066
South, East and South-East Asia	87843	96338	86252	99990	131123	94365
(a) China	40180	44237	43751	40319	40772	46846
(b) India	2525	3619	2633	2168	2319	3403
(c) Indonesia	6194	4677	-356	-2745	-4550	-3277
(d) Korea	2325	2844	5412	9333	9283	3198
(e) Malaysia	7296	6324	2714	3895	3788	554
(f) Philippines	1520	1249	1752	578	1241	1792
(g) Singapore	8608	10746	6389	11803	5407	8609
(h) Thailand	2271	3626	5143	3561	2813	3759

Source : World Investment Report (WIR), 2002; UNCTAD.

ANNEXURE 1.4
Selected Indicators of External Sector

Sl. No.	Item	Years								
		1990-91	*1996-97*	*1997-98*	*1998-99*	*1990-00*	*2000-01*	*2001-02*	*2002-03*	*2003-04**
	(1)	*(2)*	*(3)*	*(4)*	*(5)*	*(6)*	*(7)*	*(8)*	*(9)*	*(10)*
1.	Growth of Exports—BOP (%)	9.0	5.6	4.5	-3.9	9.5	19.6	0.0	16.9	12.5
2.	Growth of Imports—BOP (%)	14.4	12.1	4.6	-7.1	16.5	7.0	-2.8	13.5	20.8
3.	Exports/Imports—BOP (%)	66.2	69.7	69.7	72.1	67.8	75.8	78.0	80.3	74.2
4.	Import cover of FER (No. of months)	2.5	6.5	6.9	8.2	8.2	8.6	11.3	13.8	16.2
5.	External assistance (net)/TC (%)	26.3	10.6	9.7	10.4	8.3	4.3	10.2	-19.1	-10.3
6.	ECB (net)/TC (%)	26.8	27.3	42.6	55.4	2.9	39.7	-14.3	-18.2	-21.2
7.	NR deposits/TC (%)	18.3	32.1	12.0	12.2	14.2	24.6	25.1	23.2	19.9
8.	Short-terms debt/FER (%)	146.5	25.5	17.2	13.2	10.3	8.6	5.1	6.0	5.7
9.	Debt service payments as % of current recipts	35.3	23.0	19.5	18.8	17.1	16.2	13.4	15.8	18.1

* Calculated on the basis of figures upto Apr.-Dec. 2003-04.

Notes : (i) TC : Total Capital Flows (Net).
(ii) ECB : External Commercial Borrowing.
(iii) FER : Foreign Exchange Reserves, including gold and SDRs.

Source : *Economic Survey*, 2003-04.

Indian Exports : A Critique

2.1 THE NEW HORIZON

The volume of International trade has been growing more quickly than the volume of world production since World War II. The volume of international trade and the number of players in it have increased dramatically over the last decade. Today, every nation and an increasing number of companies buy and sell goods in the international market place. A number of developments around the world have helped to fuel this activity. One of the most important trends in the late 20th century has been the lowering of barriers to facilitate easy movement of goods and services across national borders. Internationalisation of business has benefited both nations and companies. Birla Group, Reliance, Arvind Mills, Infosys, Asian Paints, Wipro, Satyam, Ranbaxy and many more are busy in globalising their operations. The global business is carried out in several ways. One easy way is through exports and imports. Exports are goods and services produced in one country but marketed in other country. Imports are goods and services produced in one country but bought by another country.

India's contribution to world trade is trival but prospects of India, emerging as a significant player are bright. This chapter focuses on Indian exports and finer details of it.

2.2 EXPORT PERFORMANCE

Export performance has been great, Indian exports crossed the $ 50 billion mark in 2001-02 and $ 60 billion in 2003-04. During the fiscal year 2003-04 exports recorded an impressive 17.1% growth, on top of the 20 per cent increase clocked in the preceding year. In a year when the rupee appreciated by about 6 per cent against the dollar, the performance of export sector is commendable. The medium-term export strategy till 2007 had projected a 12 per cent annual growth for Indian exporters to corner 1 per cent share in global exports. The Government has set an export target of 16 per cent for the fiscal year 2004-05 which would push up India's merchandise exports to $ 73.4 billion at the end of March 2005.[1]

2.2.1 Month-wise Export-Import Performance (2003-04)

Month-wise data (2003-04) revealed that exports growth was particularly robust in December, February and March. During these months export surged by 51.5%, 34.9% and 41.9% respectively. The value of exports at $ 7.3 billion in March was all time high in a month[2,3] (Table 2.1a).

2.2.2 Terms of Trade and Index Numbers of Foreign Trade

The concept of terms of trade has been developed to measure the distributions of gains from trade in international trade theory over more than a century.

The net terms of trade, which measure the relative change in export and import prices, have been fluctuating with an average annual increase of 1.5 per cent during the 1990s. However, with depressed prices for exports and high prices of oil, it has been deteriorating since 1999-2000, it worsened by 4.5 per cent in 2000-01, and further by 2.4 per cent in 2001-02 (Graph 2.1). Inspite of the deterioration in the price terms of trade, the income terms of trade measuring the import purchasing power of exports have consistently improved every year during the 1990s, except in 1996-97. On an average, the annual growth in income terms of trade has been 11.7 per cent, partly fueled by strong export growth in volume terms with exports volume growing by 23.9 and 3.8 per cent in 2000-01 and 2001-02, the import purchasing power of exports increased by 18.3 and 1.5 per cent respectively in these two years (Table 2.1b).

TABLE 2.1a
Foreign Trade—Monthly Data :2003-04

	Exports ($ mln.)	Imports ($ mln.)	Trade bal. ($ mln.)	Exports (% chg.)	Imports (% chg.)	Exports (Rs. crore)	Imports (Rs. crore)	Trade bal. (Rs. crore)	Exports (% chg.)	Imports (% chg.)
Mar.-2003	5161	5902	-741	23.7	32.1	24541	28062	-3521	21.6	29.9
Apr.-2003	3879	5556	-1677	-3.6	31.1	18338	26269	-7931	-6.2	27.6
May-2003	4729	5945	-1216	17.9	13.9	22233	27947	5714	13.9	10.1
Jun.-2003	4314	5573	-1259	11.5	30.8	20116	25987	-5871	6.4	24.9
Jul.-2003	4442	5711	-1269	—	17.0	20501	26356	-5855	-5.2	10.9
Aug.-2003	4547	5677	-1130	5.2	16.5	20857	26038	-5181	-0.5	10.2
Sep.-2003	5268	6088	-820	22.4	19.5	24101	27853	-3752	15.8	13.1
Oct.-2003	5474	6943	-1469	17.5	23.9	24796	31453	-6657	10.3	16.3
Nov.-2003	4693	6345	-1652	18.5	24.8	21309	28811	-7502	11.8	17.7
Dec.-2003	5840	7363	-1523	51.5	47.8	26558	33487	-6929	43.4	39.9
Jan.-2004	5128	6592	-1464	8.7	18.1	23264	29909	-6645	3.1	12.0
Feb.-2004	5610	6833	-1223	34.9	47.3	25339	30864	-5525	27.9	39.6
Mar.-2004	7323	7098	225	41.9	20.3	32902	31892	1010	34.1	13.6
	Apr.-Mar.	Apr.-Mar.	Apr.-Mar.	Apr.-Mar.	Apr.-Mar.	Apr.-Mar.	Apr.-Mar.	Apr.-Mar.	Apr.-Mar.	Apr.-Mar.
2002-03	52856	60313	-7457	20.2	16.9	255137	291133	-35996	22.1	18.7
2003-04	61882	75600	-13718	17.1	25.3	283605	346474	-62869	11.2	19.0

Source : *Monthly Review of the Indian Economy*, Centre for Monitoring Indian Economy, May, 2004.

GRAPH 2.1

Trend Line for Terms of Trade from 1969-70 to 2002-03

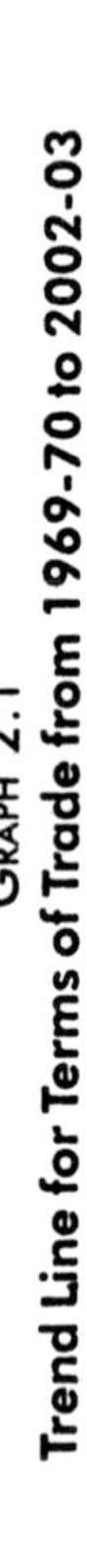

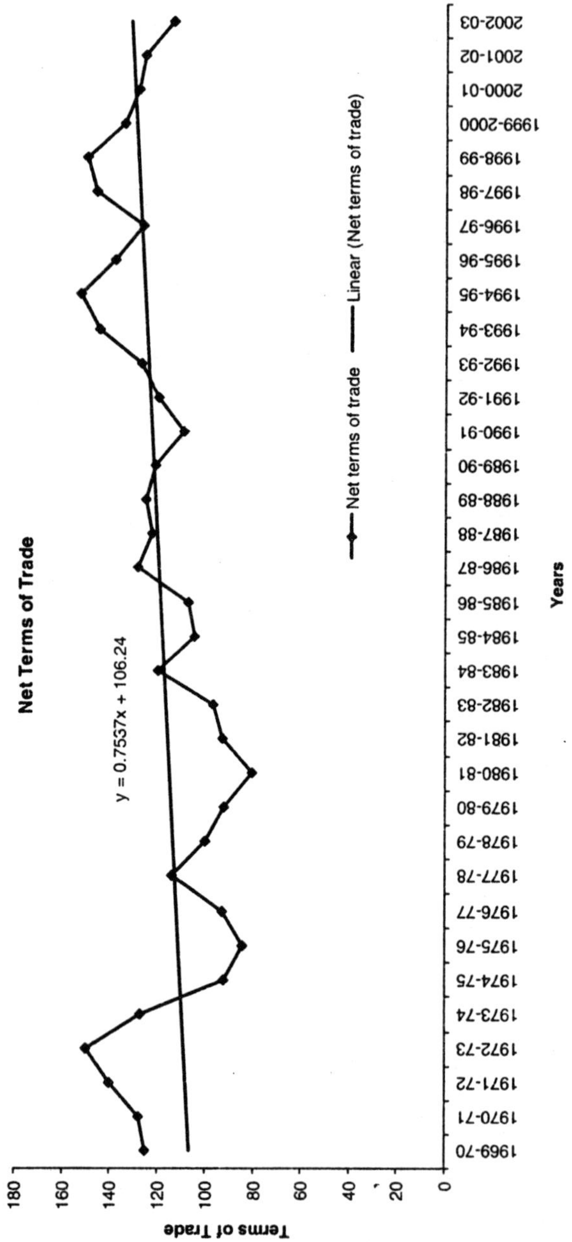

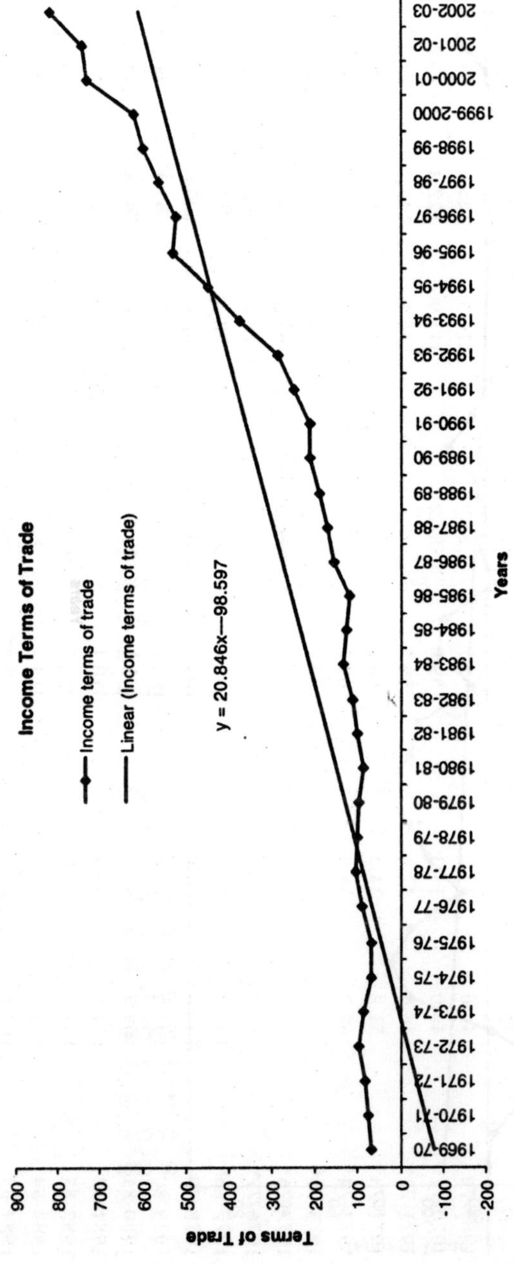
Income Terms of Trade
Income terms of trade
Linear (Income terms of trade)
y = 20.846x—98.597
Terms of Trade
Years
900
800
700
600
500
400
300
200
100
0
-100
-200
1969-70
1970-71
1971-72
1972-73
1973-74
1974-75
1975-76
1976-77
1977-78
1978-79
1979-80
1980-81
1981-82
1982-83
1983-84
1984-85
1985-86
1986-87
1987-88
1988-89
1989-90
1990-91
1991-92
1992-93
1993-94
1994-95
1995-96
1996-97
1997-98
1998-99
1999-2000
2000-01
2001-02
2002-03

TABLE 2.1b
Terms of Trade and Index Numbers of Foreign Trade
(Base : 1978-79 = 100)

Year	*Unit Value Index*		*Volume Index*		*Terms of Trade*		
	Exports	*Imports*	*Exports*	*Imports*	*Gross*	*Net*	*Income*
(1)	(2)	(3)	(4)	(5)	(6)	(7)	(8)
1969-70	44.0	35.2	55.7	64.9	116.5	125.0	69.6
1970-71*	45.0	35.3	59.0	67.2	113.9	127.4	75.2
1971-72*	46.0	32.8	59.2	80.6	136.1	140.2	83.0
1972-73*	51.2	34.2	66.5	76.7	115.3	149.7	99.6
1973-74*	62.2	48.9	69.5	87.2	125.4	127.2	88.4
1974-75*	78.0	85.5	73.7	77.2	104.7	92.3	68.4
1975-76*	83.9	99.1	81.7	76.0	93.0	84.7	69.2
1976-77*	89.4	96.3	96.8	76.1	78.6	92.9	89.9
1977-78*	100.3	88.0	93.2	100.0	107.3	114.0	106.2
1978-79	100.0	100.0	100.0	100.0	100.0	100.0	100.0
1979-80	105.4	114.1	106.2	116.4	109.7	92.4	98.1
1980-81	108.5	134.2	108.1	137.9	127.6	80.8	87.3
1981-82	124.1	133.1	110.1	150.6	136.8	93.2	102.6
1982-83	132.0	136.3	116.7	154.6	132.4	96.8	113.0
1983-84	151.0	125.8	113.0	185.4	164.1	120.0	135.6
1984-85	169.8	161.7	120.8	156.1	129.2	105.0	126.8

1985-86	170.8	158.8	111.3	182.3	163.8	107.6	119.8
1986-87	179.4	139.4	121.3	212.3	175.0	128.6	156.0
1987-88	195.4	160.0	140.0	204.8	146.3	122.1	170.9
1988-89	232.2	185.5	152.1	224.2	147.4	125.2	190.4
1989-90	276.6	228.4	174.9	227.8	130.2	121.1	211.8
1990-91	292.5	267.7	194.1	237.7	122.5	109.3	212.2
1991-92	369.5	309.1	208.6	228.0	109.3	119.5	249.3
1992-93	421.5	331.0	222.9	282.0	126.5	127.3	283.8
1993-94	474.1	327.2	257.5	329.1	127.8	144.9	373.1
1994-95	494.6	324.6	292.7	408.3	139.5	152.4	446.0
1995-96	484.2	351.0	384.3	514.8	134.0	137.9	530.0
1996-97	504.7	399.8	411.8	511.8	124.3	126.2	519.7
1997-98	589.4	404.2	386.0	562.1	145.6	145.8	562.8
1998-99	611.7	407.8	399.2	644.2	161.4	150.0	598.8
1999-2000	604.5	450.5	461.0	704.8	152.9	134.0	618.7
2000-01	624.3	487.5	571.4	697.7	122.1	128.1	732.0
2001-02	618.0	492.9	592.7	732.8	123.6	125.4	743.0
2002-03	619.6	545.6	721.6	802.4	111.2	113.6	819.7

* Converted from the original base with the help of linking factors.

Notes : 1. Gross terms of trade implies volume index of imports expressed as a percentage of volume index of exports.
2. Net terms of trade implies unit value index of exports expressed as percentage of unit value index of imports.
3. Income terms of trade implies the products of net terms of trade and volume index of exports expressed as a percentage.

Source : DGCI and S.

The unit value index and volume index for exports and imports have been given in Table 2.1b, taking the base year 1978-79. The unit value index for exports for 2002-03 was 619.6 and for imports 545.6 and volume index for exports for the same period was 721.6 and for imports was 802.4.

The *correlation coefficient* was also calculated between the exports volume index and import volume index which came out to be 0.98456. This shows that export volume index and import volume index are positively correlated and there is great degree of correlation between the two aspects.

2.3 COMMODITY COMPOSITION

The export performance of principal commodity groups during the last few years are reviewed in the following description.

2.3.1 Agricultural and Allied Products

Agriculture and allied products comprises a wide variety of products covering cereals, pulses, nuts, fruits, vegetables, guargum meal, dairy products meat and meat products, sugar, mollases, tobacco and spices etc.

During April to Nov. 2002 the exports of this group showed a marginal increase of 0.09 per cent from Rs. 10,075 crores during April to Nov. 1999 to Rs. 10,084 crores during April to Nov. 2000.

During April to Sept. 2002 the exports recorded a growth of 8.94%, as a result of which, the volume of exports rose from Rs. 8,766 crores in 2001-02 to Rs. 9,550 crores during 2002-03 (Table 2.2).

In the year 2002-03 and 2003-04 exports of agricultural and allied products registered 15.62% and 1.24% change respectively, i.e. from 5572.1 US $ million in 2002-03 to 5641.1 US $ million in 2003-04 (Table 2.3). The items which have indicated a significant increase during 2003-04 as compared to the corresponding period of previous year are cotton raw including waste, fresh fruits and vegetables, groundnuts, cereals, sesame and niger seeds and wheat, etc.

Export growth of this segment have been below the overall commodities' exports growth rates on an average. Consequently, this segment's share in overall commodity exports has been

Table 2.2
Export of Principal Commodities from India

S.No.	Commodities	Apr.-Mar. 1998-99	Apr.-Mar. 1999-2000	2000-01	2001-02	% change	Apr.-Sept. 2001	Apr.-Sept. 2002	% change
	(1)	(2)	(3)	(4)	(5)	(6)	(7)	(8)	(9)
I.	Plantations	3992.79	3129.83	3161	2814	-11.0	1510	1386	-8.21
	1. Tea	2264.79	1765.76	1976	1719	-13.01	880	853	-3.07
	2. Coffee	1727.92	1364.07	1185	1095	-7.59	630	533	-15.40
II.	Agri and Allied Products	16819.03	15499.67	17398	18827	8.21	8766	9550	8.94
	1. Cereal	6290.82	3113.54	3397	4620	36.00	2066	2963	43.42
	(a) Rice	6280.76	3105.35	2943	3174	7.85	1372	2086	52.04
	(b) Wheat	1.35	0.00	415	1330	220.48	641	838	30.73
	(c) Others	8.67	8.15	39	116	197.44	53	39	-26.42
	2. Pulses	223.02	404.90	537	369	-31.28	173	180	4.05
	3. Tobacco	761.77	992.93	871	808	-7.23	384	537	39.84
	(a) Unmanufactured	572.29	800.14	661	582	-11.95	268	394	47.01
	(b) Manufactured	189.49	192.79	210	226	7.62	116	143	23.28
	4. Spices	1632.51	1701.94	1619	1497	-7.54	786	838	662
	5. Nuts and Seeds	2099.79	3008.55	2797	2513	-10.15	1228	1276	3.91

(Contd.)

TABLE 2.2 (Contd.)

(1)	(2)	(3)	(4)	(5)	(6)	(7)	(8)	(9)
(a) Cashew incl. CNSL	1629.06	2453.63	1883	1652	-12.27	903	1056	16.94
(b) Sesame and Niger seed	328.53	371.71	598	610	2.01	265	176	-33.58
(c) Groundnut	139.67	183.21	316	251	-20.57	60	44	-26.67
6. Oil Meals	1941.68	1603.22	2045	2263	10.66	593	437	-26.31
7. Guargum Meal	727.70	818.64	603	403	-33.31	209	192	-8.13
8. Castor Oil	672.12	1061.95	953	626	-34.31	341	303	-11.14
9. Shellac	65.29	81.55	128	73	-42.97	36	35	-2.78
10. Sugar and Mollasses	24.44	37.83	511	1782	248.73	1121	660	-41.12
11. Processed food	1318.16	1634.38	2166	2427	12.05	1177	1291	9.69
(a) Fruits and Vegetables	540.35	641.50	1072	1191	11.10	551	617	11.98
(b) Processed Fruit and Juices	64.58	67.30	558	512	-8.24	259	266	2.70
(c) Misc. Processed Items	713.22	925.59	536	724	35.07	367	408	11.17
12. Meat and Meat Products	788.11	780.94	1470	1193	-18.84	515	689	33.79
13. Floriculture Products	105.98	90.61	133	127	-4.51	60	91	51.67
14. Spirit and Beverages	70.72	70.16	168	126	-25.00	77	58	-24.68
III. Marine Products	4368.57	5113.74	6367	5897	-7.38	3036	3187	4.9
IV. Ores and Minerals	3758.71	3928.93	5297	6020	13.65	2593	4699	81.22
1. Iron Ore	1615.51	1150.74	1634	2034	24.48	726	2044	181.54

2. Mica	43.33	40.91	64	56	-12.50	19	20	5.26
3. Processed Minerals	1065.02	1004.02	1724	1675	-2.84	750	1425	90
4. Others Ores and Minerals	893.87	1622.46	1707	1965	15.11	1006	1123	11.63
5. Coal	141.02	110.80	168	290	72.62	92	87	-5.43
V. Leather Manufacturers	6986.75	6666.26	8914	9110	2.20	4778	4610	-3.52
1. Footwear	2520.41	2583.80	2841	3002	5.67	1497	1470	-1.8
2. Leather and Mfrs.	4466.34	4082.50	6073	6108	0.58	3281	3140	-4.3
VI. Gems and Jewellery	24945.13	33089.02	33734	34845	3.29	15787	21687	37.37
VII. Ports Goods	308.08	279.50	309	328	6.15	167	182	8.98
VIII. Chemical and Allied Products	17521.61	20516.43	27247	28860	5.92	13880	17029	22.69
1. Basic Chemis. Pharma and Cosmetics	11168.10	12764.47	16831	17630	4.75	8359	10632	27.19
2. Plastic and Linoleum	1992.80	2543.72	4318	4709	9.06	2359	2810	19.12
3. Rubber, Glass and other Products*	3310.62	7007.02	4397	4695	6.78	2210	2682	21.36
4. Residual Chemicals and allied products	1058.54	1201.23	1701	1826	7.35	952	905	-4.94
IX. Engineering Goods	16007.15	18947.44	26658	27406	2.81	12976	16241	25.16
X. Electronics Goods	2115.10	2454.36	4899	5586	14.02	2844	2788	-1.97
XI. Project Goods	300.72	68.16	123	88	-28.46	16	159	893.75
XII. Textiles	35014.39	40097.31	49215	46094	-6.34	22903	26192	14.36

(Contd.)

TABLE 2.2 (Contd.)

(1)	(2)	(3)	(4)	(5)	(6)	(7)	(8)	(9)
1. Readymade Garments	18363.56	20808.67	25478	23877	-6.28	11642	13394	15.05
2. Cotton yarn, fabrics made-ups etc.	11661.47	13601.87	16030	14655	-8.58	7507	8086	7.71
3. Manmade textiles made-ups etc.	3027.61	3733.72	4858	5079	4.55	2511	3170	26.24
4. Natural silk textiles	752.18	1000.38	1404	1327	-5.48	652	838	28.53
5. Wool and Woolen manufactures	313.93	248.69	291	249	-14.43	127	124	-2.36
6. Coir and Coir manufactures	316.58	190.27	221	295	33.48	169	188	11.24
7. Jute manufactures	581.58	513.71	933	612	-34.41	295	392	32.88
XIII. Handicrafts	2663.53	2904.55	3055	2618	-14.30	1323	1807	36.58
XIV. Carpets	2286.71	2627.65	2658	2433	-8.47	1205	1182	-1.91
1. Hand-made (excl. silk)	1721.74	2204.68	2042	1788	-12.44	876	918	4.79
2. Mill made (excl. silk)	430.89	380.07	505	473	-6.34	233	222	-4.72
3. Silk Carpet	134.08	42.90	111	172	54.95	96	42	-56.25
XV. Cotton Raw Incl. Waste	206.90	80.69	224	43	-80.80	14	18	28.57
XVI. Petroleum Products	376.24	129.91	8646	10107	16.90	4662	6120	31.27
XVII. Unclassified items	1723.30	7323.53	5666	7942	40.17	3084	5473	77.46

TABLE 2.3

Commodity Composition of Exports : April-January

	US $ million		*% change*		*% Share in total*	
	2002-03	2003-04	2002-03	2003-04	2002-03	2003-04
(1)	(2)	(3)	(4)	(5)	(6)	(7)
All Commodities	42872.6	48867.8	18.78	13.98	100.00	100.00
Agricultural and Allied Products	5572.1	5641.1	15.62	1.24	13.00	11.54
— Basmati rice	326.3	305.5	9.94	-6.38	0.76	0.63
— Cashew	372.7	297.0	17.53	-20.32	0.87	0.61
— Cashewnut shell liquid	1.7	0.2	81.32	-87.28	—	—
— Castor Oil	101.9	104.7	-7.07	2.69	0.24	0.21
— Coffee	160.9	179.1	-14.24	11.33	0.38	0.37
— Cotton raw incl. waste	5.8	47.5	12.46	721.52	0.01	0.10
— Floriculture products	31.0	35.7	51.72	15.17	0.07	0.07
— Fresh fruits	67.7	118.3	8.96	74.68	0.16	0.24
— Fresh vegetables	107.4	141.0	11.55	31.28	0.25	0.29
— Fruits/vegetable seeds	17.0	8.2	55.17	-51.47	0.04	0.02
— Groundnuts	28.6	94.3	-37.57	229.33	0.07	0.19
— Guargum meal	79.9	92.4	15.40	15.54	0.19	0.19
— Marine products	1221.6	1066.1	14.36	-12.73	2.85	2.18

(*Contd.*)

TABLE 2.3 (Contd.)

(1)	(2)	(3)	(4)	(5)	(6)	(7)
— Meat and preparations	246.7	271.4	19.82	10.01	0.58	0.56
— Misc. processed items	149.3	178.8	29.84	19.80	0.35	0.37
— Non-basmati rice	696.0	396.1	251.89	-43.09	1.62	0.81
— Oil meals	248.5	479.1	-25.988	92.78	0.58	0.98
— Other cereals	15.7	38.2	-19.83	143.52	0.04	0.08
— Poultry and diary products	55.8	64.5	-4.91	15.43	0.13	0.13
— Dairy products	26.1	26.7	-22.71	2.30	0.06	0.05
— Poultry products	29.7	37.7	19.23	26.96	0.07	0.08
— Processed fruits and juices	102.1	56.8	8.11	-44.35	0.24	0.12
— Processed vegetables	42.4	50.6	25.72	19.26	0.10	0.10
— Pulses	63.1	54.7	-1.84	-13.29	0.15	0.11
— Seasame and Niger seeds	71.9	123.4	-34.77	71.58	0.17	0.25
— Niger seeds	12.3	6.7	69.70	-45.48	0.03	0.01
— Sesame seeds	59.6	116.7	-42.11	95.70	0.14	0.24
— Shellac	14.4	29.0	14.57	100.68	0.03	0.06
— Spices	287.6	263.8	9.69	-8.30	0.67	0.54
— Spirit and beverages	20.0	21.2	-7.92	6.11	0.05	0.04
— Sugar and mollasses	259.7	245.5	-20.41	-5.46	0.61	0.50
— Mollasses	7.6	4.2	-29.22	-45.36	0.02	0.01

— Sugar	252.1	241.3	-20.11	-4.26	0.59	0.49
— Tea	300.4	290.9	-7.11	-3.16	0.70	0.60
— Tobacco manufactured	48.4	46.8	22.68	-3.30	0.11	0.10
— Tobacco unmanufactured	115.1	130.4	35.37	13.24	0.27	0.27
— Wheat	312.3	410.0	40.26	31.29	0.73	0.84
Ores and Minerals	1664.6	1685.0	66.99	1.22	3.88	3.45
— Coal	38.5	44.7	-15.18	15.95	0.09	0.09
— Iron ore	720.7	725.6	125.05	0.67	1.68	1.48
— Mica	7.1	13.2	-29.83	85.43	0.02	0.03
— Processed minerals	462.6	458.0	68.86	-0.98	1.08	0.94
— Other ores and minerals	435.7	443.5	25.54	1.79	1.02	0.91
Manufactured Goods	32918.8	36285.7	19.75	10.23	76.78	74.25
— Leather and leather manufactures	1560.3	1604.4	-4.35	2.83	3.64	3.28
— Finished leather	436.4	410.1	11.64	-6.04	1.02	0.84
— Footwear of leather	338.9	409.0	5.08	20.67	0.79	0.84
— Leather goods	361.6	378.9	4.59	4.79	0.84	0.78
— Leather garments	235.1	251.0	-31.05	6.77	0.55	0.51
— Leather footwear component	151.2	114.4	-24.98	-24.35	0.35	0.23
— Saddlery and harness	37.0	41.0	25.78	10.97	0.09	0.08
— Chemicals and related products	4371.4	4825.8	22.70	10.39	10.20	9.88
— Cosmetics/toiletries	236.8	253.7	8.40	7.13	0.55	0.52

(Contd.)

TABLE 2.3 (Contd.)

(1)	(2)	(3)	(4)	(5)	(6)	(7)
— Drugs, pharm. and fine chemicals	2173.4	2403.9	27.35	10.61	5.07	4.92
— Dyes, intermediates, etc.	597.6	783.4	27.32	31.09	1.39	1.60
— Inorg./org./agro-chemicals	846.0	888.6	27.81	5.04	1.97	1.82
— Paints/enamels/varnishes	200.1	203.3	5.33	1.60	0.47	0.42
— Residual chem. and allied product	317.6	292.9	0.41	-7.78	0.74	0.60
— Engineering goods	7239.1	9291.4	26.26	28.35	16.89	19.01
— Aluminium other than products	138.0	132.7	10.04	-3.84	0.32	0.27
— Electronic goods	1034.5	1322.4	3.79	27.82	2.41	2.71
— Ferro alloys	43.9	49.4	25.13	12.71	0.10	0.10
— Iron and steel bar/rods	192.9	239.7	43.82	24.28	0.45	0.49
— Machine tools	102.1	98.2	16.82	-3.83	0.24	0.20
— Machinery and instruments	1662.6	2079.4	15.66	25.07	3.88	4.26
— Manufactures of metals	1538.1	1816.2	14.12	18.08	3.59	3.72
— Non-ferrous metals	229.2	334.4	117.97	45.92	0.53	0.68
— Prim. & semi-fin. iron and steel	1216.5	1613.4	94.75	32.63	2.84	3.30
— Project goods	45.4	71.6	204.47	57.67	0.11	0.15
— Residual engineering items	25.0	39.7	-4.64	58.56	0.06	0.08
— Transport equipment	1010.9	1494.3	26.63	47.82	2.36	3.06

Textiles (Excl. RMG)	4932.6	484.8	12.60	-0.97	11.51	10.00
— Yarns, fabrics, madeups	4216.6	4145.0	12.60	-1.70	9.84	8.48
— Cotton yarn fab. madeups, etc.	2797.7	2472.3	8.47	-11.63	6.53	5.06
— Manmade yarn fab. madeups, etc.	1117.6	1332.0	25.93	19.19	2.61	2.73
— Natural silk yarn fab. madeups	259.1	295.7	10.45	14.14	0.60	0.61
— Woollen yarn fab. madeups, etc.	42.3	45.1	-2.90	6.57	0.10	0.09
— Jute mfg. excl. floor coverings	135.5	168.9	40.15	24.64	0.32	0.35
— Jute hessian	61.9	72.4	84.14	17.04	0.14	0.15
— Jute yarn	35.8	40.9	-9.26	14.34	0.08	0.08
— Other jute manufactures	37.8	55.5	60.06	46.83	0.09	0.11
— Carpets	460.8	439.5	3.13	-4.62	1.07	0.90
— Carpet handmade	348.6	419.1	6.30	20.22	0.81	0.86
— Carpet millmade	96.8		12.68		0.23	
— Silk carpets	15.4	20.4	-53.30	32.53	0.04	0.04
— Other textiles excl. RMG	119.7	131.4	29.46	9.77	0.28	0.27
— Coir and coir manufactures	60.5	61.9	14.37	2.32	0.14	0.13
— Floor covering of jute	21.1	23.2	63.54	10.02	0.05	0.05
— Manmade staple fibre	35.2	45.3	79.16	28.54	0.08	0.09
— Silk waste	2.9	1.0	-58.70	-64.87	0.01	-
— Readymade garments (RMG)	4596.3	4534.6	10.98	-1.34	10.72	9.28
— RMG of cotton incl. accessories	3539.8	3413.0	17.69	-3.58	8.26	6.98

(*Contd.*)

TABLE 2.3 (Contd.)

(1)	(2)	(3)	(4)	(5)	(6)	(7)
— RMG of manmade fibres	613.6	587.2	-8.30	-4.31	1.43	1.20
— RMG of silk	109.9	119.8	-14.22	8.94	0.26	0.25
— RMG of wool	196.1	234.9	-10.46	19.75	0.46	0.48
— RMG of other textile materials	136.2	179.8	16.57	31.48	0.32	0.37
— Other manufactured goods	10219.2	11144.7	27.10	9.06	23.84	22.81
— Computer software	33.8	35.8	88.25	5.89	0.08	0.07
— Footwear of rubber/canvas, etc.	23.9	55.7	11.85	132.71	0.06	0.11
— Gems and jewellery	7350.1	8113.0	26.53	10.38	17.14	16.60
— Glass/glassware/ceramics/cement	364.0	452.7	23.75	24.34	0.85	0.93
— Handicrafts excl. handmade carpets	633.6	329.8	35.44	-47.94	1.48	0.67
— Paper/wood products	337.6	430.1	28.60	27.40	0.79	0.88
— Plastic and linoleum products	1017.3	1199.8	25.37	17.95	2.37	2.46
— Rubber manufactured products	395.8	453.2	32.19	14.50	0.92	0.93
— Sports goods	63.0	74.6	11.09	18.43	0.15	0.15
— Petroleum and crude products	1927.7	2820.7	9.69	46.32	4.50	5.77
— Other commodities	789.4	2435.3	-23.37	208.52	1.84	4.98

Source : Centre for Monitoring Indian Economy, May 2004.

declining from an average of 16.6 per cent over the last ten years to 12.3 per cent during 02-03 (Graph 2.2).

GRAPH 2.2
Global Presence—Share of Major Commodities in Total Exports

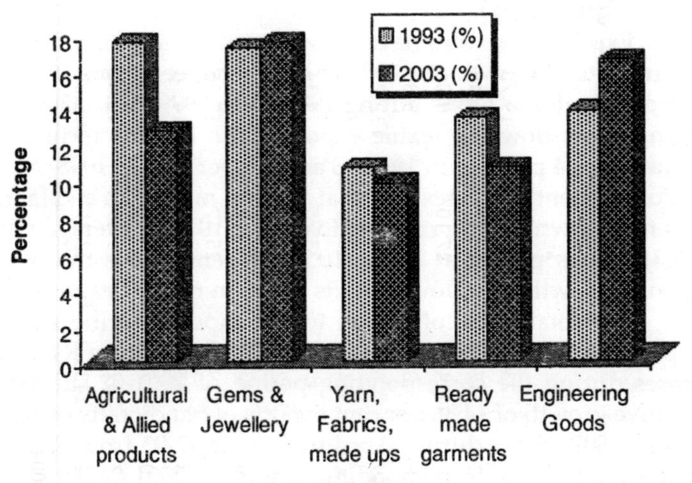

Source : CMIE.

2.3.2 Gems and Jewellery

Gems and Jewellery was and is a major export item accounting for about 17.53 per cent of our total exports during April to Nov. 2000. The exports of gems and jewellery during April to Nov. 2000 was valued at Rs. 22,462 crores as compared to Rs. 20,364 crores during the corresponding period of 1999, showing a positive growth rate of 10.3 per cent.

The exports of gems and jewellery during April to Sept. 2002-03 was valued at Rs. 21,687 crores as compared to Rs. 15,787 crores in 2001-02, showing a robust growth of 37.37 per cent.

Gems and Jewellery exports grew by 10.4 per cent to $ 8.1 billion during April-Jan. 2003-04. According to the gem and jewellery export data, nearly 80 per cent of exports is on account of cut and polished diamonds while plain gold jewellery contributes roughly 15 per cent to exports.[4]

Gems and jewellery accounts for 17 per cent of total goods exports. The compounded annual growth rate over the last 10 years or so is still a firmly double-digit growth at 11.9 per cent, higher than 11.6 per cent growth in total merchandise exports over the period (Graph 2.2).

2.3.3 Textiles (Yarn, Fabrics, Madeups, Readymade garments)

Exports of textiles have shown an increase at a compound annual rate of growth of 18.95 per cent in rupees terms and 10.96 per cent in dollar terms during 1992-93 to 1999-2000. There had been a slow down in textile exports, with exports recording a growth of 4.4 per cent in 1997-98 and 1.8 per cent in 1998-99. The major segment under textiles, that of yarn, made-ups and fabrics, has not shown much progress. Even at a 10 year average (1993-2003), it has grown at about 10.7 per cent below the overall exports growth, thus lowering its share in overall exports.

The total value of Indian textile exports during April to September, 2002-03 went up to Rs. 26,192 crores from Rs. 22,903 crores during the corresponding period of 2001-02 showing a positive growth of 14.36 per cent exports of handicrafts increased to Rs. 1,807 crores during April to Sept. 2002-03 from Rs. 1,323 crores during the corresponding period of 2001-02 showing a growth of 36.58 per cent.

The increase in exports of manmade yarn, fabrics, madeups was significant at 19 per cent during April-Jan. 2003-04.

Ready made garments accounts for approx. 42 per cent of the total textile exports of the country (2000-01). They represent value added and less import intensive sub-sector, thus deserving a special place. Total exports of ready made garments in 2003-04 is 2061.49 US $ million. Ready made garment segment grew at a ten year average growth of 9.4 per cent.

Share of textiles in exports of all commodities was 24.91 per cent (Chapter 50-63) in 2002-03 (April/Aug.) whereas in 2003-04 Apr./Aug. it is 20.97 per cent (*Source* : Texprocil/"India Trade, CMIE"/DGCI and S, Kolkata).

2.3.4 Engineering Goods

The main items of export under this group are manufactures of metals, machinery and instruments, primary and semi-finished iron and steel and transport equipment.

Exports of Engineering goods amounted to Rs. 16,241 crores during April to Sept. 2002-03 as against Rs. 12,976 crores during April-Sept., 2001-02 showing an impressive growth of 25.16 per cent.[5,6]

Engineering goods is a rapidly rising segment in Indian exports, accounting for 16 per cent of overall goods exports at present. Exports of all the major commodities falling under the engineering goods group performed well during April-January 2003-04 (9291.4 US $ million). Machinery and instruments grew by 25 per cent, manufactures of metals by 18 per cent, non-ferrous metals by 46 per cent, primary and semi-finished iron and steel by 33 per cent and transport equipment by 48 per cent. Also exports of electronic goods grew by 28 per cent in this period.

2.3.5 Petroleum and Crude Products

In April-March 1999-2000, the exports of petroleum and crude products were Rs. 129.91 crore. In the year 2000-01 it reached to Rs. 8,646 crore and to Rs. 10,107 crore in 2001-02.

Exports of petroleum and crude products were $ 2.8 billion against $ 1.9 billion in April, January 2002-03, an increase of 46.3 per cent.

2.3.6 Chemicals and Allied Products

All the four sub-groups under this head viz. Basic chemicals, pharmaceuticals and cosmetics, plastics and lenoleum, rubber, glass and other products and residual chemicals and allied products have registered over 20 per cent growth during April-Nov. 2000 as compared to April-Nov. 1999. Exports of chemicals and allied products registered a growth of 22.69% during April-Sept. 2002-03 over the same period of 2001-02 in rupee terms. Three out of the four sub-groups registered positive growth during April-Sept. 2002-03 as compared to the corresponding period of 2001-02, however residual, chemicals and allied products showed a negative export growth of 25.16 per cent and exports of this segment were 292.9 US $ million in 2002-04 as against 317.6 US $ million in 2002-03.

Tables 2.2 and 2.3 shows/depicts the trends in India's export of principal products/groups during the last few years. Graph 2.2 represents the share of major commodities in total exports in 2003 *vis-a-vis* 1993.

Tables 2.4 and 2.5 shows 15 major commodities ranked by export volume and export growth. Also 15 $\times$ 15 product country matrix of India's exports provides a glimpse of India's trade with 15 major countries in 15 major commodities (See Annexure 2.1)

2.4 PROJECT EXPORTS

Project exports have been one of the fastest growing export items in the list of Indian exports. From a little over Rs. 8,800 crore in financial year 2002, project exports have grown by over 17.2 per cent and registered earnings to the tune of Rs. 23,933 crore in fiscal 2003.

Project exports are broadly divided into three categories, namely civil engineering construction projects, industrial turnkey projects and consultancy services.

Construction contracts involve civil works as well as supply of associated equipment, erection and commisioning. The major difference between a turnkey and construction contract is that the former has a much larger component of machinery and equipment. Consultancy contracts involve deployment of personnel, furnishing of know-how and management skills.

Details of the value of contracts secured in respect of project exports during the last 6 years are shown in Table 2.6.

IRCON, Larsen and Toubro, Bharat Heavy electricals, Engineers India, KEC Punjab Lloyd and Jyoti structures are the major players dominating the project export scenario. A visible trend in project exports is the increasing profile of the private sector. L and T occupied the top slot in 2003-04 with export projects worth over Rs. 1,600 crores. In the recent past, IRCON has bagged a prestigeous contract for doubling of the Ipoh-Padang Besar railway line in Malaysia. The total value of projects secured by BHEL, KEC International and Voltas is around Rs. 4,200 crore. There are reason for this. The Indian construction industry is generally pretty fragmented. Only a handful of firms have the kind of strong finances required to take additional risks abroad.[7]

Major markets abroad include Kuwait, Iraq, Afghanistan, Qatar, Bahrain and Saudi Arabia in the middle-east, the SAARC countries in general, the Phillippines, Indonesia and Vietnam in

TABLE 2.4
15 Major Commodities Ranked by Export Volume

(*Values in Rs. Crores*)

Sl. No.	*Commodities*	*2001-02 (Apr.-Sept.)*	*2002-03 (Apr.-Sept.)*	*% share in total exports* 2002-03 (Apr.-Sept.)	*% share in total exports* 2002-03 (Apr.-Sept.)
	(1)	(2)	(3)	(4)	(5)
1.	Gems and Jewellery	15793.16	21687.30	15.99	17.73
2.	RMG Cotton incl. accessories	8237.40	10303.67	8.34	8.42
3.	Cotton yarn, fabrics, madeups, etc.	7450.20	8085.74	7.54	6.61
4.	Petroleum crude and products	4662.77	6119.33	4.72	5.00
5.	Drugs, pharmaceuticals and fine chemicals	4523.78	5727.02	4.58	4.68
6.	Machinery and instruments	3877.66	4528.02	3.93	3.70
7.	Other commodities	2308.09	4361.04	2.34	3.57
8.	Manufactures of metals	3687.73	4208.20	3.73	3.44
9.	Marine products	2997.69	3187.43	3.03	2.61
10.	Manmade yarn, fabrics, madeups	2482.03	3169.85	2.51	2.59
11.	Transport equipments	2199.54	2903.17	2.23	2.37
12.	Plastic and Linoleum products	2406.62	2809.80	2.44	2.30
13.	Electronic goods	2799.19	2788.39	2.83	2.28
14.	Primary and Semi-finished iron and steel	1737.99	2645.15	1.76	2.16
15.	Inorganic/organic/agro-chemicals	1788.04	2335.95	1.81	1.91
	Total of 15 commodities	66951.91	84860.06	67.77	69.38
	Total of all commodities	98787.90	122310.25	100.00	100.00

Source : Nabhi's Exporter's Manual, Nabhi Publication, 2004.

TABLE 2.5
15 Major Commodities Ranked by Export Growth

(Value in Rs. Crores)

S. No.	Commodities	2001-02 (Apr.-Sept.)	2002-03 (Apr.-Sept.)	% Growth
1.	Other commodities	2308.09	4361.04	88.95
2.	Primary and semi-finished iron and steel	1737.99	2645.15	52.20
3.	Gem and Jewellery	15793.16	21687.30	37.32
4.	Transport equipments	2199.54	2903.17	31.99
5.	Petroleum crude and products	4662.77	6119.33	31.24
6.	Inorganic/organic/agro-chemicals	1788.04	2335.95	30.64
7.	Manmade yarn, fabrics, madeups	2482.03	3169.85	27.71
8.	Drugs, Pharmaceuticals and fine chemicals	4523.78	5727.02	26.60
9.	RMG cotton incl. accessories	8237.39	10303.67	25.08
10.	Machinery and instruments	3877.66	4528.02	16.77
11.	Plastic and Linoleum products	2406.62	2809.80	16.75
12.	Manufactures of metals	3687.73	4208.20	14.11
13.	Cotton yarn, fabrics, madeups, etc.	7450.23	8085.74	8.53
14.	Marine products	2997.69	3187.43	6.33
15.	Electronic goods	2799.19	2788.39	0.39
	Total of 15 commodities	66951.91	84860.06	26.75
	Total of all commodities	98787.90	122310.25	23.81

Source : Nabhi's Exporter's Manual, Nabhi Publication, 2004.

TABLE 2.6
Project Exports

(Value in Rs. Crore)

	1995-96	1996-97	1997-98	1998-99	1999-00	2000-01	2001-02
Civil Construction*	312	338	431	1493	1539	1225	1544
Turkey**	712	861	1240	1760	1731	1535	3051
Consultancy Services***	1800	2000	2700	3000	3644	4241	4303
Total	2,824	3,199	4,371	6,353	6,914	7,001	8,898

Source : * Overseas construction council of India.
** Exim Bank of India.
*** Federation of Indian Export Organization.
— Nabhi Publication, 2004.

the Asian region; South Africa, Turkey, Sudan and Tanzania in Africa and some CIS countries.

'Project exports' is an indicator of the technological advancement and industrial capabilities of a country. Given the huge market, it has great potential of earning precious foreign exchange but adequate international exposure is necessary to bag more high value contracts.

2.5 SERVICE EXPORTS

If there is any sector that does India proud consistently, it has to be services. Not only it is the highest growing sector in the domestic economy, but it also has a stellar exports story to tell. In 1993-2003, India's services export grew at a compounded annual growth rate (CAGR) of as much as 17.3 per cent which for once is even higher than China's growth rate of 15 per cent.

Technological advancements in the IT and related fields have considerably enlarged the scope for global service trade. It has not only lowered the cost of service transactions through utilising newer medium of transportation like satellite links but also reduced the direct contact between sellers and buyers. Further, the advancements have created scope for trade in many newer services like medical transcriptions, e-commerce, business process outsourcing (BPO) along with financial services, entertainment and tourism.

India's service exports are found to have grown at an impressive pace since the mid-eighties as evident from the following indicators:[8]

— A huge jump in total exports of services from $ 5 bn. in 1993 to $ 25 billion in the year 2003.

— Its share in current account transactions exceeded 20 per cent level as against 18.8 per cent in the second half of eighties.

— The country's share in global service trade has already exceeded 1%, 14% in 2001.

With rise in share of world service exports over the decade, India is on the list of the top 20 services exporters in the world.

For the year 2003 Indian exports of services was $ 25 billion as compared to $ 5 billion in 1993.[9]

India's service exports are found to have grown at an impressive pace since the mid-eighties. With software development, increasing out sourcing of back office processes (Business Process Outsourcing) and call centre operations by US and European firms, exports of Indian services have been rising at a very rapid rate. According to the latest world Investment Report 2004, published by UNCTAD, while exports of software continue to dominate the share of services exports, the share of information technology (IT), enabled services (ITES) has also grown significantly from $ .6 billion in 1999-2000 to $ 3.6 billion in 2003-04.

The trends in the export of the services are presented in Table 2.7 for the year 1997-98 to 1999-2000. A study of these

TABLE 2.7
Exports of Services

(Value in billion dollars)

Services	*1997-98*	*1998-99*	*1999-2000*
A. Software services (computer software and services, Telecom and project Exports and Video film software)	2.57	3.81	4.99
B. Other Services			
(i) Travel	2.91	2.99	3.04
(ii) Transportation	1.84	1.92	1.74
(iii) Insurance	0.24	0.22	0.24
(iv) Govt. services (a)	0.28	0.59	0.58
(v) Communication	0.17	0.60	1.06
(vi) Construction	0.10	0.15	0.39
(vii) Financial	0.29	0.28	0.36
(viii) Management	0.55	0.59	0.64
(ix) Misc. (b)	1.27	3.19	3.65
Total (B)	7.65	10.53	11.70
Total Services (A+B)	10.22	14.34	16.69

Notes : (a) Not elsewhere classified.
(b) Includes advertising, royalties, newsagency services, etc.
(i) *Economic Survey*, 2000-01 (Govt. of India).
(ii) Data from Issues of *RBI Bulletin*.

Source : P.K. Khurana, Export Management, 2001, Galgotia Publishing Company.

trends reveal that India's export of services has touched the record level of USD 16.69 billion in 1999-2000 as against of USD 2.55 billion in 1990-91.

2.5.1 Software Exports

India's share in the world software and services market has increased to 2.4 per cent in 2003-04 and compared to 2.09 per cent in 2002-03 and 1.82 per cent in 2001-02. Software has been identified as a thrust area by Government of India both for exports as well as in the domestic sector.

According to the estimates of the National Commission of software and service companies (NASSCOM) exports of software and services rose to $ 12 Bn. or Rs. 55,510 crore in 2003-04 (Table 2.8). Nasscom estimates show that the export intensity (ratio of exports to total sales) of the Indian software and service industry has risen from 58 per cent to 78 per cent between 1996 and 2004. During the 1990, exports grew and the growth in demand peaked in 1999 and 2000, when IT firms grew at an exorbitant rate of 50 per cent. From 33 per cent in 2000-01, the share of software services in total exports of services has slowly crept up and now stands at 44 per cent. However, the growth of IT exports has fallen they account for 21 per cent of the total exports.[10]

TABLE 2.8
Exports of Software and Services

Year	*Value (Rs. Crore)*	*Share in India's Exports (%)*
2003-04	55,510	19.0
2002-03	46,100	18.0
2001-02	36,500	17.0
2000-01	28,350	13.8
1999-00	17,150	10.6
1998-99	10,940	7.6
1997-98	6,530	4.9
1996-97	3,900	3.2

Source : Economic Times, 1 Oct. 2004.

The rise in exports of software and services is also because of diversification into other markets like Japan and East Asian nations. According to Electronics and computer software export promotion council (EPC) India exported software and services worth Rs. 3,110 crore in 2003-04 against Rs. 2,065 crore in 2002-03 to Japan and other East Asian nations. Export picked up from 51 crore in 2002-03 to Rs. 71 crore in 2003-04 to Latin America and same was with US and Canada, despite campaign in US against BPO, an absolute growth of 21 per cent, i.e. Rs. 35,777 in 2003-04 from Rs. 29,658 crore in 2002-03 was recorded. Currently US and UK account for more than 80 per cent of the country's exports of software and ITES. Therefore, India is constantly looking to diversity its exports of services in an attempt to de-risk itself. One major problem area for service sector is the lack of sufficiently disaggregated data.

2.6 EXPORTS EXPECTATION OF INDUSTRY

A strong global economic recovery has ensured that Indian firms can be buoyant about their prospects for exports.[11] Manufacturers of consumers non-durables and capital goods seem far more confident as compared to services providers and Intermediate goods industries. Over 60 per cent companies expect their exports to rise (Table 2.9).

TABLE 2.9

Assessment of Exports in the Next 6 Months

(% of respondents)

Sector	Will Increase			No Change	Will Decrease
	0-5%	6-10%	>10%		
1. Consumer durables	39.0	11.9	13.6	32.2	3.4
2. Consumer non-durables	30.8	19.2	26.9	21.2	1.9
3. Intermediates	24.7	18.7	13.3	37.3	6.0
4. Capital goods	30.3	19.7	18.4	25.0	6.6
5. Services	28.6	26.2	9.5	31.0	4.8
6. All sectors	29.3	18.7	15.8	31.1	5.0

Source : ET-NCAER Business Confidence Index (BCI) Survey (June and July, 2004). Results based on 582 responses.

2.7 INDIAN EXPORTS BY REGION

Trade data for April-Oct. 2004 revealed increase in exports to all major trade destinations. While the European union accounted for 22 per cent of the country's exports, the US had 17.4 per cent. The growth in exports to these two destinations were placed at 22.7 per cent and 24 per cent respectively and exports to China expanded at even faster pace of 71.9 per cent in April-Oct. 2004.[12] US is India's biggest importer however the share of US in India's total exports has declined from 21.2 per cent during April-Nov. 2002 to 19.1 per cent during April-Nov. 2003 (and again rose in April-Oct. 2004).

India needs to push up export growth to maintain its high GDP growth. Over dependence on any one market can cost us dearly, therefore newer export destinations must be explored with more than one fifth share in India's total export, the US remains our biggest export destination. And the exploration of newer markets so far has remained limited to increasing exports to our immediate neighbours only. India's exports to Asian countries, excluding Middle East countries has increased by 15 per cent during April-Nov. 2003 (Table 2.10) and that with Hong-Kong and China has prospered immensely.[13]

The major trading partner in 2003-04 was USA, contributing 11.6 per cent share in total trade (exports and imports), in 2004-05 (April-Oct.) was also USA, contributing 11.1 per cent share and next was UK contributing 3.7 per cent share in total trade. Exploration of new markets, focusing on developed European countries to retain its share (viz. UK, Germany, France, Denmark and Italy) is necessary to push up Indian export growth.

2.8 IMPORT INTENSITY OF EXPORTS

The import intensity of exports has steadily declined in recent years. The import intensity of exports (measured as number of times exports measured as number of times imports as percentage of sales over exports as percentage of sales) has declined from 2.27 times in 1995-96 to 1.61 in 2002-03 (CMIE). Table 2.11 shows the import intensity of exports (times) from 1996-97 to 2002-03 for major industry groups. To study the

Table 2.10
India's Exports by Countries : April-January

			US $ million		*% change*		*% Share in total*	
	Apr.-Nov. 2001	*Apr.-Nov. 2002*	*2002-03*	*2003-04*	*2002-03*	*2003-04*	*2002-03*	*2003-04*
(1)	*(2)*	*(3)*	*(4)*	*(5)*	*(6)*	*(7)*	*(8)*	*(9)*
World	34296.1	28540.8	42872.6	48867.8	18.78	13.98	100.00	100.00
Africa	1980.9	2059.6	2578.7	2935.0	5.7	13.82	6.01	6.01
— Egypt	377.8	198.1	238.9	279.4	-43.12	16.93	0.56	0.57
— Kenya	106.4	132.6	165.9	167.7	23.65	1.08	0.39	0.34
— Mauritius	120.4	114.2	143.1	151.9	-0.40	6.15	0.33	0.31
— Nigeria	370.6	288.5	362.7	451.8	-21.40	24.57	0.85	0.92
— South Africa	236.9	326.4	409.4	389.3	41.13	-4.90	0.95	0.80
America	6612.8	8633.2	10752.8	10510.9	28.67	-2.25	25.08	21.51
— Brazil	145.5	290.3	343.1	227.8	89.75	-34.18	0.81	0.47
— Canada	375.1	466.8	574.2	603.0	17.80	5.03	1.34	1.23
— Mexico	153.5	182.8	225.2	196.4	14.20	-12.76	0.53	0.40
— USA	5548.0	7270.1	9095.0	8957.3	29.79	-1.51	21.21	18.33
Asia (Excl. Middle-East)	7366.4	7821.6	12311.4	15065.3	31.86	22.37	28.72	30.83
— Bangladesh	685.8	687.2	833.4	1288.6	5.30	54.62	1.94	2.64

(Contd.)

TABLE 2.10 (Contd.)

(1)	(2)	(3)	(4)	(5)	(6)	(7)	(8)	(9)
— China	594.3	1079.8	1483.5	2190.4	95.78	47.65	3.46	4.48
— Hong Kong	1521.2	1631.4	2007.3	2499.8	4.25	24.53	4.68	5.12
— Indonesia	327.8	524.8	661.0	900.6	55.59	36.25	1.54	1.84
— Japan	1025.4	1296.1	1583.1	1367.4	24.73	-13.62	3.69	2.80
— Korea DPR (North)	0.00	118.2	158.4	115.7	15.62	-26.95	0.37	0.24
— Korea Republic (South)	285.3	421.0	549.3	559.7	4322	1.90	1.28	1.15
— Malaysia	512.4	521.6	637.1	695.8	-5.12	9.22	1.49	1.42
— Nepal	143.5	183.2	238.9	537.7	36.10	125.04	0.56	1.10
— Philippines	149.6	371.0	425.3	258.8	110.38	-39.16	0.99	0.53
— Singapore	610.5	980.8	1193.8	1656.9	50.86	38.80	2.78	3.39
— Sri Lanka	369.2	588.9	733.1	1015.1	43.53	38.47	1.71	2.08
— Taiwan (Taipei)	230.1	365.5	462.4	417.9	54.07	-9.64	1.08	0.86
— Thailand	398.5	498.7	606.7	611.7	20.20	0.82	1.42	1.25
— Vietnam	124.3	185.3	266.2	330.3	60.00	24.08	0.62	0.68
Middle-East	3226.3	4423.7	5518.4	7067.0	34.62	28.06	12.87	14.46
— Iran	148.2	365.0	489.7	729.1	142.13	48.89	1.14	1.49
— Iraq	107.5	170.9	195.4	51.5	29.69	-73.62	0.46	0.11
— Israel	252.8	416.6	490.5	569.2	47.08	16.04	1.14	1.16

— Kuwait	137.9	143.8	190.1	236.3	9.96	24.28	0.44	0.48
— Saudi Arabia	540.0	615.0	771.9	839.8	16.05	8.79	1.80	1.72
— UAE	1619.8	2190.7	2718.4	3776.7	32.81	38.93	6.34	7.73
Europe	7620.7	8754.2	11004.3	12660.6	13.41	15.05	25.67	25.91
— European Union	63910.0	7414.5	9350.2	10640.0	15.07	13.79	21.81	21.77
— Belgium	871.2	1101.8	1349.4	1370.2	19.36	1.54	3.15	2.80
— Denmark	97.3	112.0	144.6	174.0	15.17	20.32	0.34	0.36
— France	611.3	666.7	863.7	971.8	9.56	12.52	2.01	1.99
— Germany	1138.9	1345.3	1699.9	1940.7	17.38	14.16	3.97	3.9
— Italy	792.5	846.1	1095.4	1308.7	9.06	19.47	2.56	2.68
— Netherlands	556.0	653.8	838.6	995.9	18.04	18.76	1.96	2.04
— Spain	444.5	505.5	657.2	780.3	16.29	18.72	1.53	1.60
— Sweden	102.9	108.2	139.4	167.2	5.60	19.95	0.33	0.34
— UK	1453.7	1676.3	2067.3	2351.5	14.45	13.75	4.82	4.81
— Other European Countries	1229.8	1339.7	1654.1	2020.6	4.83	22.16	3.86	4.13
— Russia	527.2	490.9	598.5	573.5	-13.22	-4.18	1.40	1.17
— Switzerland	270.6	231.4	292.8	375.2	13.80	28.16	0.68	0.77
— Turkey	129.7	247.1	311.4	401.4	81.73	28.92	0.73	0.82
Oceania	338.0	408.8	507.4	572.4	19.88	12.81	1.18	1.17
— Australia	277.0	336.5	418.7	468.0	19.49	11.78	0.98	0.96

Source : *CMIE*, May 2004 and *The Economic Times*, 15 March, 2004.

GRAPH 2.3
India's Major Trading Partners (2002-05)

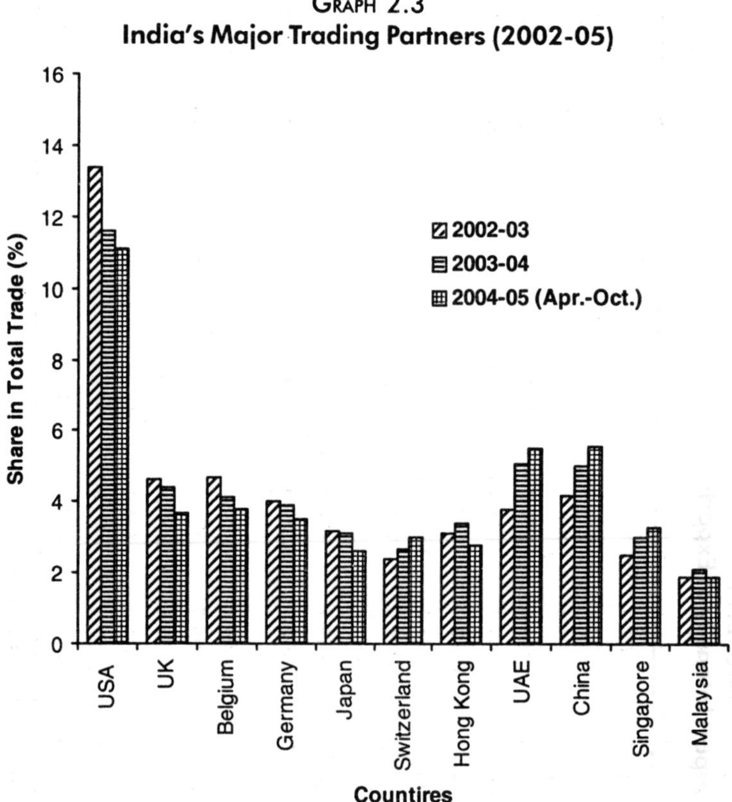

Source : *Economic Survey*, 2004-05.

economic impact it is necessary to discuss the trend of import intensity of exports. As rupee has been appreciating from last year (2002-03), the situations seems to be more complex. The immediate impact of appreciation of rupee is on exports. The exports of goods with low impact content will suffer the most. Indian companies seem to suffer heavily from rupee appreciation as import intensity of exports is declining in recent years. The share of exports in sales has increased by 4 per cent points from 8.5% in 1996-97 to 12.1 per cent in 2002-03. The share of imports in sales has nearly stagnated at around 20 per cent up by only 0.7 per cent points from 19.4 per cent to 20.1 per cent during this period.

TABLE 2.11
Import Intensity of Exports

Industry Groups	*Import Intensity of Exports (Items)*						
	1996-97	*1997-98*	*1998-99*	*1999-00*	*2000-01*	*2001-02*	*2002-03*
(1)	*(2)*	*(3)*	*(4)*	*(5)*	*(6)*	*(7)*	*(8)*
Food Products	0.45	0.52	0.67	0.63	0.62	0.62	0.82
— Tea and coffee	0.17	0.16	0.20	0.25	0.24	0.18	0.15
— Sugar	0.63	0.67	0.87	1.19	0.16	0.12	0.17
— Veg. oil and products	1.00	1.19	2.04	1.69	1.91	2.55	4.14
Beverages and Tobacco	0.89	0.38	0.74	0.58	0.59	0.57	0.43
— Tobacco products	0.64	0.32	0.73	0.55	0.57	0.56	0.40
— Beer and alcohol	2.25	1.35	0.80	0.79	0.52	0.63	1.61
Textiles	0.51	0.49	0.41	0.39	0.38	0.46	0.41
— Cotton textiles	0.28	0.34	0.33	0.31	0.31	0.40	0.32
— Synthetics textiles	2.00	1.55	1.11	0.86	0.86	1.07	0.97
— Textile processing	0.42	0.34	0.48	0.55	0.50	0.44	0.45
Chemicals	5.16	4.78	4.51	6.01	4.81	3.80	3.74
— Alkalies	1.16	2.26	1.06	1.86	1.27	1.68	0.98

(Contd.)

TABLE 2.11 (Contd.)

(1)	(2)	(3)	(4)	(5)	(6)	(7)	(8)
— Fertilisers	28.13	33.64	36.15	22.98	21.59	20.50	17.34
— Paints and varnishes	12.09	16.46	4.74	3.36	1.94	7.58	6.11
— Drugs and Pharma	0.88	0.86	0.82	0.74	0.73	0.59	0.60
— Soaps and detergents	3.04	3.70	6.29	4.19	2.44	1.89	2.10
— Polymers	3.56	3.08	3.65	3.33	2.59	2.67	2.01
— Plastic products	1.26	1.12	0.86	0.76	0.73	0.76	0.67
— Petroleum products	14.57	16.09	19.24	29.21	9.90	13.62	10.62
— Tyres and tubes	1.22	1.16	1.15	1.34	1.37	1.18	0.99
Non-metallic Mineral Products	1.02	0.94	0.84	0.95	0.93	0.83	0.81
— Cement	1.35	1.32	1.66	2.07	2.13	1.31	0.86
Ferrous Metals	1.70	1.44	1.48	1.12	1.26	1.23	0.86
— Pig and sponge iron	7.12	5.28	5.94	6.29	5.98	5.11	5.79
— Steel	1.97	1.66	1.90	1.36	1.43	1.63	0.85
— Castings and forgings	0.39	0.32	0.20	0.29	0.30	0.34	0.27
— Metal products	0.85	0.74	0.78	0.59	0.79	0.60	0.76
Non-ferrous Products	1.60	1.26	1.75	1.52	1.21	1.26	1.12
— Aluminium and products	0.67	0.47	0.53	0.46	0.40	0.47	0.91

Machinery	2.15	1.55	1.30	1.10	0.92	0.84	0.83
— Non-electrical machinery	2.34	1.65	2.02	1.63	1.65	0.83	0.89
— Industrial machinery	1.71	1.15	1.14	1.04	1.01	0.71	0.67
— Electrical machinery	2.01	1.56	1.45	1.67	1.46	1.32	1.30
— Wires and cables	6.36	2.06	2.88	3.88	2.53	3.14	2.03
— Domestic Elect. appliances	1.51	1.20	2.51	2.34	3.24	1.55	0.97
— Air condi. refri.	6.48	5.96	4.27	5.40	5.13	3.38	2.51
— Electronics	2.12	1.51	1.10	0.93	0.78	0.79	0.78
— Consumer electronics	2.20	3.65	4.73	4.10	6.65	5.23	4.75
— Computer soft/hardware	0.94	0.78	0.62	0.60	0.54	0.54	0.56
Automobile	3.42	2.54	3.12	3.44	2.83	2.40	1.72
— Commercial vehicles	1.23	1.12	1.21	0.78	0.61	0.58	0.73
— Passenger cars, MUV	4.92	3.50	3.57	5.32	4.68	5.07	2.66
— Two/three wheelers	1.90	1.91	2.22	2.85	3.17	2.89	1.57
Automobile Ancillaries	1.72	1.44	1.43	1.52	1.46	1.19	1.04
Mics. Manufacturing	1.17	1.41	1.13	1.30	1.49	1.50	1.37
— Paper and paper products	2.55	3.33	3.70	2.41	2.75	1.86	1.64
— Leather products	0.28	0.27	0.29	0.37	0.30	026	0.28
Diversified	2.02	2.18	1.97	1.54	0.99	1.99	2.31
Manufacturing	2.27	2.01	1.88	2.08	1.85	1.61	1.66

Source : Trends, *The Economic Times*, 18 April, 2004.

The worst affected will be the textile (0.41) food products and the non-metallic mineral products industries, each of which has less than *'one'* import intensity of exports. The opening up of food products industry to global players has increased its import intensity of exports during this period but it was still low at 0.83 times. However, the hardening of rupee against the dollar has helped Indian refinaries take advantage of the global volatility in crude and petroleum products to register a 40 per cent growth in exports.[14]

2.9 EXPORT ROAD MAP

— India's merchandise exports to $ 73.4 Billion at the end of March 2005.[15]

— Exports would reach a level of $ 150 Billion in 2009-10.

— Government is banking on a 10 per cent growth in chemicals during the fiscal.

— Textile Ministry has increased projection for 2004-05 to double digit growth levels since all export quotas are to be phased out from January 2005. The Government aims to increase the value of textile and apparel exports to US $ 50 Billion by 2010.

— For Petroleum products, exports are estimated to grow 50 per cent during the current fiscal.

— Gems and Jewellery EPC and the council for leather exports are projecting growth rates of around 10 per cent.

— Engineering Export promotion council has forecast a 20% growth to $ 12 billion. In case of capital goods the EPC is targetting a growth of 22 per cent. Consumer goods exports are also projected to rise 19-20% to around $ 2.5 billion.

In conclusion, to achieve the target of exports of worth $ 150 Bn. by 2009-10 and to cross $ 70 Bn. mark in 2004-05, there is continuous need for India to move up the value added ladder and improve the attractiveness of its locational advantages, developing high quality infrastructure, giving due consideration on exploration of new markets and strengthening corporate strategies and working out more sophisticated and comprehensive policy approaches and working strongly on export promotions[16] gives the potential of improved export competitiveness for promoting development the need for India to preserve sufficient policy space to pursue its development objectives also has to be recognised which will be discussed in the next chapter.

Notes and References

1. 'Government sets export growth target at 16 percent', Economic Bureau, *Business Standard,* 2 July, 2004.
2. A change in the system of collecting data partly accounted for this high growth in March. In addition to the good performance of exports, the high growth in march was due to the efforts to streamline data collection and a change in the method of reporting data by customs. The reporting system is now based on 'Let Export Order' instead of 'Export General Manifest'; seven more days in the month of March were taken into account (till 31st instead of 23rd of March).
3. *Monthly Review of the Indian Economy,* May, 2004, CMIE, Mumbai.
4. Padmapriya, J., 'It's the shine of gold within and glitter of rocks outside India', *The Economic Times,* 5 Aprilm, 2004.
   Exports of diamonds have reached high scale over the last 40 years. From just 13 million $ in 1966-67 diamond exports reached $ 2,500 million in 1991-92 and to $ 7100 million in 2002-03. On the other hand, Gold jewellery exports was quite insignificant till the 90s and has only now picked up momentum. The exports of gold was $ 1,512 million in 2002-03.
5. Nabhi's Exporter's Manual and Documentation, Nabhi Publication, 2002.
6. Nabhi's Exporter's Manual and Documentation, Nabhi Publication, 2004.
7. Bhandhari, Amit, 'Private firms lead in project exports', *The Economic Times,* New Delhi, 21 April, 2004.
8. A recent study by Boston consulting Group has estimated that service exports from India may reach $ 140 Bn. to $ 365 Bn. by 2020. It has further pointed out that by that time India would be the only major country with a surplus workforce, *The Economic Times,* New Delhi, 29 April, 2003.
9. Prem Singh, Manika, 'Service Sector Exports : Here India beats top dogs hollow', *The Economic Times,* New Delhi, 13 August, 2004.
10. Chaudhuri, Arjun Ray, and Reena Chaudhari, 'HiTech Redeemer', *The Economic Times,* New Delhi, 1 October, 2004, page 7.
11. Based on the ET-NCAER Business Confidence Index (BCI) Survey carried out in the months of June and July 2004. The results are based on 582 responses.
12. 'Exports up 24 per cent in April-Oct.', *The Economic Times,* New Delhi, 17 Nov., 2003.

13. Mahanti, Tushar K., 'Exports to US decline, Asian neighbours help India achieve target', *The Economic Times*, New Delhi, 15 March, 2004.
14. Rupee Appreciation : Winsome Loses one, commodity Inc. was hard put to match import party, price but petro exports were fuelled by 40 per cent, *The Economic Times*, New Delhi, 6 April, 2004.
15. Chaudhuri, Arjun Ray, 'On the Runway', *The Economic Times*, New Delhi, 5 March, 2004.
16. Mehta, Pradeep Kumar, 'The Exim Policy 2003-04, Tool for promoting exports', *Foreign Trade Review*, Vol. 37, Nos. 3 and 4, Oct. 2002-March, 2003, IIFT, New Delhi.

Annexure 2.1

India's First 15 Product Groups and First 15 Countries Matrix of Exports: Apr.-Sept., 2002-03

(Value in US $ million)

S. No.	First 15 product Groups of Total Exports April-Sept. (2002-03)	USA	UAE	UK	Hong Kong	German F. Rep.	Japan	Singapore	Belgium	Unspecified
(1)	(2)	(3)	(4)	(5)	(6)	(7)	(8)	(9)	(10)	(11)
1.	Gems and Jewellery	1476.09	268.03	87.43	598.26	19.05	212.27	158.24	470.30	661.65
2.	RMG Cotton Incl. Accessories	667.92	139.90	194.95	2.04	188.28	30.90	13.71	28.97	1.78
3.	Cotton Yarn, Fabrics, Madeups, etc.	304.80	45.40	81.32	56.05	71.53	55.12	9.57	30.17	1.41
4.	Petroleum Crude and Products	89.54	243.37	13.56	0.00	0.01	44.59	216.30	0.09	16.25
5.	Drugs, Pharmcutes and Fine Chems.	179.09	14.78	37.10	32.54	70.64	17.64	23.59	7.30	16.20
6.	Machinery and Instruments	124.15	67.79	49.68	7.12	72.07	19.39	31.95	9.56	1.75
7.	Other Commodities	155.28	72.84	43.63	13.07	48.37	22.44	48.08	23.07	8.29
8.	Manufactures of Metals	200.63	95.88	84.59	9.49	28.23	6.03	24.65	8.11	0.74

(Contd.)

ANNEXURE 2.1 (Contd.)

(1)	(2)	(3)	(4)	(5)	(6)	(7)	(8)	(9)	(10)	(11)
9.	Marine Products	205.52	17.87	32.98	6.12	6.12	184.82	8.05	17.70	0.74
10.	Manmade Yarn, Fabrics, Madeups	30.08	122.79	30.72	2.28	6.66	4.48	25.99	17.81	1.61
11.	Transport Equipments	80.40	12.33	29.19	1.02	25.18	2.15	5.18	1.80	0.28
12.	Plastic and Linoleum products	65.30	35.85	24.27	26.77	14.83	1.83	7.33	9.47	0.32
13.	Electronic Goods	134.57	30.62	33.91	45.25	31.71	21.53	54.19	2.26	6.71
14.	Primary and Semi-Finished Iron and Steel	108.85	32.99	1.43	14.50	2.17	4.76	4.57	7.60	2.15
15.	Inorganic/Organic/ Agro-Chemical	38.67	20.27	16.71	4.15	13.36	9.62	12.85	11.03	0.91
	Export product groups to destination country	3860.91	1220.7	761.48	818.67	598.20	637.57	644.25	645.25	720.81
	#	74.03	77.68	61.81	82.54	60.46	66.59	79.54	83.41	98.07

(Contd.)

ANNEXURE 2.1 (Contd.)

(Value in US$ million)

Sl. No	First 15 product Groups of Total Exports Apr.-Sept. (2002-03)	China PR	Italy	France	Nether land	Bangla-desh	Saudi Arabia	Sub-Total of Exports to 15 countries	Total export of the Product Gp	% Share of Product in India's Total Exports
(1)	(2)	(12)	(13)	(14)	(15)	(16)	(17)	(18)	(19)	(20)
1.	Gems and Jewellery	0.21	15.72	11.30	4.54	0.31	1.53	3984.95	4446.09	17.73
2.	RMG Cotton Incl. Accessories	0.13	61.59	125.27	89.81	0.47	39.36	1585.10	2112.34	8.42
3.	Cotton Yarn, Fabrics, Madeups, etc.	31.90	76.06	28.76	18.59	79.79	8.52	899.00	1657.65	6.61
4.	Petroleum Crude and Products	3.29	0.06	9.40	0.00	1.97	9.66	648.08	1254.56	5.00
5.	Drugs, Pharmcutes and Fine Chems.	40.09	15.76	12.05	21.72	16.57	5.96	511.05	1174.09	4.68
6.	Machinery and Instruments	13.56	19.20	17.40	16.10	19.77	19.99	489.47	928.28	3.70
7.	Other Commodities	18.75	16.68	21.60	17.15	10.58	25.71	545.55	894.05	3.57
8.	Manufactures of Metals	16.33	17.24	10.05	9.04	10.24	20.85	542.10	862.72	3.44

(Contd.)

Annexure 2.1 (Contd.)

(1)	(2)	(12)	(13)	(14)	(15)	(16)	(17)	(18)	(19)	(20)
9.	Marine Products	25.40	11.09	6.07	5.60	0.10	0.50	528.69	653.46	2.61
10.	Manmade Yarn, Fabrics, Madeups	2.29	26.64	10.65	1.78	12.80	37.91	334.49	649.85	2.59
11.	Transport Equipments	2.57	26.45	16.09	26.55	33.35	3.60	266.13	594.97	2.37
12.	Plastic and Linoleum products	62.61	18.87	7.19	12.35	14.51	12.99	314.50	576.03	2.3
13.	Electronic Goods	11.15	5.14	8.73	38.10	12.21	4.04	440.12	571.65	2.28
14.	Primary and Semi-Finished Iron and Steel	82.88	14.62	1.92	4.27	16.94	18.35	317.98	542.28	2.16
15.	Inorganic/Organic/ Agro-Chemical	43.34	22.65	15.01	20.97	7.47	11.20	248.21	478.89	1.91
	Export product groups to destination country	354.49	347.76	301.49	286.58	237.07	220.18	11655.42	17396.00	
	#	51.70	54.82	60.52	59.69	51.38	48.74			

Note : Exchange rate 1 US$ = 48.7784 Rs.
Percentage share of 15 product groups in total exports to destination.

Source : Exporter's manual, Nabhi Publication, 2004.

3

The Exim Policy (2002-07)

Trade policy governs exports from and imports into the country. It is one of the various policy instruments used by countries to attain the goal of economic development. The role of trade policy as a tool of economic development has attained considerable significance in India, specially in the post-reform periods. This has happened because the economy has witnessed a tremendous upsurge in the wake of globalization and driven by a fiercely competitive market system. This chapter examines (at length) the basic framework of five year trade policy (2002-07). For a better synergy between development and trade policies, its tenure is extended to five years and made co-terminus with the development plan of the country. Two long-term trade policies (1992-97) and (1997-2002) have completed their tenure and the third one is currently in operation (2002-07). This is in contrast to the fact that two of the three earlier trade policies each for the duration of three years, during 1985-92, were terminated prematurely for one reason or another.[1]

3.1 EXIM POLICY, 2002-07—AN INTRODUCTION

In exercise of the powers conferred under section 5 of the Foreign Trade (Development and Regulation Act), 1992 (No. 22 of

1992). Exim Policy (2002-07) came into force with effect from 1st April, 2002 and shall remain into force upto 31st March, 2007, co-terminus with the tenth five year plan (2002-07). The principal objectives of this policy are:

(i) To facilitate sustained growth in exports to attain a share of atleast 1 per cent of global merchandise trade.
(ii) To stimulate sustained economic growth by providing access to essential raw materials, intermediates, components, consumables and capital goods required for augmenting production and providing services.
(iii) To enhance the technological strength and efficiency of Indian agriculture, industry and services, thereby improving their competitive strength while generating new employment opportunities, and to encourage the attainment of internationally accepted standards of quality.
(iv) To provide consumers with good quality goods and services at internationally competitive prices while at the same time creating a level of playing field for the domestic producers.
(v) The objectives will be met through the co-ordinated efforts of the State Governments and all the departments of the Government of India in general and the Ministry of Commerce and Industry and the Directorate General of Foreign Trade and its network of regional offices in particular, with a shared vision and commitment and in the best spirit of facilitation, in the interest of promotion of trade in goods and services.[2]

3.2 MAIN FEATURES OF EXIM POLICY (2002-07)

3.2.1 General Provisions Regarding Imports and Exports (As amended upto 15th Dec. 2003)

(a) Exports and Imports Free Unless Regulated

Exports and Imports shall be free, except to the extent they are regulated by the provisions of the exim policy or any other law for the time being in force.

(b) Compliance with Law and Interpretation of Policy

Every exporter or importer shall comply with the provisions of the foreign trade (Development and Regulation) Act, 1992, the rules and orders made thereunder. The provisions of this policy and terms and conditions of any licence/certificate/permission granted to him, as well as provisions of any other law for the time being in force. All imported goods shall also be subject to domestic laws, rules, orders, regulations, technical specifications, environmental and safety norms as applicable to domestically produced goods.

No import or export of rough diamonds shall be permitted, unless the shipment parcel is accompanied by Kimberley Process (KP) Certificate required under the procedure specified by the Gem & Jewellery Export Promotion Council (GJEPC).

(c) Exemption from Policy/Procedure

Any request for relaxation of the provisions of the policy or of any procedure, on the ground that there is genuine hardship to the applicant or that a strict application of the policy or the procedure is likely to have an adverse impact on trade, may be made to the Director General of Foreign Trade for such relief as may be necessary. The Director General of Foreign Trade may pass such orders or grant such relaxation or relief, as he may deem fit and proper. The Director General of Foreign Trade may, in public interest, exempt any person or class or category of persons from any provision of this Policy or any procedure and may, while granting such exemption, impose such conditions as he may deem fit. Such request may be considered only after consulting Advance Licensing Committee if the request is in respect of a provision of Chapter 4 of exim policy which discusses duty exemption scheme (excluding any provision relating to Gem & Jewellery sector) of the policy/procedure. However, any such request in respect of a provision other than Chapter 4 as given above may be considered only after consulting Policy Relaxation Committee.

(d) Restricted Goods

Any goods, the export or import of which is restricted under ITC(HS) may be exported or imported only in accordance with a licence/certificate/permission or a public notice issued in this behalf.

(e) Terms and Conditions of Licence/Certificate Permission

Every licence/certificate/permission shall be valid for the period of validity specified in the licence/certificate/permission and shall contain such terms and conditions as may be specified by the licensing authority which may include :

(i) The quantity, description and value of the goods,
(ii) Actual User condition;
(iii) Export obligation;
(iv) The value addition to be achieved; and
(v) The minimum export price.

(f) State Trading

Any goods, the import or export of which is governed through exclusive or special privileges trained to State Trading Enterprise(s), may be imported or exported by the State Trading Enterprise(s) as specified in the ITC(HS) Book subject to the conditions specified therein. The Director General of Foreign Trade may, however, grant a licence/certificate/permission to any other person to import or export any of these goods.

(g) Importer-Exporter and Code Number

No export or import shall be made by any person without an Importer-Exporter Code (IEC) number unless specifically exempted. An Importer-Exporter Code (IEC) number shall be granted on application by the competent authority in accordance with the procedure specified in the Handbook (Vol. 1).

(h) Export of Samples

Export of samples shall be governed by the provisions given in Handbook (Vol. I).

(i) Export of Gifts

Goods, including edible items, of value not exceeding Rs. 1,00,000 in a licensing year, may be exported as a gift. However, items mentioned as restricted for exports in ITC(HS) shall not be exported as a gift, without a licence/certificate/permission, except in the case of edible items.

(j) Export of Spares

Warranty spares, whether indigenous or imported, of plant, equipment, machinery, automobiles or any other goods may be exported upto 7.5 per cent of the FOB value of the exports of such goods along with the main equipment or subsequently but within the contracted warranty period of such goods.

(k) Denomination of Export Contracts

All export contracts and invoices shall be denominated either in freely convertible currency or Indian Rupees but the export proceeds shall be realised in freely convertible currency only. Contracts for which payments are received through the Asian Clearing Union (ACU) shall be denominated in ACU Dollar. The Central Government may relax the provisions of this paragraph in appropriate cases. Export contracts and Invoices can be denominated in Indian rupees against Exim Bank/ Government of India line of credit.

(l) Export Promotion Council

The basic objective of export promotion councils is to promote and develop the exports of the country. Each Council is responsible for the promotion of a particular group of products, projects and services.

(m) Registration-cum-Membership Certificate

Any person, applying for (i) a licence/certificate/ permission to import/export, (except items listed as restricted items in ITC(HS) or (ii) any other benefit or concession under this policy shall be required to furnish Registration-*cum*-Membership Certificate (RCMC) granted by the competent authority in accordance with the procedure specified in the Handbook (Vol. I) unless specifically exempted under the policy.

3.2.2 Promotional Measures

(a) Central Assistance to States

The State Governments shall be encouraged to fully participate in encouraging exports from their respective states. For this purpose, suitable provisions shall be made in the Annual Plan of the Department of Commerce for allocation of funds to the states on the twin criteria of gross exports and the rate of growth of exports from different states. The states shall utilise this amount for developing complementary and critical infrastructure such as roads connecting production centres with the ports, setting up of Inland Container Depots and Container Freight Stations, creation of new State level export promotion industrial parks/zones, augmenting common facilities in the existing zones, equity participation in infrastructure projects and any other activities as may be notified by DGFT from time to time.

(b) Market Access Initiative

Financial assistance shall be available under the scheme to the export promotion councils, industry and trade associations and other eligible entities, as may be notified from time to time, on the basis of the competitive merits of proposals received in this regard for the following purposes which *inter-alia* includes marketing studies, setting up showrooms abroad, brand promotion, sales promotion, publicity campaigns and participation in trade fairs and exhibitions.

(c) Towns of Export Excellence

A number of towns in specific geographical locations have emerged as dynamic industrial locations handsomely contributing to India's exports. These "Industrial Clusters" (Tirupur for hosiery, woollen blankets in Panipat, woollen knitwear in Ludhiana) rooted in history symbolise the bursting forth of the free market spirit and are essentially collective response to common problems of competitiveness. Some have become globally renowned manufacturing bases. It is necessary to grant recognition to these industrial cluster items with a view to maximise their export profiles and help in upgrading them to move up in the higher value markets.

(d) Special Focus on Cottage and Handicraft Sector

The following facilities shall be extended to this sector:

(i) The unit in this sector shall be eligible for funds from Market Access Initiative (MAI) scheme (as given in paragraph 3.2 of this policy). Funds shall be earmarked for this sector in the MAI scheme. The funds shall be utilised for developing their web site for virtual exhibition, among other activities.

(ii) Under the EPCG scheme, these units will not be required to maintain average level of exports [as given in paragraph 5.5 (ii) of this policy].

(iii) These units shall be entitled to the benefit of export house status on achieving lower average export performance of Rs. 5 crore during the preceding three licensing years (as given in paragraph 3.7.2 of this policy); and

(iv) The units in handicraft sector shall be entitled to duty free imports of specified items upto 3 per cent of FOB value of their exports.

(e) Agri Export Zones

— AEZ would be set-up for end to end development for export of specific products from a geographically contiguous area.

— AEZ would be identified, managed and cordinated by the State Government, who may evolve a comprehensive package of services provided by all State Government agencies, State agriculture universities and all institutions and agencies of the Union Government for intensive delivery in these zones.

Such services which would be managed and co-ordinated by State Government would include provision of pre/post-harvest treatment and operations, plant protection, processing, packaging, storage and related research and development, etc. APEDA will supplement, within its schemes and provisions, efforts of State Governments for facilitating such exports.

— Units in AEZ would be entitled for all the facilities available for exports of goods in terms of provisions of the respective schemes.

(f) Test Houses

The Central Government will assist in the modernisation

and upgradation of test houses and laboratories in order to bring them at par with international standards.

(g) Quality Complaints

The Regional Sub-Committee on Quality Complaints (RSCQC) set-up at the Regional Offices of the Directorate General of Foreign Trade shall investigate quality complaints received from foreign buyers. The guidelines for settlement of quality complaints, in particular, and such other complaints, in general (which is given in Appendix-37 of Handbook Vol. I).

If it comes to the notice of the Director General of Foreign Trade or he has reason to believe that an export or import has been made in a manner gravely prejudicial—

(i) to the trade relations of India with any foreign country;
(ii) to the interest of other persons engaged in exports or imports; and
(iii) has brought disrepute to the credit or the goods of the country.

The Director General Foreign Trade may take action against the exporter or importer concerned in accordance with the provisions of the act, the rules and orders made thereunder and this policy.

(h) Status Certificate

Export Performance Level

The applicant is required to achieve the prescribed average export performance level.

However, units in Small Scale Industry/Tiny Sector/Cottage Sector/Unit registered with KVICs or KVIBs/Units located in North Eastern States, Sikkim and J&K/Units exporting handloom, handicrafts, hand knotted carpets, silk carpets/exporters holding golden status/exporters exporting to countries in Latin America and CIS/sub-Saharan Africa, units having ISO 9000 (Series) or ISO 14000 (Series) or HACCP Certification or WHOGMP or SEI CMM level 2 and above certification status, shall be entitled for export house status on achieving average FOB/FOR value of Rs. 5 crore during the preceding three

TABLE 3.1
Status Provided to the Exporters According to the Export Performance Level

Category	*Average FOB/FOR value during the preceding three licensing years, (in Rupees)*	*FOB/FOR during the current licensing year (in Rupees)*
Export House	15 crore	45 crore
Trading House	100 crore	300 crore
Star Trading House	500 crore	1500 crore
Superstar trading house	2000 crore	6000 crore

Source : Exim Policy (2002-07), Government of India.

licensing years of FOB/FOR value of Rs. 15 crore during the current licencing year. The same threshold limit shall be applicable to the service exporters and agri exporters (other than grains) for obtaining Export house status.

Export made on re-export basis shall not be counted for the purpose of recognition.

The exports made by a subsidiary of a limited company shall be counted towards export performance of the limited company for the purpose of recognition. For this purpose, the company shall have the majority share holding in the subsidiary company.

(i) Special Strategic Package for Status Holders

The status holders shall be eligible for the following new/ special facilities :

- Licence/certificate/permissions and Customs clearances for both imports and exports on self-declaration basis;
- Fixation of Input-output norms on priority;
- Priority Finance for medium and long-term capital requirement as per conditions notified by RBI;
- Exemption from compulsory negotiation of documents through banks. The remittance, however, would continue to be received through banking channels;

- 100 per cent retention of foreign exchange in EEFC account; and
- Enhancement in normal repatriation period from 180 days to 360 days.

(j) Validity Period

All status certificates issued or renewed on or after 1.4.2002 shall be valid from 1st April of the licensing year during which the application for the grant of such recognition is made upto 31st March, 2007, unless otherwise specified. On the expiry of such certificate, application for renewal of status certificate shall be required to be made within a period as prescribed in the Handbook (Vol. 1). During the said period, the status holder shall be eligible to claim the usual facilities and benefits.

The status certificates expiring on 31st March, 2002 shall be deemed to have been extended upto 31st March, 2004. However, further renewal shall be granted on achieving the threshold limit prescribed in the Policy.

(k) Service Exports

"Services" include all the 161 tradable services covered under the General Agreement on Trade in Services where payment for such services is received in free foreign exchange.

(l) Electronic Data Interchange

In an attempt to speed up the transactions, to reduce physical interface and to bring about transparency in various activities related to exports, electronic data interchange would be encouraged. Applications received electronically shall be cleared within 24 hours.

3.2.3 Duty Exemption/Remission Scheme

The duty exemption scheme enables duty free import of input required for export production.

Duty Exemption Schemes are also known as indirect tax rebate schemes. The basic feature of these schemes is that the duty leviable on raw materials used in the manufacture of export product is waived off and is not collected at all. An advance licence is issued under duty exemption scheme.

3.2.3.1 Advance Licence

An advance licence is issued to allow duty free import of inputs, which are physically incorporated in the export product.

Advance licensing scheme is applicable to nearly 6000 exports products for which the names of the products and major raw material have been specified by the DGFT. Advance licence can be issued for physical exports, intermediate supplies (to be supplied to the ultimate exporter) and for deemed export (for deemed exports exemption from basic customs duty and additional customs duty only). Advance Licence shall not be transferable even after completion of export obligation. The period of fulfilment of export obligation under advance licence shall be prescribed in the Handbook (Vol. 1). An advance licence holder may avail the facility of back-to-back inland letter of credit.

In the case of an Advance Licence, the drawback shall be available in respect of any of the duty paid materials, whether imported or indigenous, used in the goods exported, as per the drawback rate fixed by Ministry of Finance (Directorate of drawback).

Standard Input-Output Norms (SIONs) (which constitutes the basic building block of all the major export promotion schemes) for 403 new products have been notified. Advance licences shall be issued with a positive value addition.[3]

3.2.3.2 Duty Free Replenishment Certificate (DFRC)

- DFRC is issued to a merchant exporter or manufacturer-exporter for the import of inputs used in the manufacture of goods without payment of basic customs duty, and special additional duty, under this scheme, import of raw materials can be affected after exports.
- The basic difference between the advance licensing scheme and the DFRC is that the former provides for prior import of raw materials for the manufacture of the export product whereas the latter provides for import of raw material against exports already affected.
- DFRC shall be issued a minimum value addition of 33 per cent (which was later reduced to 25 per cent). DFRC

shall be issued only in respect of export products covered under the SIONs as notified by DGFT.[4]

- DFRC shall be issued for import of inputs as per SION as indicated in the shipping bills. The validity of such licences shall be 18 months. DFRC and or the material(s) imported against it shall be freely transferable.
- The export products, which are eligible for modified VAT, shall be eligible for CENVAT credit.
- The exporter shall be entitled for drawback benefits in respect of any of the duty paid materials whether imported or indigenous, used in the export product as per the drawback rate fixed by Directorate of Drawback (Ministry of Finance).[5]

3.2.3.3 Duty Entitlement Passbook Scheme

The objective of DEPB is to neutralise the incidence of customs duty on the import content of the export product. The neutralisation shall be provided by way of grant of duty credit against the export product.

- Under DEPB, an exporter may apply for credit, as a specified percentage of FOB value of exports, made in freely convertible currency. The credit shall be against such export products and at such rates as may be specified by the DGFT by way of public notice issued in this behalf, for import of raw materials, intermediates, components, parts, packaging material, etc.
- The DEPB shall be valid for a period of 12 months from the date of issue.
- The DEPB/or the items imported against it are freely transferable.
- Normally the exports made under the DEPB shall not be entitled for drawback. However, the additional customs duty/excise duty paid in cash on inputs under DEPB shall be adjusted as CENVAT credit or Duty drawback as per the rules framed by the Deptt. of Revenue.

- Exporters of Gem and Jewellery are eligible to import their inputs by obtaining REP Licences from the Licensing authorities in accordance with the procedure specified in this behalf.

Changes therein after

The changes in DEPB rates for import of various products as announced by the Government.[6,7] For the DEPB rates for products made of steel, has been increased with retrospective effect. The credit for a wide range of engineering items has been increased.[8] (In case of plastic suit cases made of HDPE or PP, the Government has increased the DEPB rate to 12 per cent as compared to the 10 per cent (Feb. 2004).

The Finance Ministry plans to issue DEPB credit to Exporters in demat form. De materialisation of DEPB credit would have procedural advantages since all custom houses are networked and verification of the pass book can be done through the Electronic data interchange (EDI).[9]

The average DEPB credit disbursal is around Rs. 7,000 crore per annum and over 50% of the country's exports are through the DEPB facility.

- Initially the Government had said that imports and exports under the DEPB scheme should be routed through the same port. This noun was subsequently eased.[10]
- The Government has nominated the Exim Facilitation Committee (EFC) of the DGFT to distribute import entitlement under Tariff rate quota (TRQ) for import of corn, infant milk food, skimmed milk powder and certain edible oils at concessional duty (imports should be completed by March 31, 2005).[11]

DEPB is a unique and effective instrument of export promotion to provide raw material to the exporter at notional international prices.

3.2.4 Export Promotion Capital Goods Scheme

The Export Promotion Capital Goods (EPCG) scheme was one of the several export promotion initiatives launched by the Government in the early 1990s to boost exports.

The basic purpose of the scheme was to allow exporters to import machinery and equipment at affordable prices so that they can produce quality products and sell them in the international market.[12]

As per the Exim policy 2002-07, the scheme allows the import of new capital goods (including CKD/SKD) thereof as well as computer software systems at 5 per cent custom duty subject to an export obligation equivalent to 5 times CIF value of capital goods to be fulfilled over a period of 8 years reckoned from the date of issuance of licence over a period of 8 years. However, in respect of EPCG licences for Rs. 100 crore or more, the same export obligation shall be required to be fulfilled over a period of 12 years.

The scheme covers manufacturer exporters with or without supporting manufacturer(s)/vendor(s), merchant exporters tied to supporting manufacturer(s) service providers.

- *Export Obligation*—The export obligation shall be fulfilled by the export of goods capable of being manufactured or produced by the use of the capital goods imported under the scheme. In case of any firm/ company acquiring a unit which is under BIFR and licences issued to units in the agricultural export zones, a period of 12 years reckoned from the date of issuance of the license would be permitted for the fulfilment of export obligation.

Service industries like hotels can also avail EPCG imports and fulfil the export obligation through the foreign exchange earned by them.

3.2.5 Export Oriented Units (EOUs), Units in Export Processing Zones (EPZs), Electronics Hardware Technology Parks (EHTPs) and Software Technology Parks (STPs)

Units undertaking to export their entire production of goods and services may be set-up under the Export Oriented Unit (EOU) Scheme, EPZ Scheme, EHTP Scheme or STP Scheme. An EOU/EPZ/EHTP/STP unit may export goods and services including agro-products, partly processed jewellery, sub-assemblies and components. It may also export by products, rejects, waste scrap arising out of the production process.

An EOU/EPZ/EHTP/STP unit may import without payment of duty all types of goods, including capital goods, as defined in the policy provided they are not prohibited items of imports in the ITC (HS). Further details of EOU/EPZ/EHTP/STP units is covered in the Chapter 8.

3.2.6 Special Economic Zones

- Special Economic Zones (SEZ) is a specifically delineated duty free enclave and shall be deemed to be foreign territory for the purposes of trade operations and duties and tariffs.
- Goods going into the SEZ area from Domestic Tariff Area (DTA) shall be treated as deemed exports and goods coming from the SEZ area into DTA shall be treated as if the goods are being imported.
- SEZ units shall be entitled for reimbursement of central sales tax, exemption from payment of Central Excise Duty on all goods eligible for procurement (as per paragraph 7.2 of the policy) and reimbursement of duty paid on fuels or any other goods procured from DTA as per the rate of drawback notified by the DGFT from the date of such notification.
- SEZ unit shall be a positive net foreign exchange (NFE) earner NFE earning shall be calculated cumulatively for a period of 5 years from the commencement of commercial production.
- SEZ units can capitalize import payable.
- SEZ units can sell all products including gems and jewellery through exhibitions and duty free shops or shops set-up abroad.
- Codification of SEZ rules to facilitate investment. Restriction of one year period for remittance of export proceeds removed for SEZ units. (Detailed description on SEZ is covered in Chapter 8).

3.2.7 Deemed Exports

'Deemed exports' refers to those transactions in which the goods supplied do not leave the country.

Deemed exports shall be eligible for any/all of the following benefits in respect of manufacture and supply of goods qualifying as deemed exports subject to the terms and conditions as given in Handbook (Vol. 1) :

(a) Advance Licence for Intermediate supply/deemed export.
(b) Deemed Exports Drawback
(c) Refund of Terminal Excise duty.

3.3 EXIM POLICY (2003-04)

Exim Policy (2003-04) anounced by the then Commerce and Industry Minister Arun Jaitley on 31st March 2004. Clearly has generated new hope in dealing with globalised world inspite of uncertainty created by Iraq war.[13] As now the quantitative restrictions (QR) are gone, the challenge lies in identifying the drivers which could help India boost its exports.

The main features of Exim Policy (2003-04) are as follows :

- The EPCG scheme has been changed to make imports easier. Instead of fixing the export obligation against the value of the import, the policy fixed it against the import duty—the importer would have to export goods valued eight times the import duty saved. A back of the envelope circulation shows that this virtually cuts the export obligation by one-fourth.
- Second hand imports under the EPCG scheme has been permitted. Second hand capital goods are the main vehicles of investment in the country. Removal of actual user condition opens the door to trading activity.[14]
- Ten export clusters to be developed.
- Services exporters can import 10% of their overseas sales at zero duty.[15]
- Duty free import entitlement upto 10% of the average export during the past 3 years will be provided to service provider. To hotels it would be 5%. This facility would provide a big boost to key segments like healthcare, tourism and professional services.[16]

- Special scheme being formulated for boosting service exports.
- Duty free Hardware imports upto $ 10,000 allow oil companies with marketing licences allowed to import petro-products directly.
- Income Tax concessions contemplated for companies investing in agriculture export processing zones.[17]
- EOU norms have been relaxed. EOUs will only be required to be net foreign exchange earner in order to avail the benefits of this scheme.
- Sops have been provided for gems and jewellery, hardware and software units while sick units have been provided extension of export obligation.
- Sales to SEZs from DTA would be treated as exports, sales to DTA from SEZ to be exempted from special additional duty (SAD).[18]
- Reduction of transaction costs through EDI (Electronic Data Interchange) implementation programme to facilitate on line approvals to exporters from 23 EDI ports.
- The new exim policy (2003-04) has taken a good note of global developments and appears to be path breaking in terms of technology identifying services other than IT, as a vital source of earning foreign exchange. Redrafted EPCG appears to be more logical and attractive. Inspire of all these path breaking initiatives, the policy has failed to seize the opportunity to consolidate numerous notifications and circulars relating to export incentive schemes. It also did not accord priority to procedural simplifications. There is no revamp of the negative list. The 69 or so items moved out of the list are largely to meet the criticism at WTO, on remaining QRs. The proper thrust on drugs and pharmaceutical products seems to be grossly inadequate.

3.4 MINI EXIM POLICY, 2004

Mini Exim Policy, 2004 announced on 28th Jan. 2004 by the then commerce minister Arun Jaitley has doted out numerous sops to exporters and the domestic industry which he called as 'trade facilitation measures' to bring cheers to exporters.[19] The main features of Mini Exim Policy, 2004 are as follows :

- Gold and Silver can now be imported by anyone without having to go through canalising agencies like state trading companies or banks.[20] This will make precious metal cheaper as the need to pay charges ranging from 0.1 per cent to 0.7 per cent of the value to the canalising agencies has been eliminated.
  Gold imports are allowed under baggage rules. A passenger coming into the country after a minimum stay of 6 months abroad is entitled to bring 10 kgs of gold and 100 kgs of silver. The duty has to be paid in convertible foreign currency.
- Repayment at ports under EPCG—The Commerce Ministry will be looking at all rupee payments received for port handling services as export obligations under the EPCG scheme. The ceiling on export of gifts has been raised to Rs. 5 lakh from Rs. 1 lakh/year.[21]
- Duty free full imports have been permitted with actual user conditions under the Duty Free Replenishment Certificate (DFRC) scheme. An advance licence for intermediate supplies has been allowed against DFRC schemes.
- The Equity base of the Export Credit Guarantee Corporation (ECGC) has been raised to Rs. 800 crore from Rs. 500 crore. New insurance account will be opened to underwrite big projects.
- Automobiles priced above $ 40,000 can be imported without having to go through costly homologation and difficult procedures prescribed by regulatory authorities.[22]
- Gold credit card scheme was announced for credit worthy exporters with good track record to obtain export credit without difficulty at best terms.[23]
- Hotels and restaurants earning foreign exchange can make duty-free imports.
- Simpler quality norms have been prescribed for import of various items including food products.

- The Government has announced a series of procedural simplifications for exporters in order to reduce transaction costs and introduce transparency into the system. They include—
- Digital signatures.[24]
- Electronic Fund Transfer.
- Message exchange with community partners like customs and banks.
- Enforcement of the bar on import of harmful azo dyes has been rationalised by the mini Exim Policy. If the imports are used for export of value added products, the testing procedures would now be more lenient, with only 25 per cent of samples to be drawn for testing by customs instead of 100 per cent at present.
- The extension of the deemed export status items with nil customs duty by the Mini-exim policy will mean that companies producing life-saving drugs,[25] IT equipments like CD-ROMS, Audio, VCD/DVDs, mega power projects and those making machineries for petroleum refining operations can now enjoy export benefits at par with those in special economic zones.
- It can be said that trade facilitation has finally got its due. In a welcome recognition of the fact that high transaction costs are a major obstacle to trade, the exim policy has focused on a string of measures to facilitate trade by reducing transaction costs. The basic thrust all through is to reduce procedural hassles so that Indian exporters can compete on an equal footing with exporters overseas. The only surprising omission is regarding special economic zones (SEZs) a regular feature in earlier Exims.

3.5 NEW FOREIGN TRADE POLICY (2004-09)

New Foreign Trade Policy (NFTP) 2004-09 is a significant step towards furthering the reforms process started a decade ago. It aims to boost foreign trade and double India's share of foreign trade from 0.7 per cent in 2003 to 1.5% by 2009.[26]

Some of the important steps proposed by New Foreign Trade Policy, 2004-09 are as follows :

- Sectors with significant export prospects coupled with potential for employment generation have been identified as thrust sectors. Special Focus Initiatives have been prepared for Agriculture, Handicrafts, Handlooms, Gem and Jewellery and leather and footwear sectors.
- The threshold limit of designated 'Towns of export excellence' was reduced from Rs. 1000 crores to Rs. 250 crores in the thrust sectors.
- A new scheme to accelerate growth of exports called 'Target plus' has been introduced. Exporters who have achieved a quantum growth in exports would be entitled to duty free credit based on incremental exports substantially higher than the annual export target fixed.
  Rewards will be granted based on tiered approach. For incremental growth of over 20%, 25% and 100%, the duty free credits would be 5%, 10% and 15% of FOB value of incremental exports.
- A new rationalized scheme of categorization of status holders as star export house has been introduced, designating them from one star to five star, depending on their total imports during the current and previous three years. The entry level for qualifying for status is (now) Rs. 15 crores in 3 years.
- The DEPB scheme would be continued till April 2005. EPCG scheme has been made more flexible.
- EOUs shall be exempted from service tax in proportion to their exported goods and services and shall be permitted to retain 100 per cent of export earning in EEFC accounts.
- A new scheme to establish free trade and warehousing zones has been introduced to create trade-related infrastructure to facilitate the import and export of goods and services with freedom to carry out trade transactions in free currency.
- Validity of all licences and entitlements issued under various schemes has been increased to a uniform 24 months.

- Time bound introduction of Electronic Data Interface (EDI) for export transactions. 75 per cent of all export transactions to be on EDI within six months.
- Enhanced delegation of powers to Zonal and Regional offices of DGFT for speedy and less cumbersome disposal of matters.
- The number of returns and forms to filed have been reduced. This process shall be continued in consultation with customs and excise.[27]

Experts feel that for the first time, an equal thrust has been given to both export promotion as well as import liberalisation in the foreign trade policy. The reforms in the trade policy continue on the lines of liberalisation, transparency and globalization. This will help boost foreign trade and support, overall economic development. The trade friendly environment is also in line with WTO framework for reducing quantitative restrictions and cutting tariffs.

3.6 EXIM POLICY, 2002-07 : A CRITICAL APPRAISAL

The pressure to succeed in competitive export markets is indeed a powerful inducement to innovate, upgrade technology, ensure quality standards and enforce cost efficiency.[28] But it is equally a fact that to successfully face up to the demands of the international market on any significant economy-wide scale, a competitive domestic economic environment conducive to technological adaptation, innovation and productivity enhancement is imperative. Given insufficiency of the required policy and institutional changes, as has been the experience of the Indian Economy in the recent period, micro-export policies, however finely and minutely crafted, cannot be expected to significantly impinge on the growth of the economy.

The 2002 survey by the CII has painted a grim picture of exports. Only 5 of the 48 export industries had 'excellent' growth as compared to 9 in the previous year. High growth was achieved by 9 industries compared to 11 in the previous year, while 34 industries registered moderate growth or a decline.[29]

The performance in Feb. 2002 has virtually doused the government's hope of achieving atleast the scaled down export target of 3 per cent. Against this background, the Government had necessarily to take measures to boost exports at all cost. Having launched a major change in 2001 in removing QRs on imports, 2002 had to have a policy of giving more concessions and smoothening out the creases in the existing policy.

The measures are more or less based on giving up taxes and continuation of the same scheme.[30] Basically it includes—removal of export QRs, giving extra facilities to SEZ, boost to agricultural exports by transport subsidy, reduction of examination of exports and adopting a common eight digit code as in customs.[31] A host of fresh sops have been announced for SEZs, EOUs, entitling domestic suppliers to drawback, DEPB benefits, central sales tax exemption and service tax exemption. Focus Africa and Focus CIS are not new ideas. The provision that old machinery can be relocated from abroad on licence is also an existing practice. Only the licensing provision has been done away with. The Finance Ministry is set to forgo revenues of around Rs. 33,000 crore in 2003-04 on account of incentives given to exporters under various export promotion schemes.[32]

Table 3.2
Duty Foregone on Export Promotion Schemes

(Value in Rupees crore)

	2001-02	*2002-03**	*2003-04*
DEPB	5,600	7,000	11,500
Duty Drawback	3,000	4,000	Drawback-3,000, DFRC-600
EPCG	2,000	3,500	3,400
Advance Licence	7,800	9,000	10,000
EPZ, 100% EOU and SEZ	6,300**	8,000	1,300*** EOU/EHTP-9,400
Total	24,700	31,500	39,200

* 2002-03 estimated Revenue loss.
** Does not include SEZ.
*** Only for SEZ.

Source : Custom notification and IEC, India and *The Economic Times*, 23rd August 2004, p. 9.

Key Issues

- It is very clear that while the policy is designed to tap India's export potential, a lot depends on how policy is going to be implemented. Therefore, there is need to concentrate on implementation.[33]
- The licence and customs classification should be made to match with drawback classification. For this the commerce minister should appoint a joint committee having technical and administrative personnel who would devise it within 6 months.
- Reduction of transaction costs due to corruption at different levels needs to receive some attention.
- All EPZs should have been converted into SEZs. There is no rationale for having different type of zones.
- There are still provisions for savage penalties for non-performance in exports even when the reasons are genuine. This makes entrepreneurs to face double injury, losing the market and also having to pay penalty. A proper approach should be to make the manufacturing more efficient and competitive in real terms.
- Improving the infrastructure and changing the labour law at least in the SEZs.
- A forum should be created for issuing of recommendation letters by the DGFT for the so-called doubtful cases where clearance is held by customs, signed by DGFT himself.
- Other issues like electronic fund transfer, digital signatures, relaxed import norms, export promotion measures and focus on service sector have already been considered in Exim Policy, 2003-04 and Mini Exim Policy (2004).

There is no doubt that foreign trade holds the key to India's long-term growth. Therefore, it is imperative that the Government removes hurdles such as procedural hassles and red tape that can delay speedy implementation.

Notes and References

1. Mehta, Pradeep Kumar, 'The Exim Policy, 2003-04', Tools for promoting Exports, Foreign Trade Review, IIFT, Vol. 37, Nos. 3 & 4, Oct. 2002-March 2003.
2. Exim Policy, 2002-07, Govt. of India (1st April 2002).
3. Value Addition = $\frac{A-B}{B} \times 100$

   Where

   A = is the FOB value of the export realised/FOR value of the supply received.

   B = is the CIF value of the importer inputs covered by the licence + any other imported materials used on which the benefit of duty drawback is being claimed.
4. DFRC shall not be issued in respect of SIONs which are subject to "actual user" condition or where the input is allowed with prior import condition or where the norms allow import of Acetic anhydride, Ephedrine and Pseudo Ephedrine in HB (Vol. III). However DFRC may be issued for SIONs allowing import of Acetic Anhydride, Ephedrine and Pseudo Ephedrine, provided these items are specifically deleted from the list of import items.
5. Drawback Manual, 2003-04.
6. DEPB rates have been revised for Bare Aluminium conductors to 9% from 6%. Kitchenware & Tableware to 20% from 13%.
   (This benefit will be available to exports made between April 2003 and Feb. 8, 2004). Forged steel ball to 11 per cent from 6% and likewise. (*Source* : DEPB on steel items, Engg. goods liked, 29 Feb., 2004, *The Economic Times*, New Delhi).
7. Goyal, Arun 'Jas shocking, DEPB rate cut hurts Exporters', *The Economic Times*, New Delhi, 20 Feb., 2004.
8. 'DEPB on Steel items, Engg. Goods', G. Ganapatty Subramaniam, 29 Feb. 2004, *The Economic Times*, New Delhi.
9. Ramakrishnan, Hema and G. Ganapathy Subramaniam, 'MOF Plans to issue DEPB credit to Exporters in Demat form', *The Economic Times*, New Delhi, 10 Aug., 2004.
10. 'Row over Scrapping of DEPB relief on Supplies to SEZs', *The Economic Times*, New Delhi, 27 Feb., 2004.
11. 'DGFT Panel to dole out import entitlement at concessional duty', *The Economic Times*, New Delhi, 23 May, 2004.
12. 'What is the purpose of EPCG Scheme?' *The Economic Times*, New Delhi.
13. "Everything but Iraq Embedded", Team ET, *The Economic Times*, New Delhi, 1st April, 2003, p. 1.
14. Goyal, Arun, "CG Import Opened under DTA, EPCG Windows", Export Import Notes, Academy of Business Studies, *The Economic Times*, New Delhi, 1st April, 2003, p. 6.

15. "Chambers Say Thumbs up to thrust on Services" *The Economic Times*, New Delhi, 1st April, 2003, p. 7.
16. 'New catalyst to promote service export', *The Economic Times*, New Delhi, 1st April, 2003, p. 7.
17. "I-T Sops to boost AEZ investment", *The Economic Times*, New Delhi, 1st April, 2003, p. 7.
18. "DTA access granted to All", 'Focus on growth engine that can pull others alone', 'IT hardware units can now diversify into software', *The Economic Times*, New Delhi, 1st April, 2003, p. 6.
19. 'No Hem in Jaitly's Mini', Team ET, *The Economic Times*, New Delhi, 29th Jan., 2004, p. 1.
20. In 1997, the Government authorised 3 canalising agencies—MMTC, STC and HHEC—and 8 banks including SBI, Bank of Nova Scotia, HSBC, ICICI, etc. to import gold and silver for sale in the domestic market.
21. "Capital Goods Export rooms eased', EPCG Scheme, *Business Standard*, 29 January, 2004, p. 8.
22. Gupta, Nandini Sen, 'Eases Exim Worms help own most coveted foreign cars', *The Economic Times*, New Delhi, 30th Jan., 2004, p. 4.
23. Ramakrishnan, Hema and K.G. Narendra Nath, 'Goods, Services used as inputs for exports to get tax brakes', *The Economic Times*, New Delhi, 22 Aug., 2004.
24. 'Electronic Signatures to reduce cost', Economy Bureau, *Business World*, New Delhi, 28th Jan., 2004.
26. Sugandhi Priyanka, 'India's New Foreign Trade Policy (2004-09)', *Chartered Financial Analyst*, Oct. 2004, p. 10.
25. 'Domestic Trade to Enjoy Export Status', *Business Standard*, 29 January, 2004.
27. www.foreignpolicy.com
28. Mukhopadhya, Sukumar, 'Exim Policy, 2002-07', Focus must shift to Action', *Economic and Political Weekly*, April 13, 2002, pp. 1389-90.
29. 'Exim Policy Expecting too much', *Economic & Political Weekly*, April 6, 2002, p. 1296.
30. Rao, N. Janardhan, 'Exim Policy, 2002-07 Implementation is the key', *Chartered Financial Analyst*, June 2002, p. 18.
31. This incidentally was a suggestion given by report of the NIPFP in 1997. The common digit will remove difference with customs. It has the advantage of making export policy and customs classification non-controversial and Transparent.
32. Export Trading Houses in India, Custom Notification & IEC, India.
33. *Ibid.*

Studies on Export and Export Promotion Institutions

This chapter concerns with earlier research work conducted on export promotion and precisely on institutions boosting the exports. The contribution of various research work around the globe on the relevant subject is noteworthy and has explored new opportunities for the country's exports.

Deepak Nayyar (1975) has done pioneering work on Indian exports. In his study titled 'Indian exports and export policies in 1960s' he found that commodity composition influence export competitiveness. In case of India, it has been pointed out that it could not possibly increase its share of world exports as the 'commodity composition' of its export was an 'unfortunate one'. Even when India started exporting non-traditional products. Such exports were largely based on slow moving products. He also suggested improvements in the export policy of India.[1]

Garry Pursell (1987) found that in India, any individual manufactured product which is exported will typically benefit from a variety of export incentives and hence it is of considerable interest to have a measure of combined impact of all incentives. The researcher explained the concept of effective protection and how it can be used to quantify and analyse the Indian export incentives.[2]

$$\text{Effective protection coefficient} = \frac{V_{ad}}{A_{aw}} = \frac{\text{Value added in Domestic Prices}}{\text{Value added in world prices}}$$

$$\text{Effective subsidy coefficient (ESC)} = \frac{\text{(FOB price – actual cost of R.M) + other subsidies}}{\text{(FOB price – cost of raw-material at world prices)}}$$

According to Garry Pursell, if the Government wished to make exports equally profitable as import subsidisation profits, for the same products, it could set the incentives so that the effective subsidy for exports is equal to effective protection in the domestic market.

B.P. Mathur (1985) in his work titled 'Industrial Exports and Developing countries—India's Search for countervailing power' found that an obvious solution of growth for India is to move into the fields of industrial exports.[3] His area of focus was on :

(a) Proper segmentation of international market.
(b) Use of Joint venture strategy to enter into the foreign market.
(c) Creation of 'institutional agencies' in the shape of 'aid and creditcorporation' and 'corporation for promoting Joint ventures'.

Studies conducted by *Joint Advisory group*[4] at the International Trade Centre UNCTAD/GATT (1975) and Guide to Evaluation of Trade promotion programmes, at International Trade Centre UNCTAD/GATT (1987) gave ways to evaluate the export promotion programmes. ITC states the following reasons as underlying their evaluation :

(a) To examine activities carried out under a given programme, in order to ascertain the magnitude of the result achieved and the effectiveness of the programme.
(b) To uncover implementation problems and identify possible solutions.

(c) To accumulate experience from the implementation of particular activities and of programme as a whole.
(d) To measure the impact of programme and ascertain whether the results justify the implementation of the programme.
(e) To help in defining activities that will contribute more positively to the effectiveness of programs.

The studies also focused on the matter of impact of trade promotion programmes. According to this research study two broad goals underlie government efforts in providing export promotion support : first at macro-level, generating a favourable trade balance or reducing a trade deficit, and second, at the micro-level, enhancing the international competitive competence of domestic industries and companies.

Rolf Seringhaus Ontario (1988)[5] found that the impact of Government export promotion is seen to occur at several different levels, ranging from the broadest possible effect on a country's trade position to the highly specific result an exporter may realize using a particular export programme.

Also Seringhaus gave framework for evaluation of government export promotion research focusing on government assistance construct comprising global measure. This research included all export marketing assistance services or program offered by government. Second were narrow global measures which included similar purpose services like providing information for export planning and market entry and individual measures like individual assistance provided by specific institution viz. Canadian Trade Commission Service. Specific measure included specific assistance provided by a specific programme.

H.C. Olson (1975) in his work titled 'Studies in Export Promotion' studied the impact of the export promotion programme on firm behavior.

According to Olson, Government export promotion programmes act as a independent variable and actual or future export volume of a company as a dependent variable. Export promotion programme builds the decision base in the company, which makes company able to judge the merit of embarking on a related course of export action, as a result of which the firm decides to act accordingly, organises its important activities and finally makes export sales.[6]

FIG. 4.1
Export Promotional Support and Firm Behaviour

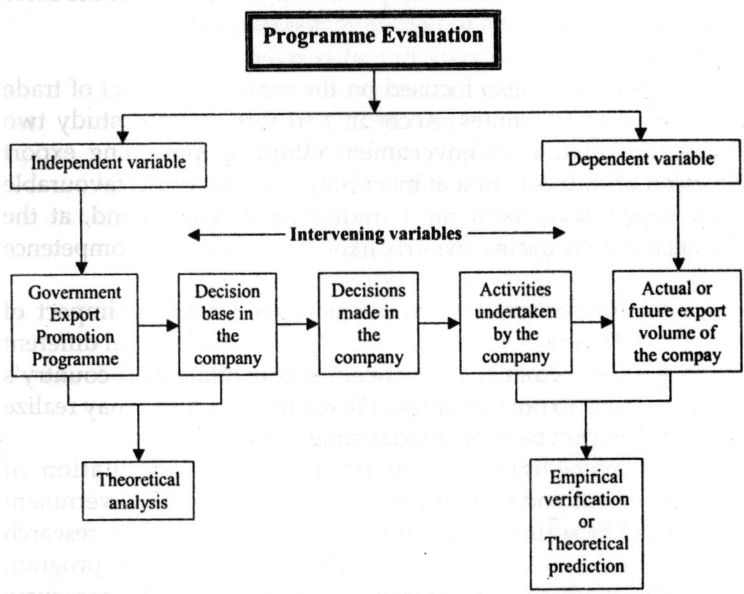

Source : Adapted from H.C. Olson, Studies in Export Promotion, Stockholm, Almquit and Wiksell International, 1975, p. 31.

The actual or future export volume of a company will decide the effectiveness of export promotion programme launched by government.

Bibek Debroy (1989) in his research work titled 'China's External Trade—A review' threw light on reform process started in China and how it has helped China's external sector, i.e. foreign trade. Extended reforms in China have been instituted since 1978 which have been based on 3 broad planks of first were the reforms in rural economic organisation, viz. birth control, changes and reforms in legal policy framework. Second, there were reforms in urban economic organisation to make industry more flexible and increase production, and thirdly, reforms in external trade sector focusing on decentralisation and transparency. Reforms in foreign trade have helped China to gain fast growth.[7]

To achieve impressive growth in foreign trade is to have overall reforms. Consistency and coordination in reforms process is next important aspect. The parameter of judging the foreign trade of any country is not only dependent on reforms and improvement in one part but also overall synergy between institutions and policies is required.

M. Dattatreyulu's paper on 'Framework for Exporting Industries in India—India's Export to West Germany' talks about the need of suitable framework to promote competitive efficiency. This paper deals with the working of various organisations connected with India's exports like :

- Empowered Committee/Cabinet Committee on Exports,
- Co-ordination Committee/Representative of Ministries and Export Promotion agencies,
- Export Service promotion agencies,
- Inter-Ministerial Committee on JV abroad,
- Commodity Board, and
- EPCs, IIFT, TDA, FIEO, etc.

The work of coordination committee was given special emphasis in the research paper and the focus was that if exports were to be promoted the procedural delays should be removed at all cost.

V.R. Panchmukhi, C.J. Batliwala, K.C. Reddy, V.L. Rao, Philip Thomas and *I.R. Mukharji's (1991)* Joint Research Work on 'Export Financing Aspects in India' studied the following aspects :

- Focus on export Financing, i.e. Export Financing has become very crucial for the growth of exports in India. Various schemes have been drawn by RBI, Exim Bank, Commercial Banks and ECGC in order to help exporters to build a competitive edge.
- The research paper aimed to estimate the credit requirements of exporters using various mathematical techniques.

- This research work has done thorough analysis on the then existing export promotion policies.
- It provided comprehensive information on specific rules/conditions relating the disbursement of credit.

Researchers recommended special credit schemes for small exporters. According to them, export incentives should be extended to indirect exports and government and exporters must focus on quality upgradation.

RIS's [(Research and Information System) for the non-aligned and other developing countries] work on 'Export financing in India' (1991) was focused on the network of institutions and institutions providing export finance for the promotion of exports in India. According to this research study bureaucratic control should be reduced and decanalisation of exports is necessary.

M.R. Narayana's (1992) research on 'Export subsidies in India : Need for a strategic approach' says that the persisting trade imbalances, mounting external debt and its servicing burden, depleting foreign exchange reserves have often led to considering export promotion as a policy alternative for India.[9] However, our continuing reliance on industrial market economies for exports underlines the importance of competition in product quality and price. This research's main focus was on subsidised export financing from Exim bank and export credit (interest) subsidy schemes of 1968. The analytical results of this research work showed that the underlying imperfect market structure of India's export trading is characterised by Cournot's duopoly, the impact of export subsidies can be favourable in terms of larger market share for home exporting firms. The results of this work offered strong economic support for the strategic export policy, yet to be formulated in India, or justification for the current export policy if only the subsidised exporting domestic firm's behaviour is strategic. The research study provided the economic basis for empirical estimation of export earning by a strategic export subsidisation policy as compared to the existing non-strategic policy.

O.P. Sharma's (1992) work on 'Export competitiveness—Some conceptual issues' threw light on the word *'competitiveness'*. The concept of competitiveness has been dealt differently at different times in the empirical work on international trade flows.

There is no single measure of competitiveness.[10] At best, it is a composite concept because different measures (price, export shares, profitability and unit cost etc.) give different results. The research identified several measures of competitiveness which were quantifiable, which included—export market shares, specialisation of industrial structure, costs and exchange rates and profitability and financial structure of Industrial labour force This research made a modest attempt at elucidating some of the relevant issues involved in understanding the concept.

Vijaya Katti's (1992) study on 'Construction Industry and Consultancy Services and Exports : Problems and Prospects' dealt with details of consultancy exports in agriculture, engineering, processing and management, etc. and the facilities extended by the Exim bank alongwith the Government's policy measures for the development of consultancy services. The possible areas of co-operation with developing countries have also been explained in this paper.[11]

S.P. Agarwal's (1992) research work on 'Role of Consultants in Export of Technologies and Manufactured Product', emphasized that exports of technologies and technology-intensive manufacturing products must be encouraged for sustained earnings of foreign exchange, apart from the traditional exports of commodities and low-value added manufactured items. One such measures relates to promoting use of consultancies and professional services in a large measure by the manufacturers and exporters and strengthening the consultancy capabilities in emerging areas of technology. However, the consultants have generally kept themselves away from export production systems where they can contribute substantially in enhancing technical and managerial capabilities of exporters, in terms of vital aspects like quality, cost and delivery schedules. Consultants can provide effective and workable linkages between industry, R&D institutions, academic institutions and the Government as well as the consumer markets, besides developing the back-up infrastructural facilities conducive for a concerted export offer.[12]

Enhancing Competitiveness of Potential Export Sectors in Developing countries' lessons from experience, UNCTAD Secretariat, UNCTAD/TTP/90 (23rd Oct. 1992). According to it, for developing countries EPZs may be an initial step towards export-oriented industrialization, Labour intensive processes and component specialization in EPZs within vertically transitional industries constitute a relatively easy avenue through which developing countries with infant industrial export sectors could expand manufactured exports and realise immediate foreign earning requirement for development. The developing countries should assess on a continuous basis the benefits and costs of export incentives, of support measures in the context of sectoral development and of the operations of EPZs. The most appropriate institution to evaluate the costs and benefits of support measures would be a national authority, external to, and sufficiently independent from, the political executive and the demands of pressure groups in the private sector.

The findings of S. Shiva Ranu's work on 'consultancy and project exports : overseas entry strategy' (1992) is as follows :

According to the research work,[13] Indian project exporters exhibit the following pattern :

- Indian project exporters have been successful in the competitive projects abroad.
- Turnkey projects are perceived as a very good opportunity for Indian exporters, specifically the growth segment is "consultancy".
- Indian exporters have been able to participate in global and multilateral funded projects.
- They have been able to diversify into new markets and new project areas at a response to changing global scenario.

P.K. Jain's (1984) research work on 'Export marketing : problems, procedure and prospect' throws light on India's export trade, engineering goods industries, 4P's of marketing and market research. The aim of the research was to analyse and examine in detail, the problems of Indian engineering goods industries especially in the field of exports.[14] The research revealed the problems faced by engineering exports viz.:

- Paucity of export information available to the exporter. (There is a multiplicity of institutions which collects and further disseminate information on various aspects of marketing. It would be helpful to the exporter if one body assume the central role and the focal point of all markets data relevant to exporters).

- High incidence of the freight rate and freight disparities between regions.
- Pricing constraints.
- Poor steel supply for exports, inadequate supply of infrastructure facilities, etc.

Research work has also suggested important measures like regional diversification of engineering exports, creation of additional industrial capacity, smooth and efficient functioning of economy, co-ordinated efforts needed for promotional work and pragmatism in export obligation schemes.

R.K. Pandey's (1989) research paper on 'Export Promotional System in India—Need for a New Strategy' puts in proper perspective the role, which export promotion measures/system should play to ensure continuing expansion and diversification of India's exports in the context of the highly competitive, complex and fast changing international marketing environment.[15]

The entire export promotion system in India, according to the author, has to be overhauled and scientifically oriented to the export marketing promotion needs rather than just catering to the cost reduction/profitability enhancement objectives, which indeed have some, but very limited, contribution to the export expansion and diversification efforts of the country.

A popular method of appraising benefits from export promotion measures in India has been to compare the net foreign exchange realisation from exports with the total cost of administering export promotion measures to national exchequer—'a fiscalist approach'. The benefit analysis of export promotion system in any country should, however, necessarily be based on a comparison between domestic research cost of export promotion measures/system and the 'Domestic resource Gain' as well as 'Net Foreign Exchange Earning'.

Subrata Banerjee's (1988) research paper on 'India's foreign trade and industrial development' put emphasis on the then in practice 'import liberalization' as basic strategy of export promotion.

The basic principle of imports for industrial development and exports has to be modified, to ensure that import liberalization meets priority needs of industry, not indigenously available or likely to be developed within a short time.

The paper talks about the need in case of non-traditional goods, to bear in mind comparative advantage and build up thrust areas as likely to have a continuing and expanding market over a reasonable time-frame.

Yung-Chul Kwon's (1988) research work on 'Trade Finance as a Competitive Tool : An overview' clearly reveals the role of trade finance as an important determinant of international competitiveness. This paper deals with role of trade finance, sources of trade financing, counter-trade, trade finance risks, trade credit and collection and trade finance management and organisation.

Thus, in the context of marketing, competitiveness depends on 4Ps. However on international level, at least one other factor is involved with making a competitive offer, that is, trade financing which often makes the difference in obtaining an order, particularly when the product and price offered are competitive with those of other industrialised nations.

The research paper says that to use trade financing as a competitive tool, trade financing programmes of the Government and trade financing techniques of the individual exporters must be effective and efficient.[16]

H.B. Desai's (1984) research study on 'Indian shipping perspectives' took account of difficulties and problems business firms have to face and how they have to incur extra expenses on maintenance of special establishments at seaports, undertaking frequent journey to port cities for sorting out procedural bottlenecks with customs and port authorities and spending time and money on communication for information and advises through telex, telegrams and telephone calls.[17]

The research study's focus was on role of Delhi dry port, technological innovation, container transportation system (for faster and reliable delivery of goods, to have better protection in cargo handling cost), container freight rates and establishment of national shipping board. According to the researcher, there is need of a quantum jump in upgradation and modernisation of port infrastructure and methods of operations.

Report of Review Committee on Export promotion council headed by Shri Prabhu V. Mehta (May 1965) came out with important recommendation with the basic idea of strengthening the EPCs, particularly bearing in mind the export target and the steps that have to be taken both in the matter of releasing exportable surpluses and for meeting the growing world competition. (Some of recommendations are covered in the Chapter 7).[18]

Charles Cadwell (May 1992) (State Export Promotion and Small Business). This study examined an important avenue of assistance for the small firm looking to expand their markets abroad; state export promotion programs. Nine case studies of export promotion programs were conducted to assess the common characteristics, assistance strategies, and relative effectiveness for small business of the programs in various states of US.[19] The study made the following recommendations :

1. State legislatures should establish explicit goals for export promotion programs and should distinguish between the goals of the export programs aimed at increasing the dollar value of the exports (short-term results) and aimed at increasing the number of small business exporters (long-term export capability).
2. States should implement fees for services. Seminars and trainings should have modest participation fees.
3. Program managers should understand the limitations of export assistance and avoid over ambitious promises of dramatic economic effects from a state export assistance effort.
4. States should identify specific feedback mechanism for export promotion activity to evaluate the effectiveness of programs.
5. State should articulate the comparative advantage of various state-supported export assistance providers and increase co-ordination and joint publicity.

Mc Kendrick and Associates (1996; United States) did research work on 'The Cost of Financing Exports for Small Business'. The purpose of this study was to examine the financing issues issues faced by small exporters, including availability of trade financing and cost associated with financing and payment settlement.[20]

The study examined the prevalence and cost of working capital financing among small exporters; payment mechanisms; the cost of export finance for manufacturer's *versus* non-manufacturers and export management companies, the role of banking and finance sector in export finance markets, awareness level of export finance; and use of alternative in export finance including transaction finance firms. The major findings of this research study were :

1. Drawing on an established line of credit from a commercial bank is the lowest cost method of external financing. Financing costs are almost twice as high from non-bank financial firms as from banks, not including points or upfront fees for initiating loans.
2. Payment mechanisms such as letters of credit take a relatively deeper bite out of smaller transactions.
3. Differences in the capital structures of manufacturing and non-manufacturing firms affect their relative ability to obtain trade finance. In addition, companies not primarily in the export business, such as manufacturers, tend to pay more for export finance than companies directly involved in the exporting business.
4. The banking sector has re-emerged as a trade finance source, and many see opportunities in the small business trade finance market. The potential expansion could alleviate the most restrictive and debilitating factor in small business export finance, that is the lack of systematic access by exporters.
5. The vast majority of companies in the study used traditional banks. There was a pervasive lack of knowledge of alternate finance mechanisms such as forfaiters, factorers, transaction finance firms and public sector lending programmes. Public sector programmes and private financial institutions have not reach the small exporter with information about their programmes.

6. Small business export finance costs compare favourably with those of Germany. However, Germany's small exporters may receive higher levels of service.

A. Diamantopoulos, A. Souchon, G. Durden, C. Axinn, H. Holzmuller, H. Simmet Bloomberg (1999) did research work titled 'Mapping Export Information use: A five nation study'.[21] Main focus of this research was on the extent to which and the ways in which export information is used can play a significant role in a firm's level of export performance. The focus of this study was the investigation of export information use 'practices' across different countries. A total sample of 989 exporting companies across Austria, Germany, Newzealand, the UK and the USA was obtained, and the data analyzed using analysis of covariance to control for extraneous, firm level, variables. The results indicated that US exporters were much more 'political' in their use of information, than exporters from the other countries, while Austrian exporters tend not to use information for political purpose. Similarly, export information gathered informally tends to be used much more 'rigorously' than does information gathered from export assistance bodies.

Hadi Salehi Esfahani's (1999; University of Illinois) work on 'Institutional Requirements of Successful Export Promotion in MENA Countries' threw light on institutional environment in MENA countries for international trade.[22]

The main objective of this research work was to identify the institutional arrangements that are conducive to improved export policies and performance in MENA countries. This projects focus was on two aspects. The first part developed a theoretical framework that links export promotion instititions with export policies and performance in the context of a country's general economic and institutional characteristics. The second part examined the relevance of the framework and methodology by applying them to 5 country case studies and comparing institutions and outcomes over time and across countries. These case studies were expected to generate practical policy lessons for improving export promotion arrangements in MENA countries. This study focus was on the following set of variables— (i) indicators of export performance, (ii) level and variances of export incentives, (iii) measures of institutional export orientation, (iv) measures of administration capability, and (v) indicators of macro-economic instability.

Arvind Virmani (2000) was one of the key members of Manmohan Singh's team that put together the economic reforms package of the early 1990s and followed through with its implementation.

Some of the articles written by him during this period have been collected in the book titled 'Accelerating Growth and Poverty Reduction'. The book contains 18 essays on aspects of economic growth and poverty reduction. One of its part has covered external sector, FDI and policies to mitigate the effect of capital inflow surge. Virmani cited the myriad of controls inhibiting economic growth and the inability of the old policy regime to provide higher economic growth as important reasons why the old paradigm needed to be abandoned. Virmani formulated a rationale for the new paradigm based on the pillars of liberalisation and enlightened Government policy along with adequate safeguards in the form of countervailing power and regulatory structures.[23]

Beside the above research works, other research studies taken were :

(a) S.S. Mehta (1988)—'India's Foreign Trade, Performance and Policy Options for 90's to inject an element of realism
(b) Eric Gonsalves's work on 'Some thoughts on India's Export Strategies'—July-Sept. 1986.
(c) An overview of Lina Seminar (with UNCTC 1-4, Feb. 1988) on "Services and Development—The role of FDI and Trade' explaining the complexity of service sector by taking Brazilian and Andean case study.
(d) Brij Mohan (1990) did research on "Effectiveness of export incentives measures in India". According to him, the export sector has remained the holy cow and no country is there which has not used incentives for export orientation.
(e) M.R. Czinkota; Export Development Strategies; US Promotion Policy (1982) on strategies used by US to boost exports.

(f) R.K. Bhatia on 'Exports and growth : An absorption approach in Indian case' (1979).
(g) Studies conducted by International Trade Centre.

Luminaries like A. John Raven (viz. Streamlining the export process, 1980), Bhagwati and Srinivasan (Foreign Trade Regime and Economic Development, 1972), Manmohan Singh (Export Trade Policy and Economic Development), N. Vittal (Free trade Zones and export strategy, 1977). Deepak Nayyar (India's Exports and Export policies in the 1960s, 1976). R.L. Varshney and B. Bhattacharya (International Marketing Management—an Indian perspective, 2002), Kelkar and Sharma (Trends and determinants of India's export performance, 1976). J.R. Rao (Trends in India's Export performance and Export Promotion measures, 1980) and P.K. Khurana (Export Management) and Sanjay Lall have done commendable work on Indian exports. Institutions like Exim Bank, ECGC, IIP, IIFT, etc. have also conducted researches on related aspect. However, specific focus on institutional support did not get adequate attention so far.

Notes and References

1. Nayyar, Deepak, 'Indian Exports and Export Policies in 1960s', Cambridge, 1975, p. 340.
2. Pursell, Garry, 'How to Measure and Compare Export Incentive'?, *Foreign Trade Review*, Vol. 22, *IIFT Journal*, New Delhi, 1987.
3. Mathur, B.P., 'Industrial Exports and Developing Countries—India's Research for Countervailing Power', Ajanta Publication, 1985.
4. Guide to the Evaluation of Trade Promotion Programmes, International Trade Centre UNCTAD/GATT, Geneva 1987, p. 1; Enhancing the effectiveness of Technical Assistance in Export Promotion, Joint Advisory group on the International Trade Centre UNCTAD/GATT, Eighth Session, Geneva, 6-17 Jan. 1975, p. 2.
5. Seringhaus, R.H. Rolf, 'A Methodological Approach to the Evaluation of Government Export—Promotion Programs', Research Paper Series No. 1-88, School of Business and Economics, Wilfrid Laurier University, Ontario, 1988.
6. Olson, H.C., 'Studies in Export Promotion', ACTA Universitatis Upsaliensis, Studia Oeconomiae Negotirum to, Stockholm, Alquist and Wiksell International, 1975.
7. Debroy, Bibek, 'China's External Trade—A Review', *Foreign Trade Review*, April-June, 1989, No. 1, Vol. XXIV.
8. Panchmukhi, V.R., Batliwala C.J., Reddy, K.C., Rao V.L., Thomas Philip, Mukherji, I.N., 'Export Financing in India', Interest Publication, 1991.

9. Narayana, M.R., 'Export Subsidies in India : Need for a Strategic Approach', *Foreign Trade Review*, April-June, 1992, Vol. XXVII, No. 1, pp. 35-51.
10. Sharma, O.P., 'Export Competitiveness : Some Conceptual Issues', *Foreign Trade Review*, July-Sept. 1992, Vol. XXVII, No. 2, pp. 159-76.
11. Katt, Vyaya, 'Construction Industry and Consultancy services, Exports : Problems and Prospects', *Foreign Trade Review*, July-Sept. 1992, Vol. XXVII, No. 2.
12. Agarwal, S.P., 'Role of Consultants in Export of Technologies and Manufactured Products', *Foreign Trade Review*, Oct.-Dec. 1992, Vol. XXVII, No. 3.
13. Ranu, S. Shiva, 'Consultancy and Project Exports; Overseas Entry Strategy', *Foreign Trade Review*, July-Sept. 1992, No. 2, XXVII, pp. 143-58.
14. Jain, P.K., 'Export Marketing of Indian Goods—Problems, Procedures and Prospects', Deep & Deep Publications, New Delhi, 1984, pp. 307-25.
15. Pandey R.K., 'Export Promotional System in India, Need for a New Strategy', *Foreign Trade Review*, April-June, 1989. Vol. XXIV, No. 1.
16. Kown Chul Yung, 'Trade Finance as a Competitive Tool : An Overview', *Foreign Trade Review*, IIFT, New Delhi, April-June, 1988.
17. Desai, H.B., 'Indian Shipping Perspectives : (iv), (v) and (vi); *Foreign Trade Review* April-June 1984, Oct. Dec. 1984, Jan.-March, 1984.
18. This was followed by Conference on Export Promotion by ICICI, Bombay, Dec. 15-16, 1967.
19. Cadwell, Charles, 'State Export Promotion and Small Business', National Small Business United, Washington, D.C. May 1992.
20. Kendrick, M.C. and Associates, 'The Cost of Financing Exports for Small Business', National Technical Information Service, US Department of Commerce, US, 1996, p. 199.
21. Esfahani, Hadi Salehi, 'Institutional Requirements of Successful Export Promotion in MENA Countries', University of Illinois, (Time Frame 20 months), FORUM, Vol. 6, No. 1, April 1999.
22. Diamantopoulos, A., Souchsn, A., Durden, G., Arcinn, C., Holgmuller, H., Simmt-Blomberg H., 'Mapping Export Information Use : A Five Nation Study', Aston Business School, Aston University, June, 1999.
23. Jha, Ragbendra, 'Reforms and Growth', *Economic and Political Weekly*, July 3, 2004, p. 2975.

Research Methods on Export and Export Promotion Institutions

5.1 IMPORTANCE

Trade is not an end in itself, but means to economic growth and national development. The primary purpose of foreign trade is not the mere earning of foreign exchange, but the stimulation of greater economic activity. As internationalization and globalization proceed ever faster, developing nations and LDCs face increasing competitive pressures, with implications for their survival and growth as well as for the development of economies. Also in the current global economy, trade and investment do not behave as independent variables, but are symbiotic. Trade brings investment and investment creates new trade opportunities.

For India to become a major player in world trade, an all encompassing, comprehensive view needs to be taken for the overall development of the country's foreign trade. Coherence and consistency among foreign trade and other economic policies is important for maximizing the contribution of such policies to development. The importance of economic policies and export promoting policies is widely recognized but important aspect which needs immediate attention is that, without appropriate institutional mechanisms, export promotion policy and incentives may be subject to a reversal of their effect and so institutional support to country's export becomes altogether important.

As effectiveness of exports largely depends upon the efficiency of institutions engaged to promote the exports, it becomes important to study the institutional network supporting the exports. The challenge for countries is to improve their export competitiveness along with development of institutional capacity. Here it must not be ignored that the definition of competitiveness is also changing. The value that dominated last century's global economy and trade was productivity per time unit based on quantitative input of labour. Today, information, knowledge and creativity are emerging as core competitive elements. So as to achieve export target, the competitiveness of institutional network is altogether essential, as institutions engaged in finance, insurance, testing, quality assurance, initiating research, information dissemination and export promotion provides the infrastructure of modern industrial activity. Their importance to competitiveness is growing as a result of increasingly stringent quality, precision, tolerance, other standards and competition in international market.

The creation of synergy via a construction of networks has become a major factor in achieving competitiveness.

A trade promotion strategy designed and implemented in isolation from other economic and commercial initiatives in a country is unlikely to succeed. Creating a national export strategy is by definition a national issue involving all relevant players. A solid national export strategy has to include the effective participation of Ministries of commerce, finance, other institutions engaged in export promotion and industry as well as experienced exporters.

This book aims at highlighting the role of institutional support in India's export promotion measures. The main aim is to analyse whether, all such institutions are really working on effective lines or not. This study becomes important to understand whether trade promotion organization can stay relevant and competitive in turbulent times or not? This study tries to give an insight as how the competitiveness and strengths of various institutions can be enhanced. The need of hour is to evaluate the strength of such institutions and to create the capacity to adapt to changing trade opportunities, so as to ensure that trade development strategies contribute to overall economic development and particularly poverty reduction to explain more clearly to the general public the role of exports as engine of growth.

5.2 OBJECTIVES

The objectives of the study are as follows :

1. To give a detailed view of export promotion organisations operating in India and the services provided by them.
2. To critically evaluate the performance of network of institutional support to Indian exporters.
3. To judge the awareness level and the perception of Indian exporters towards the service providers.
4. To study and critically examine the Indian exports, trends, direction and Export-Import policy (Exim policy).
5. To trace the level of comfort exporters feel while availing the services from such institutions.
6. To study the problems faced by exporters.
7. To generate strategies for efficient working of such institutions.
8. To find out the challenges for such institutions in future.
9. To study the ease of availing the services, clearance and grants being same or different for small and large exporters.
10. Call suggestions from the exporters for improvement in the services provided by export promotion organisations.

5.3 RESEARCH PROCESS

Research is a systematic and intensive study directed towards a more complete knowledge of the subject studied. Its purpose is to find answers to questions and problems through the application of scientific method.

Before executing any research work its methodology should be laid down explicitly. The step-wise discussion of the research process adopted in this research work is as follows :

5.3.1 The Research Problem

The first step in research is formulating a research problem.[1] It is rightly said that a "problem well defined is half solved".

The problem statement of this research work is as follows :

"Role of Institutional Support in India's Export Promotion Measures".

The main aim of this research work is to evaluate the performance of major institutions or export promotion organisations. The terms 'Institutional support' is described in the subsequent chapters and major institutions/organisations have been discussed in detail in the next chapters. The term 'Export' and 'promotion measures' have also been defined earlier in Chapters 1 and 3. This research work is restricted to India as specified in the problem also.

It took two and half years (Sept. 2002- March 2005) to give this research work final shape and structure. The importance and objectives of the research work has already been discussed in the earlier section of this chapter.

5.3.2 Hypotheses Formulation

A hypothesis is a supposition made as a basis for reasoning.[2] In other words, a hypothesis is a proposition which the researcher wants to verify.

The two hypotheses in a statistical test are normally referred to as :

- Null Hypothesis (Ho)
- Alternative Hypothesis (Ha)

The null hypothesis is very useful tool in testing the significance of difference. The term 'null' means nothing or invalid. The rejection of null hypothesis indicates that the differences have statistical significance and the acceptance of the null hypothesis indicates that the differences are due to chance. As against the null hypothesis, the alternative hypothesis specifies those values that the researcher believes to hold true. In other words, the conclusion that is accepted contingent on the rejection of the null hypothesis is alternative hypothesis.[3]

Having formulated the hypothesis, the next step is to test its validity at a certain level of significance. The confidence with which a null hypothesis is accepted or rejected depends upon the significance level used for the purpose. A significance level of, say 5 per cent, means that in the long-run, the risk of making wrong decision is 5 per cent.

For the apropos research, following hypotheses have been formulated.

(Only null hypothesis have been stated below) :

1. Ho1 There is no significant difference between the status of exporter and awareness regarding ECGC policies.
2. Ho2 There is no significant difference between the zones and awareness regarding ECGC policies.
3. Ho3 There is no difference in ratings for working of exim bank in terms of financial and other assistances.
4. Ho4 Status of exporter and working of Indian Institute of Packaging are independent attributes.
5. Ho5 There is no significant difference between the status of exporter and satisfaction with process of registration with EPCs.
6. Ho6 The status of exporters and rating of working of EPCs in discharging their functions are independent attributes.
7. Ho7 There is no significant difference between the (un)satisfaction level with the process of registration with EPC and rating of working of EPCs in discharging its functions.

8.	Ho8	The zones and process of registration with EPC are independent attributes.
9.	Ho9	There is no difference in ratings for working of FIEO and chambers.
10.	Ho10	There is no significant difference between availing any assistance provided by MDA and the process of release of approved MDA grant.
11.	Ho11	There is no significant difference between availing any assistance provided by MDA and the process of release of approved MDA grant (excluding the can't say option).
12.	Ho12	There is no difference among the status of exporters with respect to overall assistances provided under MDA.
13.	Ho13	Zone-wise rating for overall assistances provided under MDA do not differ.
14.	Ho14	There is no significant difference between the status of exporter and satisfaction derived from DEPB and advance licence.
15.	$Ho15_a$	There is no significant difference between the satisfaction associated with obtaining the letter of permission/letter of Intent and with its validity period (including Can't say option).
	$Ho15_b$	There is no significant difference between the satisfaction associated with obtaining the letter of permission/letter of Intent and with its validity period (excluding Can't say option).
16.	Ho16	There is no difference in ratings for the support of local authorities.
17.	Ho17	There is no difference among the status of exporters with respect to working of aggregate supporting agencies and infrastructural support.
18.	Ho18	Zone-wise rating for aggregate supporting agencies and infrastructural support do not differ.
19.	Ho19	There is no difference among the status of exporters with respect to role of overall institutional support.
20.	Ho20	Zone-wise rating for overall institutional support do not differ.

5.3.3 Research Design

Research design is the plan, structure, and strategy of investigation conceived so as to obtain answers to research questions and to control variance.[4]

According to Green and Tull—"A research design is the specification of methods and procedures for acquiring the information needed. It is the overall operational pattern or framework of the project that stipulates what information is to be collected from which sources by what procedures."[5]

The research design of the present research work is exploratory-*cum*-descriptive. It is more of exploratory nature as exploratory study is generally based on the secondary data that are readily available. On all the major concerned institutions, literature was searched and reviewed to know about their history, operations, strengths and organisational profile. In depth interviews were held with the key officials of institutions like Export Credit Guarantee Corporation, Export promotion councils, Exim bank, Chambers and key academician to get an insight into the problems and to get an overall understanding of the research project from new perspectives. Researcher also tried to attend "Exporters' meet" being organised by the concerned institutions to get the clear picture and finer details and problems of exporters.

The research design to a certain extent was also descriptive as survey was conducted and details were collected from the exporters and institutions. Information was collected from the exporters on various dimensions (including general information) and on their perception about the working of concerned institutions.

5.3.4 Data Collection

The next important step in research methodology is data collection which starts with deriving data objective. The data objectives are derived from the research objectives and which further throws light on what data are to be obtained, from whom and to make the predictions.

While deciding upon the method of data collection to be used for the study, the researcher has two options—secondary data and primary data.

(a) Secondary Data

Any data which have been gathered earlier for some other purpose are secondary data in the hands of researcher.

For the purpose of secondary data collection related to the topic, a large number of books, earlier researches, journals, magazines, reports, Government reports, periodicals, research papers, related websites, recommendations made by concerned committees (formed by Government) were referred to. Information was collected from many rich libraries of the country including the library of Indian Institute of Foreign Trade (IIFT), New Delhi which is considered as rich source of information with respect to foreign trade.

(b) Primary Data

Primary data are the first hand data, which are collected afresh for the first time and thus happen to be original in character.

With the exploration of secondary data from various sources and examining the possibility of their use in this research study, primary data was also collected. For the purpose of primary data collection, questionnaire method have been used in this research work. Questionnaire were filled out by the exporters (respondents). Structured questionnaire was prepared to get the information from the respondents. Questionnaire were filled through personal survey, (mainly by) mail survey and telephonic survey. All three were used and to many respondents, questionnaire were faxed also. The task of conducting the survey was very tedious one. Though a sample of 100 respondents was taken earlier but the response came out to be 70 per cent (i.e. 70) that too with much persuasion and facing many difficulties. Many of the exporters were not at all interested in filling the questionnaire, many were apprehensive though it was clearly communicated that the questionnaire does not ask for any confidential aspect and that there responses will be kept completely confidential and that the questionnaire is meant for academic purpose only.

Design of Questionnaire

The questionnaire was divided into two parts. First part was meant for collecting the general information about the respondents like name, address, IEC No. (Importer-Exporter Code No.), status and type of exports involved in etc. There were total nine questions in the first part.

Specific information on various aspects including Exim policy measures, about working of Export Credit Guarantee Corporation, Exim Bank, Export promotion councils, Indian Institute of Packaging, Chambers, FIEO, role of liasioning officers and about infrastructural support and calling suggestions from exporters were included in the second part. There were total 19 questions in the second part.

Dichotomous questions which has only two answers 'yes' or 'no' were used in the questionnaire. The third alternative (i.e. can't say) was also introduced where the respondents were not having any idea. Mostly in other questions where responses involved attributes and opinions, five points scales were used, where the scoring pattern was:

Excellent	-	5 points
Good	-	4 points
Average	-	3 points
Poor	-	2 points
Very poor	-	1 point

The questionnaire is appended in the thesis (Appendix 1).

5.3.5 Sampling Design

A number of tasks and decisions are involved in sampling. The sampling process consists of making and implementing decisions with respect to defining the population, selecting the sampling frame, and sampling method, determining the sample size, developing the sampling plan and actually selecting the sample and obtaining data, and finally, validating the sampling results. The various steps with respect to the present research are:

(a) Population

A population is an aggregation of the elements.[6] Population in this study includes (all institutions supporting India's Export Promotion Measures) all exporters exporting products or services from India, irrespective of the type of commodities or services exported by them and place from where they export (in India).

(b) Sampling Frame

The frame serves, in a sense, as the boundaries that circumscribe the population. The sampling frame in this research consists of the list of exporters. Website : www.indiamart.com/ Indian exporters and Exporter's yellow pages 2003-04, Infocom Network Ltd., New Delhi, provided comprehensive list of exporters of India.

(c) Sampling Procedure

Two stage sampling procedure was followed. In the first stage important commodities (and services) were selected. It was non-probability sampling method.

The first stage sampling was purposive non-probability sampling intended to obtain a true cross-section of the population. 20 commodity groups were selected.

At the second stage, exporters from each commodity segment were selected. The second-stage sampling also included non-probability method of sampling. Since the response from all commodity group was not the same, hence no fixed number of respondents could be alloted to the commodity groups. It was more of convenience sampling.

(d) Sample Size

The sample size in the present study consists of 70 respondents (the profile of which is discussed in the later part of this chapter).

5.3.6 Data Analysis

Having gathered the data from primary or secondary sources, the next step is to proceed towards the drawing of conclusions by logical inference. At this stage those data are only individual responses incapable of interpretation until converted into significant statistical information. The classification, coding and tabulation has been done to arrange the raw data in an understandable form. Computer software has been used for statistical analysis. The pictorial presentations of the data analysed has been done through pie, bar and line charts.

5.3.6.1 Statistical Techniques Used for Analysis and Interpretations

In this study a number of statistical techniques have been

used in order to interpret the tabulated data in the best possible manner. The techniques used are as follows :

(1) *Percentage* : This is very basic technique used for analysis of all responses.

(2) *Average score* : In this research work, five point scale were used to determine the extent of satisfaction on each parameter. All assigned scores on a particular parameter were taken to be a series and were added and then divided by total number of respondents to get the average score.

(3) *Chi-square (χ^2) Test* : χ^2 test as a test of independence : with the help of c^2 test, one can find whether two or more attributes are associated or not. In order to test whether or not the attributes are associated, null hypothesis can be taken as that there is no association in the attributes under study. If the calculated value of χ^2 is less than the table value at a certain level of significance (generally 5% level) and certain degree of freedom, it can be said about the hypothesis that the attributes are not associated, holds good.

	{df	=	(C—1) (r—1)
where	df	=	degree of freedom,
	c	=	No. of columns, and
	r	=	No. of rows}

χ^2 can be calculated as = $[\Sigma(O—E)^2/E]$ where O is observed frequency and E is expected frequency.

(4) *Kolmogorav-Smirnov one-sample test* : This test is similar to χ^2 test of goodness of fit. That is, it is concerned with the degree of agreement between the distribution of observed values and expected frequencies. This test is chosen when the researcher wants to compare the distribution on an ordinal scale.

The Kolmogorov-Smirnov test focuses on the largest value of the deviations among observed and theoretical proportions. 'D' value is calculated as :

D	=	Maximum [Fo(X)—Sn(x)]
where Fo(x)	=	Theoretical cumulative distribution of choices under Ho, and
Sn(X)	=	Cumulative distribution of observed choices.

For a sample size of more than 35, the critical value of D at an a of 0.05 is $1.36/\sqrt{n}$. If the calculated D exceeds the critical value, the null hypothesis is rejected.

(5) *F-test and analysis of variance* : The F-distribution measures the ratio of the variance between groups to the variance within groups. The variance between samples measures the differences between the sample mean of each group and the overall mean weighted by the no. of observations in each group. The variance within samples measures variability around the mean of each group. If the calculated value of F is at a certain critical level (5% level of significance) for the degrees of freedom is greater than the table value, it is concluded that the difference in sample means is significant (i.e., it could not have arisen due to fluctuations of simple sampling).

(6) *Trend analysis* : The term 'trend' is very commonly used in day-to-day parlance. The concept of trend (generally) does not include short-range oscillations but rather steady movements over a long time.

The method of least squares have been used for trend analysis. The straight line trend is represented by the equation

$$Yc = a + bx$$

where, X variable in time series always represents time.

Yo is used to designate the trend values to distinguish them from the actual Y values, a is the Y intercept or the computed trend figure of the Y variable when X = 0, b represents the slope of the trend line or the amount of change in Y variable that is associated with a change of one unit in X variable.

To find the growth pattern of exports performance of various organizations, trend analysis have been used by least square method and by plotting linear graph. Correlation technique have also been used to explain the degree of association between two variables.

5.4 PROFILE OF THE RESPONDENTS

5.4.1 Breakup of the Respondents According to the Commodities

Twenty commodity group has been selected (in which responses was received) which are as follows :

TABLE 5.1
Break-up of the Respondents on the Basis of Commodities

Sl. No.	*Commodity Group*	*No. of Respondents*
1.	Agriculture products	1
2.	Automobile	1
3.	Automatic accessories	2
4.	Pharmaceuticals, Bulk drugs	5
5.	Computer and computer hardware	3
6.	Carpets	3
7.	Woollen	5
8.	Sports Good	2
9.	Gems and Jewellery	5
10.	Handicrafts	7
11.	Rubber	1
12.	Engineering and Heavy Engineering Goods	2
13.	Textiles	2
14.	Chemicals and Allied	5
15.	Fashion Jewellery and Accessories	3
16.	Marbles, Granites, Minerals, Metals	10
17.	Tea	1
18.	Phosphates and Fertilizers	4
19.	Leather	3
20.	Miscellaneous (Software, services, and other exporters)	5
	Total	70

5.4.2 Break-up of Respondents on the Basis of Status

TABLE 5.2
Break-up of Respondents on the Basis of Status

	Number of Respondents	*Percentage*
(a) 100% Export-oriented unit	6	8.57
(b) Export House	12	17.14
(c) Trading House	2	2.86
(d) Star Trading House	0	0.00
(e) Super Star Trading House	2	2.86
(f) Any other	48	68.57

Maximum respondents, i.e. 67.14 per cent are not status holders. 17.14 per cent are export houses, 8.57 per cent are Export-oriented units and only 2.86 per cent are super star trading house in the present sample.

5.4.3 Nearest Port as Mentioned by the Respondents

TABLE 5.3
Nearest Port as Mentioned by the Respondents

	Number of Respondents	*Percentage*
(a) By Road	2	2.86
(b) Cochin	2	2.86
(c) New Delhi	27	38.57
(d) Kandla	13	18.57
(e) Kolkata	2	2.86
(f) Manglore	1	1.43
(g) Mumbai	22	31.43
(h) Vishakhapattanam	1	1.43

5.4.4 Unit-wise Classification of Sample Respondents

STP/EPZ/SEZ/EHTP/FTZ unit/Any other.

Majority of the respondent, i.e. 90 percent belongs to any other category, i.e. they do not come under, any such above mentioned category.

TABLE 5.4
Unit-wise Classification of Sample Respondents

	Number of Respondents	*Percentage*
(a) STP Unit	1	1.43
(b) FTZ Unit	0	0.00
(c) EHTP Unit	3	4.29
(d) EPZ Unit	0	0.00
(e) SEZ Unit	2	2.86
(f) Any other	64	91.42

5.4.5 Profile of Respondents on the Basis of Type of Exports Involved in

94.29 per cent of respondents are involved in merchandise exports.

TABLE 5.5
Break-up of Respondents on the Type of Exports Involved in

	Number of Respondents	*Percentage*
(a) Merchandise Export	66	94.28
(b) Service Export	1	1.43
(c) Deemed Exports	2	2.86
(d) Project Exports	0	0.00
(e) Merchandise and service exports	1	1.43

5.4.6 Profile of Respondents on the basis of their export product falling into restricted category or free with terms and conditions, etc.

TABLE 5.6
Profile of Respondents on the Basis of Export Product Category

		Number of Respondents	*Percentage*
(a)	Restricted	4	5.71
(b)	State Trading Enterprises	0	0.00
(c)	Free with Terms and conditions	66	94.29
(d)	Any other	0	0.00

5.4.7 Firms certified by ISO 9000, 14000, etc.

Out of the 70 respondent surveyed 55 firms were not certified by ISO 9000, the basic quality standard. Only one firm was having 9000, 14000 and 18000. Two firms were certified by HACCP (Hazard Analysis Critical Control Point). One firm was having 'EC' certificate given by Bureau veritas. Another firm was having quarantine certificate and phytosanitary certificate from the sample surveyed (Table 5.7).

TABLE 5.7
Firms Certified by ISO 9000, 14000, 18000, etc.

	No. of Respondents
Firms certified by ISO 9000	15
Firms certified by ISO 14000	5
Firms certified by ISO 18000	2
Firms certified by ISO 9000 and 14000	5
Firm certified by ISO 9000, 14000, 18000	1
Firm having WHO GMP	1
Firms having HACCP	2
Firms not certified by any such certification	55

5.4.8 Zone-wise Classification

The respondents were classified into four zones viz., North, South, East and West. States likes Rajasthan, Punjab, Haryana and New Delhi were included in north zone. In south zone—Tamilnadu, Kerala and Andhra Pradesh were included. In east zone respondents from Kolkata and Orissa and from west zone respondents from Maharashtra and Gujarat were included.

TABLE 5.8
Zone-wise Classification of Respondents

Zones	*Number of Respondents*
North	49
South	5
West	14
East	2

GRAPH 5.1
Profile of Respondents on the Basis of Status

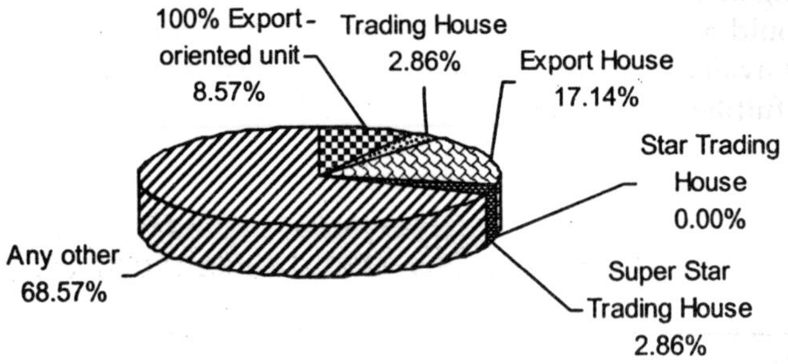

GRAPH 5.2
Unit-wise Classification

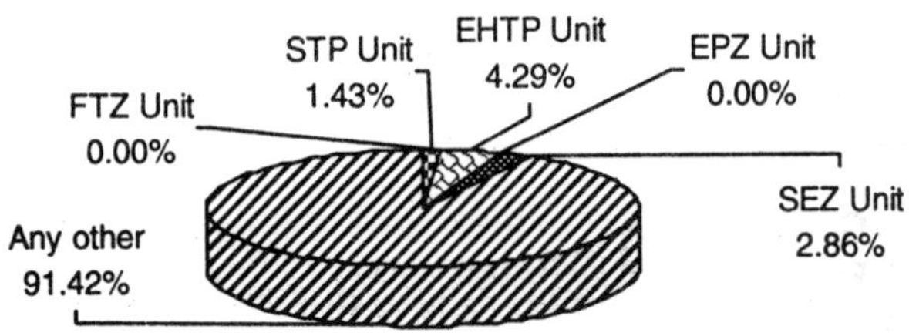

GRAPH 5.3
Profile of Respondents on the Basis of Type of Exports

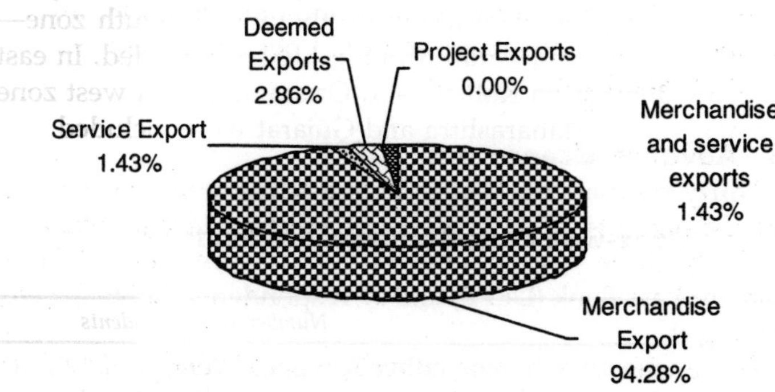

5.5 OTHER RELATED FINDINGS

5.5.1 Export Obligation to be Fulfilled with Respect to EPCG Licence

64.29 per cent of respondents said that the period for export obligation to be fulfilled should be 8 years, 31.43 per cent said it should be 10 years. One respondent gave the answer which was not available in the option, saying that export obligation should be fulfilled over 6 years.

TABLE 5.9
Export Obligation to be Fulfilled with Respect to EPCG Licence

Years	*Number of Respondents*	*Percentage*
8	45	64.29
10	22	31.43
12	1	1.43
14	1	1.43
06	01	1.43

5.5.2 Green Card Facility and Export and Import of Free Trade Sample

35 respondents (i.e. 50%) were in favour of green card

facility taken back by the Government and 35 respondents (i.e. 50%) were against this.

74.29% (52 respondents) of respondents said that they were satisfied with the conditions, quantity and other terms for export and import of free trade sample and 25.71 per cent of respondents were not satisfied with it.

5.5.3 Advance Licence and DEPB

Thirty respondents (42.86%) were advance licence holders and 40 respondents (57.14%) were not Advance Licence holders.

Thirty-three respondents (47.14%) were having Duty Entitlement Pass Book (DEPB) and 37 respondents (52.86%) were not having it.

Those who were having either Advance licence or DEPB or both were asked whether they were satisfied with advance licence and DEPB or not. 89.47 per cent respondents, i.e. 34 respondents said they were satisfied and 10.52 per cent respondents (4 respondents) said that they were not satisfied by it.

5.5.3.1 Chi-square Test

Null hypothesis can be stated as :

Ho 14: There is no significant difference between the status of exporter and satisfaction derived from DEPB and advance licence.

Chi-square value calculated at 5 per cent level of significance, degrees of freedom being 4 was 3.53. The table value (@ 5% significance, df = 4) is 9.49. Since the calculated value is less than table value, hence the null hypothesis is accepted.

5.5.4 Letter of Permission/Letter of Intent

52.85 per cent of respondents said they were satisfied with the process of obtaining letter of permission/letter of Intent issued to EOU/EPZ/EHTP/STP unit.

5.5.4.1 Validity period of Letter of Permission/Letter of Intent

58.57 per cent of respondents said they were satisfied with validity period, i.e. 3 years of letter of permission/letter of intent.

TABLE 5.10
Satisfaction Associated with Letter of Permission

Years	*Number of Respondents*	*Percentage*
Satisfactory	37	52.86
Unsatisfactory	0	0
Can't say	33	47.14

TABLE 5.11
Satisfaction Associated with the Validity Period of Letter of Permission

Years	*Number of Respondents*	*Percentage*
Satisfied	41	58.57
Not satisfied	4	5.71
Can't say	25	35.71

5.5.4.2 Chi-Square Test

Chi-square test can be used to test the hypothesis:

Ho15—There is no significant difference between the satisfaction associated with obtaining the letter of permission/LOI and with its validity period.

(a) Chi-Square value calculated at 5% level of significance and 2 degrees of freedom is 34.47 which is greater than the table value (5%, df = 2) = 5.99, hence the null hypothesis is rejected and alternative hypothesis is accepted, i.e. there is difference between the satisfaction associated with obtaining the letter of permission and with its validity period.

(b) If the option 'Can't say' is not included (Q. 24 and 25 of questionnaire), then the c^2 value at 5% level of significance and degree of freedom comes out to be 0.67. The table value (@ 5%, df = 2) is 3.84. Since the calculated value is less than tabulated value, hence in this case (without option can't say), null hypothesis is accepted.

5.5.5 Research Findings Regarding Export Documentation

None of the respondent rated export documentation of the country excellent as compared to other developed countries. 24.29 per cent of respondents rated it good, 52.86 per cent said it is fair. 21.43 per cent of respondents rated it poor and 1.43 per cent rated it very poor.

TABLE 5.12
Ratings Given by Respondents on Export Documentation Attribute

Years	*Number of Respondents*	*Percentage*
Excellent	0	0.0
Good	17	24.28
Fair	37	52.86
Poor	15	21.43
Very poor	1	1.43

5.5.5.1 Average Score

(a) Average score on this attribute was 3.0 which was less than the overall average score on institutional support 3.2. It suggests that improvements can be made on this attribute.

(b) Exporter's status and average score on this attribute.

It can be explained through the following Table 5.13.

TABLE 5.13
Exporter's Status and Average Score on Export Documentation Attribute

Status	*Average score*
100% EOU	3.17
Export House	3.08
Trading House	3.00
Super Star trading house	4.00
Others	2.92

The average score on this attribute was highest for superstar trading house and was lowest for others (2.92) not having any export status.

(c) Zones and average score on export documentation.

TABLE 5.14
Zones and Average Score on Export Documentation Attribute

Zones	*Average score*
East	3.50
North	2.98
South	3.40
West	2.86

For east zone and south zone, average score on export documentation are high and for west zone average score is just 2.86.

GRAPH 5.4
Process of Obtaining LOP

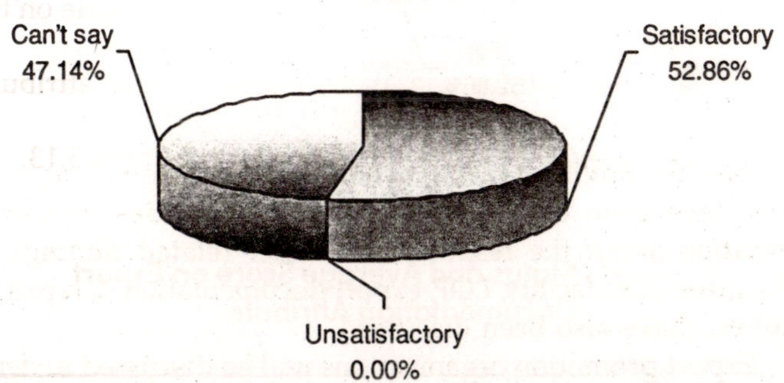

Thus these were the general findings regarding the profile of the respondent and on some other important attributes.

In this chapter complete research plan has been discussed, focussing on the importance of the study, its objectives, methodology and limitations.

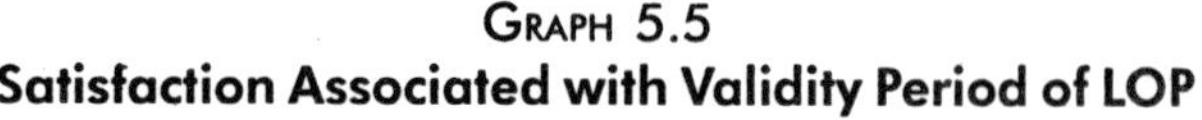

GRAPH 5.5
Satisfaction Associated with Validity Period of LOP

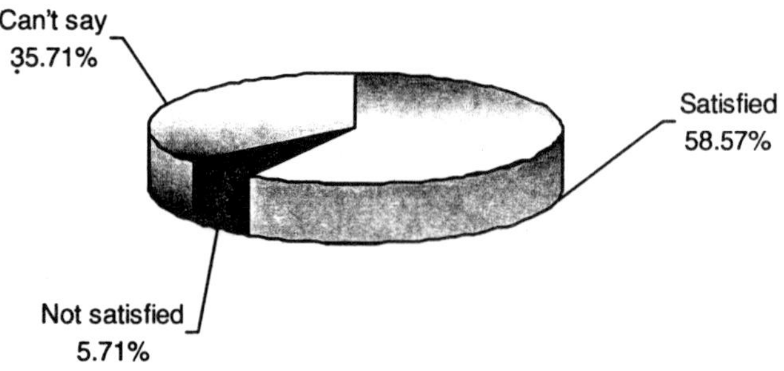

GRAPH 5.6
Rating on Export Documentation Attribute

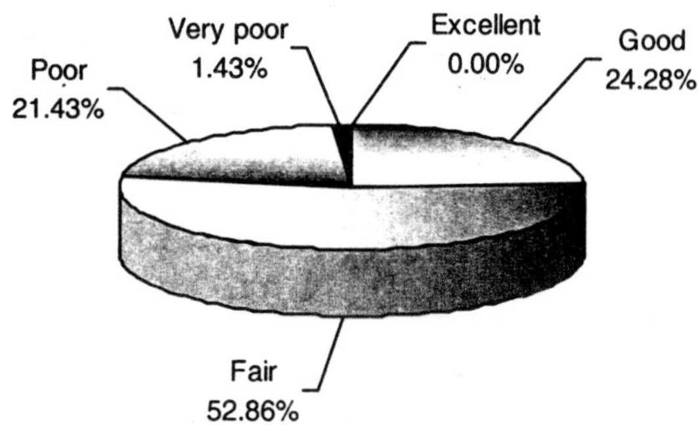

Also the profile of respondents (as evident from Graphs 5.1 to 5.3) have been discussed to get a general idea and basic information about the respondents. Other related findings on EPCG, green card facility, LOP, export documentation (Graphs 5.4 to 5.6) etc. have also been discussed.

Export promotion organizations will be discussed in detail in next few chapters.

NOTES AND REFERENCES

1. Beri, G.C., Marketing Research, Tata McGraw-Hill, New Delhi, Third Edition, 2000, p. 3, pp. 41-50.

2. Gupta, S.P., 'Statistical Methods, Sultan Chand and Sons, New Delhi, Twenty-eighth Edition, 2000, pp. A.3.2-3.4.
3. Luck, David J., Rubin Ronald S., Marketing Research, Prentice Hall of India, New Delhi, 7th Edition, 2002, pp. 428-30.
4. Kerlinger, Fred N., Foundations of Behavioural Research, Surjeet Publications, New Delhi, 1983, p. 300.
5. Green, Paul E. and Dull, Donald S., Research for Marketing Decisions, Englewood Prentice Hall, Inc., Englewood Cliffs, New Jersey, 1970, p. 73.
6. Kish, Leslie, Survey Sampling, John Wiley, New York, 1965, pp. 6-7.

Institutions Engaged in Export Promotion

6.1 INTRODUCTION

Export promotion in the developing world was reviewed against the backdrop of the particular economic and trade situation of these countries.[1] It is apparent that these countries have made substantial progress towards both export development and diversification of their exports into more sophisticated manufactured products. At the same time, the ongoing challenge of narrowing the expectation and reality gap between developed and developing countries suggests that tremendous efforts lie ahead, in economic development, export development and, in particular export promotion and so the question arises how ? one way could be to strengthen the organisational network engaged in export promotion.

This chapter and subsequent chapter deals with the institutional network, i.e. institutional support to Indian export promotion measures which is the life blood of this research study.

Institutions engaged in export effort (generally) fall in six different tiers. At the top is Department of Commerce of the Ministry of Commerce. This is the main organisation to formulate and guide India's trade policy.[2]

At the second tier, there are deliberative and consultative organizations to ensure that export problems are comprehensively dealt with after mutual discussion between the government and industry[3] (At the third tier are the commodity specific organisations which deal with problems relating to individual commodities and/or groups of commodities (EPCs and Commodity Boards). The fourth tier consists of service institutions which facilitate and assist the exporters to expand their operations and reach out more effectively to the world market (IIFT, ITPO, ECGC, EXIM Bank, etc.). The fifth tier consists of Government trading organisations specifically set-up to handle export/import of specified commodities and to supplement the efforts of the private enterprise in the field of export promotion and import management. Agencies for export promotion at the state level constitute the sixth tier.

In this chapter mainly institutions like—Export Credit Guaratee Corporation (ECGC), Export-Import Bank of India (Exim Bank), Indian Institute of Packaging (IIP), Beareau of Indian Standards, Export Inspection Council, Indian Council of Arbitration, along with the organisations at the top tier will be discussed.

6.1.1 The Top Tier

Ministry of Commerce and Department of Commerce

The Ministry of Commerce is responsible for the country's external trade and related matters such as export promotion measures, commercial relations with other countries, development and regulation of export-oriented industries and commodities and state trading. The Ministry formulates and implements policies in the sphere of foreign trade, reflected in export-import policy of India. Ministry of Commerce has also set-up Trade Point which aims at reducing transactional costs in international trade improving trade efficiency through an electronic network. It have access to approximately 500 to 1000 trade opportunities per day.

The Department of Commerce under the Ministry of Commerce is responsible for the country's external trade and all matters connected with it, such as commercial relations with other countries, general international trade policy, foreign trade (including trade negotiations, agreements and trade cooperation), state trading, trading with enemy, SEZs and EPZs, DGFT, Commodity Boards and all organisations and institutions connected with the provision of services relating to the export effect.[4]

DGFT, DGCI&S and DGAD

The Directorate General of Foreign Trade (DGFT), New Delhi is headed by Director General of Foreign Trade and is responsible for execution of Exim policy announced by the Government from time to time for promotion of exports. It also looks after monitoring of export obligation and work relating to issue of licences.

The Directorate General of Commercial Intelligence and Statistics (DGCI&S) Kolkata is the primary agency for the collection, compilation and publication of the foreign inland and ancillary trade statistics and dissemination of various types of commercial information.

The Directorate General of Anti-Dumping and Allied Duties (DGAD) came into existence in 1998 in the Department of Commerce. It is responsible for carrying out investigations and to recommend the amount of anti-dumping duty on the identified articles which would be adequate to remove injury to the domestic industry.

The Directorate of Drawback working under the Ministry of Finance, Department of Revenue determines and fixes drawback rates of items which are exported. It also formulates the procedures and documents required for claim of duty drawback.

6.2 EXPORT CREDIT GUARANTEE CORPORATION (ECGC) (YOU FOCUS ON EXPORTS. WE COVER THE RISKS)

6.2.1 Introduction

Payments for exports are open to risk even at the best of times. The risks have assumed large proportions today due to the far reaching political and economic changes that are sweeping the world. In order to provide export credit insurance support to Indian exporters, the Government of India set-up the Export Risks Insurance Corporation (ERIC) in July, 1957, as a no-profit no loss organization on the lines of Export Credits Guarantee Department (ECGD) in the UK. ERIC was transformed into Export Credit and Guarantee Corporation Limited (ECGC) in 1964. To brings the Indian identity into sharper focus, the corporation's name was once again changed to the present Export Credit Guarantee Corporation of India Limited in 1983. ECGC is wholly owned by Government of India. ECGC was registered under the companies Act, 1956. It functions under the administrative control of the Ministry of Commerce and is managed by a Board of Directors representing government, banking, insurance, trade and industry, etc.

When the Insurance Regulatory and Development Authority (IRDA) was set-up in 2000, opinions varied on whether ECGC should be brought under its purview or not.[5] Finally, new ECGC is under the ambit of insurance regulator. Under the framework of IRDA, ECGC will have to bring about some changes in its accounting and investment procedures.[6] It may be necessary for ECGC to take prior permission from IRDA to launch new product while ECGC is preparing grounds to switch over to the new IRDA—stipulated segment-wise accounting norms this year. However, investment changes are expected to take some more time.[7]

The Export promotion organization which has paid up capital of Rs. 440 crore, is expected to infuse additional capital of about Rs. 800 crore by 2007.[8]

6.2.2 Objectives of ECGC

ECGC provides a range of credit risk insurance cover to exporters against loss in export of goods and services.

- ECGC offers guarantees to banks and financial institutions to enable exporters obtain better facilities from them, and
- It provides overseas investment insurance to Indian companies investing in joint ventures abroad.

Besides the above objectives ECGC does the following :

- Offers insurance protection to exporters against payment risks.

- Provides guidance in export-related activities.
- Makes information available on different countries with its own credit ratings.
- Makes it easy to obtain export finance from banks/ financial institutions.
- Assist exporters in recovering bad debts.
- Provides information on credit worthiness of overseas buyers.
- ECGC's main focus is on credit insurance while export insurance generally focuses on covering goods services and receivables (Fig. 6.1).

FIG. 6.1
Export Insurance

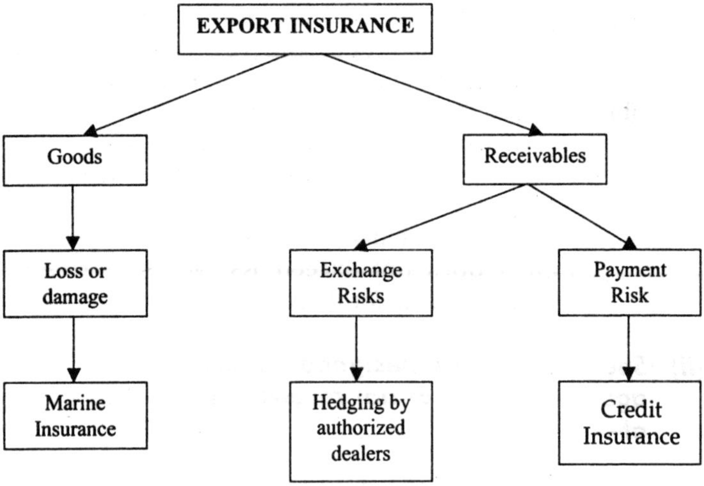

Since as discussed earlier payment for exports are open to risk even at the best time.

An out-break of war or civil war may block or delay the payment for the goods exported. Economic difficulties, balance of payment problem, embargo/exchange transfer delay, commercial risks of a foreign buyer going bankrupt can aggravate the situation. Therefore, ECGC provides export credit insurance which is designed to protect exporters from the consequences of payment risks and to enable them to expand their overseas business without fear of loss.

6.2.3. Covers issued by ECGC

(i) Standard Policies

The shipments (Comprehensive Risks) policy is commonly known as standard policy—

(a) Standard policies are issued to exporters to protect them against the payment risk involved in exports on short term credit (credit not exceeding 180 days). This policy is meant to cover all the shipments that may be made by an exporter during a period of 24 months ahead and (excluding shipments made against advance payment or those, which are supported by irrevocable letter of credit) covers commercial and political risk.

(b) The small exporter's policy is basically the standard policy, incorporating certain improvement in terms of cover, in order to encourage small exporters to obtain and operate the policy. It will be issued to exporters whose anticipated export turnover for the next 12 months does not exceed Rs. 50 lakh. Minimum premium payable for this policy is equal to Rs. 2000.

(ii) Specific policies designed to protect Indian firms against the risk of not receiving payment in respect of—

(a) Exports on deferred payment terms,

(b) Services rendered to foreign parties, and

(c) Construction work, including turnkey projects undertaken abroad (construction works policy).

Specific policy for supply contracts may take any of the following forms :

(i) Specific shipments (comprehensive Risks policy),

(ii) Specific shipments (Political risks) policy,

(iii) Specific contact (comprehensive risks) policy, and
(iv) Specific contract (Political risks) policy.

Other specific policies include :

- Specific shipment policies—short-term (To cover specific transaction) (SSP-ST),
- Buyer-wise Policies—Short-term (BP-ST) (To cover specific buyer),
- Services Policy.

Corporation have evolved 3 types of policies—

(i) Specific services contract (comprehensive risks) policy;
(ii) Whole turnover services (comprehensive risks) policy and
(iii) Whole turnover services (Political risks) policy.

(iii) Software Project Policy Covers Projects Involving for

(i) Development of software offshore to be delivered and implemented in the buyer's location;
(ii) Development of software on site of the client and supply and implementation; and
(iii) Both offshore and on-site development.

(iv) Financial Guarantees to Bank

ECGC has designed a scheme of Guarantees to bank with a view to enhancing the credit worthiness of the exporters so that they would be able to secure better and larger facilities from their bankers. To meet the varying needs of exporters, the corporation has evolved the following types of Guarantees:

(1) Packing Credit Guarantee,
(2) Export Production Finance Guarantee,
(3) Post-Shipment Export Credit Guarantee,
(4) Export Finance Guarantee,
(5) Export Performance Guarantee, and
(6) Export Finance (overseas lending) Guarantee.

(v) Special Schemes

Special schemes includes transfer guarantee meant to protect banks which add confirmation to letters of credit opened by foreign banks, insurance cover for buyers' credit, line of credit and overseas investment insurance and exchange fluctuation risk insurance.[9]

6.2.4 Underwriting Policy

(a) *Buyer underwriting* : Under the Alliance of ECGC and Dun and Bradstreet (the world's leading information provider), the corporation has provided a value-added service to its policy-holders for keeping the authenticity of business in their export transactions by providing the D and B's D-U-N-S number free of cost.[10] The other ways used by ECGC are :

- Checking the financials' credit worthiness.
- Feedback from other insurers.
- Agreement with credit Information Agencies
- ECGC's Past experience
- Exporter's Experience.

(b) *Country underwriting* : The corporation has classified almost 220 countries into its seven-fold classification for country risk assessment purposes and for determining its premium rates under the short, medium and long-term insurance covers issued by it. The classifications are based on a number of quantitative and qualitative factors encompassing economic and political parameters, rating of international credit rating agencies, bilateral relations with the country under study and above all ECGC's own experience. ECGC uses open cover (covers such countries without any restrictions subject to the usual terms and conditions) and restricted cover category (in it exporter are required to take prior approval for each shipment contract) countries with unstable economic and political environment fall under this category (Annexure 6.1 and 6.2 takes account of seven fold classification and countries transferred from restricted cover category to open cover category respectively).

6.2.5 ECGC's Performance

6.2.5.1 Business Highlights (1999-04)

During 2003-04,[11] the corporation earned a total income of Rs. 561.27 crore, registering a growth of 12.36 per cent over the total income of Rs. 499.54 crore during 2002-03. The gross premium income for the year was Rs. 445.48 crore. Growth in short-term policy premium during the year was 10.41 per cent over the previous year (Graph 6.1 and 6.2).[12]

GRAPH 6.1

Value of Business Covered

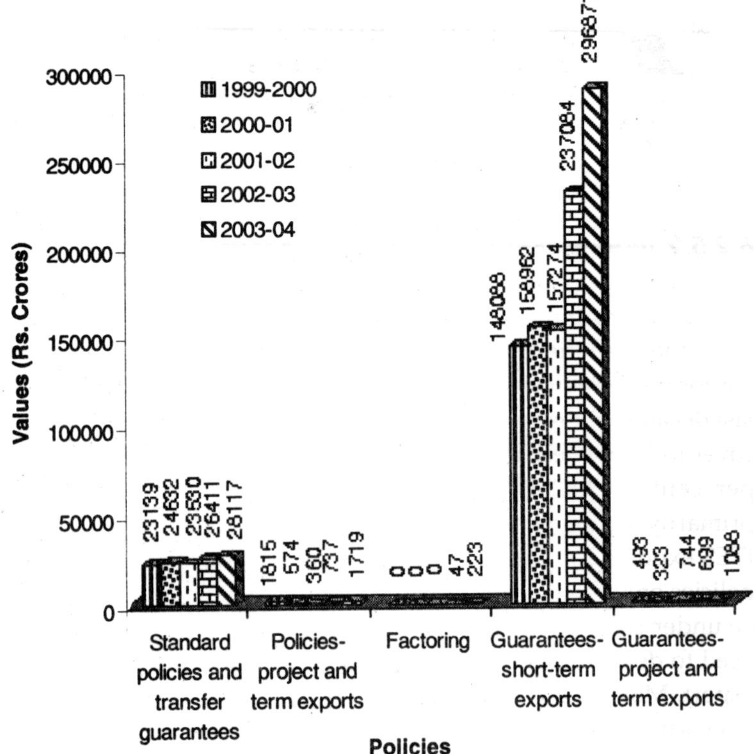

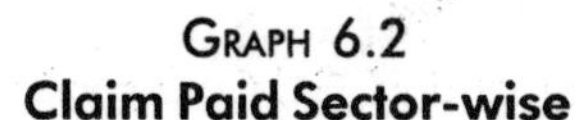

GRAPH 6.2
Claim Paid Sector-wise

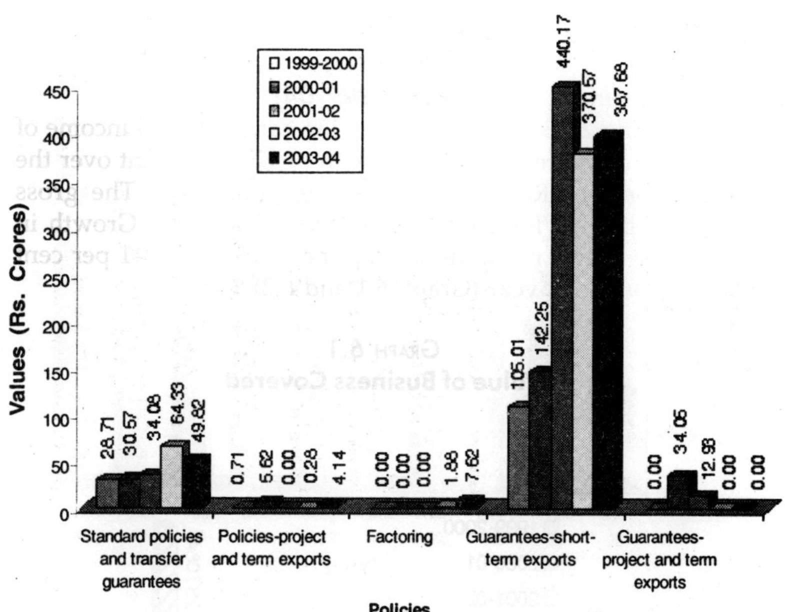

6.2.5.2 India's Exports and ECGC Coverage

In the year 2003-04 ECGC has provided short-term cover to 10 per cent of India's total exports (Graph 6.3).

One of the areas of concern is the reduction in the corporation's percentage coverage of India's export during the last decade. In 1993-94, the Corporation has provided short-term cover to 17 per cent of India's total exports, which reduced to 10 per cent in 2003-04. Though the reduction in coverage is primarily attributed to the phenomenal increase in software and ITES exports, for which the Corporation has developed specific policies only recently, the scope for growth in other sectors cannot be under-estimated. In the coming days, the Corporation would need to devise a suitable strategy for greater coverage of India's export. Moreover a significant percentage of active exporters are not corporation's policy-holders.

Graph 6.3
India's Exports and ECGC Coverage (Short-term)

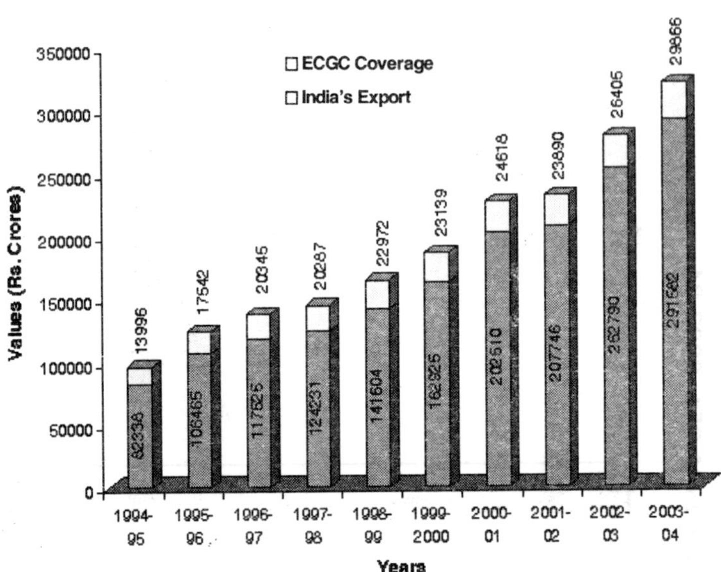

6.2.5.3 Performance of ECGC from 1994-95 to 2003-04

Total value of business covered in 2003-04 was Rs. 3,28,018 crore as compared to Rs. 1,16,929 crore in 1994-95. The total premium income in 2003-04 was Rs. 445.48 crore as compared to Rs. 164.84 crore in 1994-95. In 2003-04 a total of Rs. 449.26 crore claims were paid, which in 1994-95 was Rs. 227.52 crore. In 2003-04 worth Rs. 62.93 crore recoveries were made by ECGC.

In line with keeping pace with changing environment ECGC has taken certain steps. For its large exporters it has opened branches at Mumbai and head office (i.e. it is going for branch expansion). Also it has tied-up with National Insurance Company for Marine Cover as add-on. Given its unsatisfactory experience with individual agents, it has resorted to bancassurance.[13]

ECGC has launched its redesigned portal www.ecgcindia.com and it provides on line connectivity to exporter clients. ECGC is also member of Berne Union.

TABLE 6.1
ECGC's Performance from 1994-95 to 2003-04

(Rs. in ,Crore)

	1994-95	*1995-96*	*1996-97*	*1997-98*	*1998-99*
(1)	*(2)*	*(3)*	*(4)*	*(5)*	*(6)*
Value of Business Covered					
Standard Policies and Transfer Guarantees	13997.00	17542.00	20345.00	20287.00	22972.00
Policies—Project and Term Exports	789.00	882.00	1014.00	1184.00	1551.00
Factoring	0.00	0.00	0.00	0.00	0.00
Guarantees—Short-term Exports	101653.00	111052.00	129860.00	144716.00	141365.00
Guarantees—Project and Term Exports	490.00	642.00	345.00	327.00	843.00
Total	116929.00	130118.00	151564.00	166514.00	166731.00
Premium Income					
Standard Policies and Transfer Guarantees	52.35	64.50	74.25	75.48	86.62
Policies—Project and Term Exports	8.60	9.76	11.10	12.50	11.89
Factoring	0.00	0.00	0.00	0.00	0.00
Guarantees—Short-term Exports	97.55	128.02	146.00	171.69	192.18
Guarantees—Project and Term Exports	6.34	5.06	5.61	5.49	6.01
Total	164.84	207.34	236.96	265.16	296.70

(Contd.)

TABLE 6.1 (Contd.)

(1)	(2)	(3)	(4)	(5)	(6)
Claims Paid					
Standard Policies and Transfer Guarantees	11.10	20.66	21.87	21.50	22.87
Policies—Project and Term Exports	148.76	106.97	75.14	30.39	17.49
Factoring	0.00	0.00	0.00	0.00	0.00
Guarantees—Short-term Exports	17.84	22.72	61.55	99.01	80.72
Guarantees—Project and Term Exports	49.82	70.52	44.47	84.86	0.00
Total	227.52	220.87	203.03	235.76	121.08
Recoveries Made					
Standard Policies and Transfer Guarantees	4.18	0.72	2.15	3.88	1.07
Policies—Project and Term Exports	16.52	5.80	0.16	1.12	0.54
Factoring	0.00	0.00	0.00	0.00	0.00
Guarantees—Short-term Exports	2.67	4.08	4.98	4.31	5.81
Guarantees—Project and Term Exports	29.25	36.77	22.35	11.14	0.00
Total	52.62	47.37	29.64	20.45	7.42

(Contd.)

TABLE 6.1 (Contd.)

(Rs. in Crore)

	1999-2000	2000-01	2001-02	2002-03	2003-04
(1)	(6)	(7)	(8)	(9)	(10)
Value of Business Covered					
Standard Policies and Transfer Guarantees	23139.00	24633.00	23530.00	26411.00	28117.00
Policies—Project and Term Exports	1815.00	574.00	360.00	737.00	1720.00
Factoring	0.00	0.00	0.00	47.00	223.00
Guarantees—Short-term Exports	148088.00	158962.00	157274.00	237084.00	296870.00
Guarantees—Project and Term Exports	493.00	323.00	744.00	699.00	1088.00
Total	173535.00	184492.00	181908.00	264978.00	328018.00
Premium Income					
Standard Policies and Transfer Guarantees	87.88	96.73	101.02	110.66	116.62
Policies—Project and Term Exports	12.70	8.70	6.76	8.91	9.16
Factoring	0.00	0.00	0.00	1.09	4.61
Guarantees—Short-term Exports	200.78	218.66	224.97	245.37	302.47
Guarantees—Project and Term Exports	5.41	6.36	5.77	8.62	10.62
Total	306.77	330.45	338.52	374.65	445.48

(Contd.)

TABLE 6.1 (Contd.)

(1)	(2)	(3)	(4)	(5)	(6)
Claims Paid					
Standard Policies and Transfer Guarantees	28.71	30.57	34.08	64.33	49.82
Policies—Project and Term Exports	0.71	5.62	0.00	0.28	4.14
Factoring	0.00	0.00	0.00	1.88	7.62
Guarantees—Short-term Exports	105.00	142.25	440.11	370.57	387.68
Guarantees—Project and Term Exports	0.00	34.05	12.93	0.00	0.00
Total	134.42	212.49	487.12	437.06	449.26
Recoveries Made					
Standard Policies and Transfer Guarantees	7.02	6.47	2.27	2.09	8.65
Policies—Project and Term Exports	0.00	2.78	0.00	0.53	0.09
Factoring	0.00	0.00	0.00	0.28	3.03
Guarantees—Short-term Exports	16.18	12.20	23.89	36.97	50.56
Guarantees—Project and Term Exports	0.08	0.00	0.60	23.54	0.60
Total	23.28	21.45	26.76	63.41	62.93

Source : Export Credit Guarantee Corporation of India, Limited.

6.2.6 Research Findings Regarding ECGC

6.2.6.1 Awareness Regarding the Policies Issued by ECGC

Fifty-five respondents said that they were knowing about the standard policies, specific policies and financial guarantees issued by ECGC and 15 respondents said that they were not aware of it (Graph 6.4).

GRAPH 6.4
Awareness Regarding the Policies Issued by ECGC

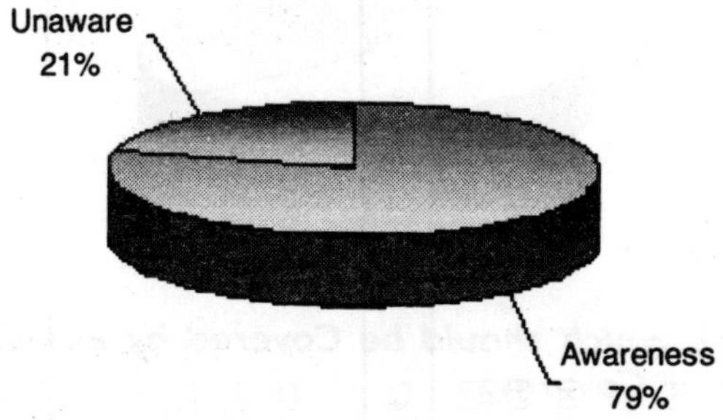

6.2.6.2 Rating of the Various Policy Schemes Issued by ECGC on the Basis of Risk Covered and Premium

Out of those respondents who said they were aware of policies issued by ECGC only 3.63 percent has rated it excellent and 61.8 percent has rated it as good.

TABLE 6.2
Rating of Various Policies Issued by ECGC

	Number of respondents	*Percentage*
Excellent	2	3.63
Good	34	61.80
Average	18	32.72
Poor	0	0.00
Very poor	0	0.00
No response	1	1.81
Total	55	100.00

6.2.6.3 Payment of Claims

2 Respondents rated it as excellent, 18 respondents said good and 32 respondents rated it as an average (Graph 6.5).

GRAPH 6.5
Rating on Payment of Claims by ECGC

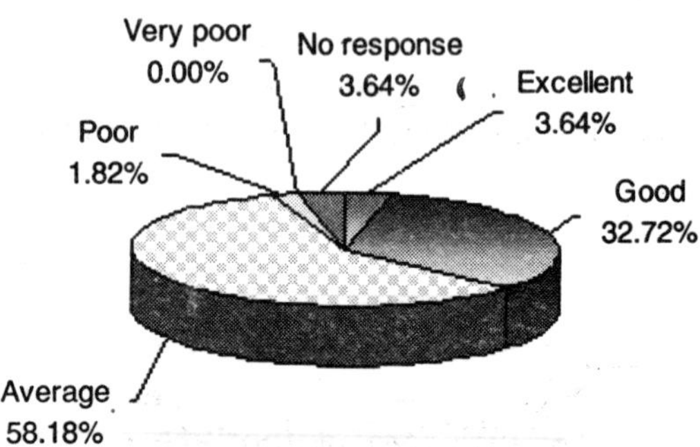

6.2.6.4 Risk which should be Covered by ECGC which it is not Covering

87.27 per cent respondents said that they don't want to suggest (i.e. there is no need to suggest) risks which should be covered by ECGC which it is not covering. 12.73 per cent respondents said 'yes', i.e. there must be some more risks which should be covered by ECGC.

6.2.6.5 Chi-Square Test

(a) Chi-Square was calculated to find whether null hypothesis will be accepted or rejected.
Ho1—There is no significant difference between the status of exporter and awareness regarding ECGC policies.
Chi-square was calculated at 5 per cent level of significance at four degree of freedom which came out to be 8.75. Since the calculated c^2 value is less than tabulated value (@ 5%, df = 4, 9.49), null hypothesis is accepted.

(b) Ho2—There is no significant difference between the zones and awareness regarding ECGC policies.

χ^2 value was calculated @ 5% level of significance at 3 degrees of freedom which came out to be 0.58. Since the calculated χ^2 value is less than tabulated value @ 5%, (df = 3, 7.81) the null hypothesis is accepted, i.e. zones and awareness regarding ECGC policies are independent attributes.

6.2.6.6 Average Score

Average score on the attribute (rating of the various policy schemes issued by ECGC) came out to be 2.86 which is less than overall average score 3.20.

Average score regarding the payment of claims by ECGC was 2.57 which is also less than the overall average score 3.20.

Overall average was calculated taking all the concerned attribute which represented the overall satisfaction regarding the working of institutions which included ECGC [Q. 16, 17 of questionnaire (Qe)], Exim bank (Q. 19 of Qe), Export promotion councils (Q. 23 of Qe), local authorities, local promotional agencies, infrastructure, export documentation, working of FIEO and chambers and Indian Institute of Packaging (Q. 27 of Qe).

6.3 EXPORT-IMPORT BANK OF INDIA (EXIM BANK)

Export Import Bank of India is the principal financial institution in the country for coordinating working of institutions engaged in financing exports and imports. Exim bank is a public sector financial institution fully owned by Government of India, created by an act of Parliament—The Export-Import Bank of India Act, 1981.

Exim Bank was set-up for the purpose of financing, facilitating and promoting foreign trade in India (Fig. 6.2).

Exim Bank of India is managed by Board of Directors with representatives from Government, RBI, ECGC, financial institutions, banks and business community. It has network of 14 offices in India (at Ahmedabad, Bangalore, Chennai, Guwahati, Hyderabad, Kolkata, Mumbai, New Delhi and Pune) and overseas (Budapest, Johannesburg, Milan, Singapore and Washington D.C.).

The organization of Exim bank can well be understood as given in Fig. 6.3.

FIG. 6.2
Evolving Vision of Exim Bank of India

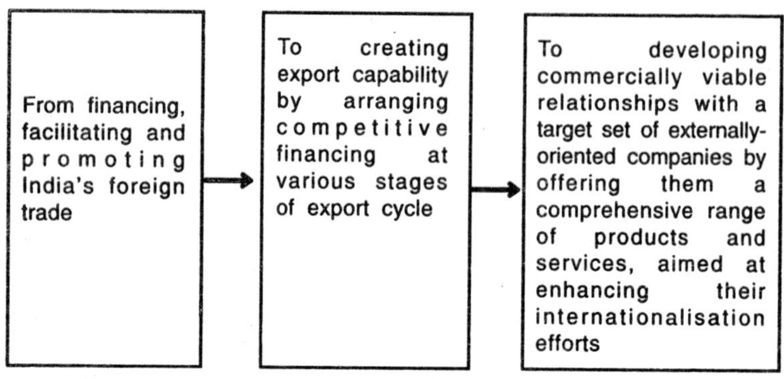

6.3.1 Exim Bank's Operation

Exim bank provides a range of analytical information and export-related services. The bank's fee based services help identify new business propositions, source trade and investment-related information, create and enhance presence through joint network of institutional linkages (Annexure 6.3) across the globe, and assists externally-oriented companies in their guest for excellence and globalisation.

The operations of the Exim bank are grouped as below :

I. Export Credits

A. For Indian Companies

(i) Pre-Shipment credit (Finance is available from Exim bank for companies executing export contracts involving cycle time exceeding six months).
(ii) Foreign currency Pre-shipment credit (It is extended, with a view to making credit available to exporters at internationally competitive rates for domestic and imported inputs of exported goods at LIBOR/EURO LIBOR-related rates of interest).
(iii) Post-shipment supplier's credit.
(iv) Finance for deemed exports.

Fig. 6.3
Organization of Exim Bank

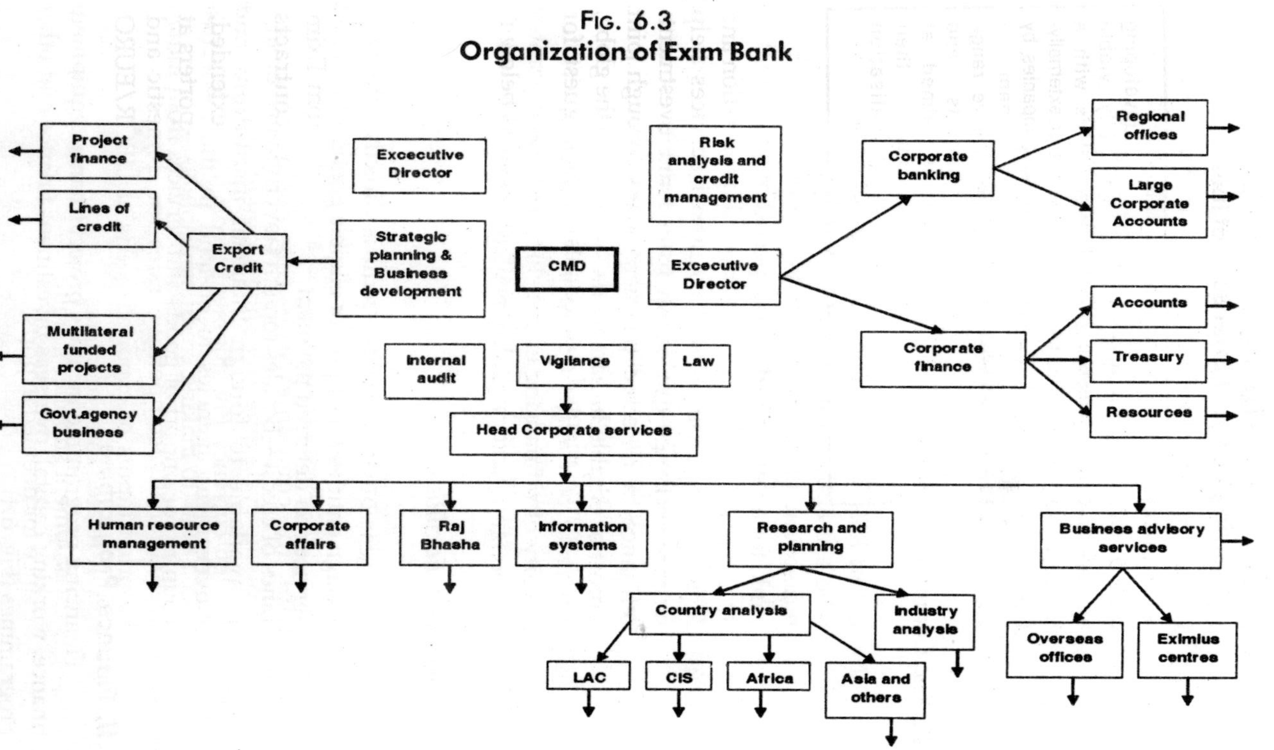

(v) Finance for consultancy and technology services.

(vi) Guarantee and L/C facilitation facilities.

(vii) Forfaiting (Forfaiting refers to the exporter relinquishing his right to a receivable due at future date in exchange for immediate cash payment, at an agreed discount, passing all risks and responsibilities for collecting the debt to the forfaiters). The role of exim bank will be that of facilitator between the Indian exporter and the overseas forfaiting agency.

B. For Commercial Banks

(i) *Export Bills Rediscounting* : Commercial banks in India who are authorised to deal in foreign exchange can rediscount their short-term export bills with Exim bank, for an unexpired usance period of not more than 90 days.

(ii) *Refinance of Export Credit* : Authorised dealers in foreign exchange can obtain from Exim Bank 100% refinance of deferred payment loans extended for export of eligible Indian goods.

(iii) *Refinance of Foreign Currency Pre-shipment Credit* : Facility of refinancing of pre-shipment credit granted in foreign currency is also available from Exim bank.

C. Overseas Facilities

(i) Overseas buyer's credit—credit is directly offered to foreign entities for import of eligible goods and related services on deferred payment.

(ii) Lines of credit—Besides foreign Governments' finance is available to foreign financial institutions and Government agencies to on-land in the respective country for import of goods and services from India.

II. Finance Programme

Financing programme includes project finance, equipment finance, working capital, overseas investment finance and other programmes (Fig. 6.4).

Fig. 6.4
Finance Programme of Exim Bank

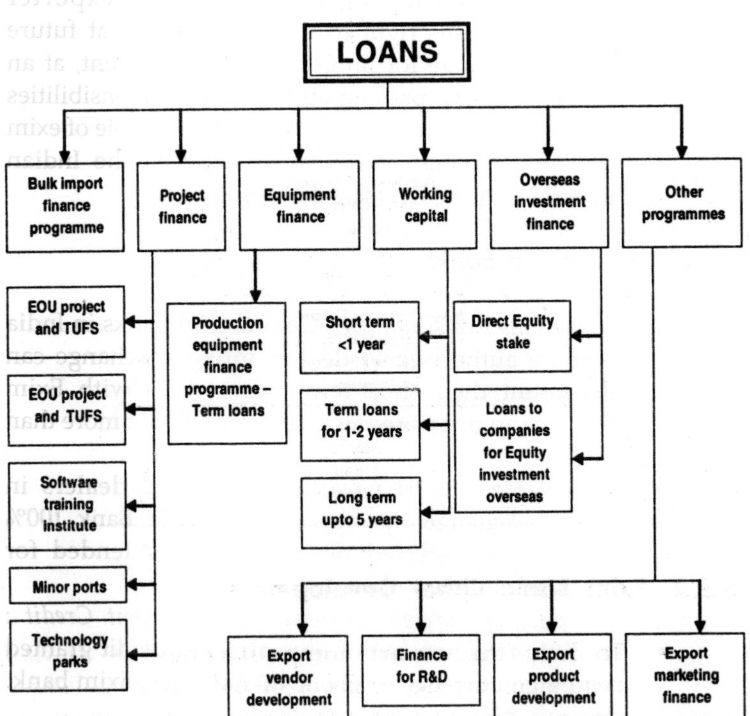

III. Export Services

Bank provides a range of information and advisory services to Indian companies to supplement their efforts aimed at globalisation of Indian business (Fig. 6.5).

IV. Supporting Groups

- Planning and Research
- Accounts/MIS/EDP
- Legal
- Co-ordination
- HRD
- Establishment

FIG. 6.5
Value Based Services Offered by Exim Bank

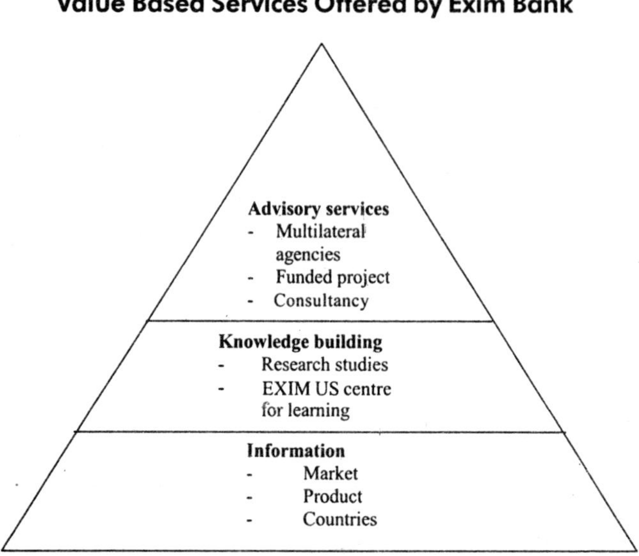

6.3.2 Exim Bank: Other Developments

- To help the export competitiveness of Indian companies the Government of India has finalised a strategic plan to bolster the capital base of the bank. The bank's capital base is Approximately 649 crore (Annexure 6.4). The Exim bank capital base is in sharp contrast to that of Japanese Exim bank which has a capital base of $ 12 billion, US Exim bank $ 1 billion and China of $ 650 million. By enhancing the capital base of the bank,[16] the Government proposes to provide an interest subsidy through the Exim bank to exporters in certain areas to be identified by the Government, to ensure that they are more competitive *vis-a-vis* their international counterparts.[17]
- Exim Bank and Central Food Technological Research Institute (CFTRI) have signed a memorandum of Understanding (MOU) to promote small and medium enterprise (SME) food processing projects in Africa and CIS region under Exim Bank's lines of credit facility.[18]

- The Government soon will provide for interest equalisation support to the Exim bank and other banks for raising resources which would be routed to overseas sovereign entities as lines of credit (Libor plus 50 basis points).
- Exim bank got stable rating (Baa3 foreign currency issuer rating)[19] from Moody which reflects that the bank has managed to develop significant expertise in this field.

At the same time, one thing which can't be ignored is Exim bank's relatively high concentration to the industrial corporate leaves it vulnerable to a possible systemic down-turn in the economy.

- Exim bank has facilitated 110 contracts of Indian exporters in 45 countries worth Rs. 6,531 crore. Also its net NPAs are under prescribed limits (which is 2.25% of total funds).

6.3.3 Research Findings Regarding Exim Bank

6.3.3.1 Rating of Working of Exim Bank in Terms of Financial and Other Assistances

Thirty-three respondents rated it as good and the 34 respondents rated it as average. Only 2 respondents rated it as cxcellent and 1 respondent as poor (Graph 6.6).

GRAPH 6.6
Rating on Working of Exim Bank

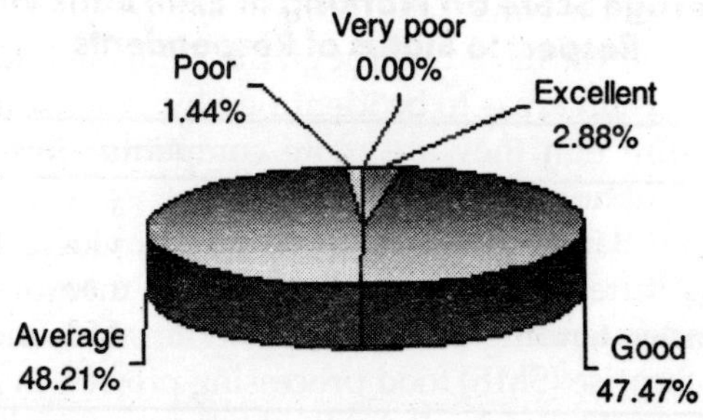

6.3.3.2 Access to Exim Bank Finance

Majority of respondents, i.e. 40 said that they can't say on this attribute. 22 respondents said it is difficult and only 8 respondents said it is easy (Graph 6.7).

GRAPH 6.7
Access to Exim Bank Finance

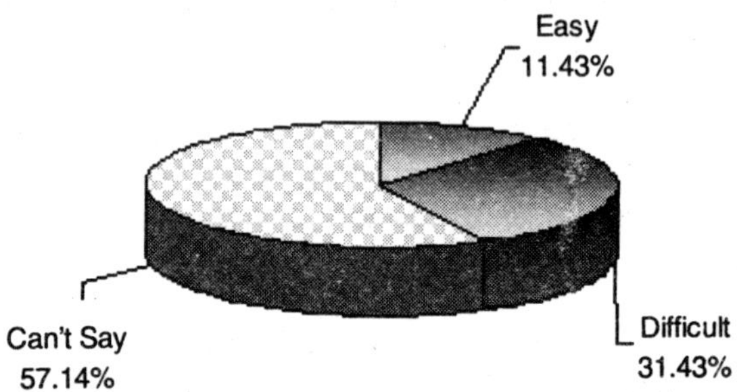

6.3.3.3 Average Score

(a) Average score concerned with rating of working of Exim bank in terms of financial and other assistances came out to be 3.51 which is greater than overall average score 3.20, thus it can be said that satisfaction level is high on this attribute.
(b) Average score on the (above) attribute with respect to status of Exporter.

Average score (on working of Exim bank in terms of financial and other assistances).

TABLE 6.3
Average Score on Working of Exim Bank with Respect to Status of Respondents

Status of Exporter	*Average Score*
100% EOU	3.33
Export House	3.67
Trading House	3.00
Super star trading house	4.50
Any other	3.48

Maximum average score has been given by super star trading house, i.e. 4.50 which on 5 point scale is close towards excellent performance.

6.3.3.4 Kolmogorov-Smirnov One Sample Test

(Since the rating very poor, poor, average, good and excellent represents a natural ordering, this test can be applied to test the preference hypothesis).

Null hypothesis can be stated as :

Ho3 = There is no difference in ratings for working of Exim bank in terms of financial and other assistances.

Kolmogorov-Smirnov D value (largest absolute difference) came out to be 1.0. The critical value at 5% significance comes out to be 0.1626 ($1.36/\sqrt{n} = 1.36/\sqrt{70} = 0.1626$). As the calculated D value exceeds critical value of 0.1626, the null hypothesis is rejected and alternative hypothesis is accepted, i.e. there is a difference in the ratings for working of exim bank in terms of financial and other assistances.

6.4 BUREAU OF INDIAN STANDARDS

6.4.1 Introduction

The Indian Standards Institution was registered as a Society under the Societies Registration Act, 1860 in January 1947 to prepare and promote standards. The Indian Standards Institution Certification Marks Act, 1952, covered the operation of the Certification Marks Scheme. Though considerable progress had been made by ISI in its multifarious activities like standards formulation, certification, setting up laboratories and promotional activities, need was felt for :

(a) providing recognition and status to the organisation to enable it to discharge its functions effectively and efficiently towards acceptance and promotion of Indian Standards;
(b) according priority to the functions in line with the national priorities;
(c) making a provision in the enactment for introduction of mandatory certification in the public interest;

(d) extending outside India services of the Institution for inspection, testing and similar other purposes; and
(e) providing more stringent punishment against misuse of Standard Mark.

Keeping these factors in view, the Bureau of Indian Standards was established with effect from 1.4.1987, under the provision of the Bureau of Indian Standards Act, 1986. The Bureau took over the functions, assets and liabilities of the Indian Standards Institution.

6.4.2 Organisation

The Bureau is a body corporate consisting of members representing the Government, industry, scientific and research institutions and other relevant interests with Minister Incharge of the Central Ministry having administrative control of the Bureau as its President and Minister of State or a Deputy Minister, if any, as Vice-President. Presently, the Bureau is under the administrative control of the Department of Civil Supplies, Consumer Affairs and Public Distribution. The Bureau is assisted in its functions by Executive Committee and the Secretary to the Government incharge of the Ministry or Department and Director General of the Bureau are *ex-officio* members of the Committee. The Bureau is further assisted in its functions by the Advisory Committee dealing with finance, certification, standards formulation, laboratories and long-range planning.

6.4.3 Functions

The functions of the Bureau include :

(a) establishment, publication and promotion of Indian Standards;
(b) inspection of article or process under Certification Scheme;
(c) establishment, maintenance and recognition of laboratories;
(d) formulate, implement and coordinate activities relating to quality maintenance and improvement in products and processes;

(e) promote harmonious development in standardization, quality systems and certification and matters connected therewith both within the country and at international level;

(f) provide information, documentation and other services to consumers and recognized consumer organisations on such terms and conditions as may be mutually agreed upon;

(g) give recognition to quality assurance systems in manufacturing or processing units on such terms and conditions as mutually agreed upon; and

(h) bring out handbooks, guides and other special publications, and for conformity to any other standard if so authorised.

Thus the main functions of the Bureau can be grouped under standards formulation, certification making, laboratory testing, promotional and international activities relating to quality standards (*Source* : Nabhi Publication, 2004).

6.5 EXPORT INSPECTION COUNCIL (EIC)

The basic object of Export Inspection Council, a statutory body under the Ministry of Commerce, is to provide for sound development of export trade through quality control and preshipment inspection. It advises the Central Government regarding measures for enforcing quality control and inspection in relation to commodities intended for export and draws up programmes for implementing those measures. The Council arranges preshipment inspection of notified commodities for export. The Council is vested with power to search and seize commodities, initiate adjudication proceedings against erring exporters and manufacturers, cancellation or withholding of the certificate issued by the inspection agencies, etc.

6.5.1 About Export Inspection Agencies

For carrying out preshipment inspection of export goods the Government of India has set-up five Export Inspection Agencies (EIA), one each at Mumbai, Calcutta, Kochi, Delhi and Chennai under the administrative control of EIC. In addition to their headquarter offices in above mentioned cities, Export Inspection Agencies have a network of 42 sub-offices located at important industrial centres and ports of shipment. These agencies have well-equipped laboratory facilities for testing all export products.

The EIAs also undertake inspection on voluntary basis, where desired, by the foreign buyers. To ensure that the export cargo meet the specific conditions prescribed in the Export Trade Policy, these agencies also carry out inspection of the products such as meat and meat products, Indian made foreign liquor, stainless steel products, etc. as required under the trade policy.

The EIAs have also been authorised by the Government of India to issue certificates of origin under the Generalised System of Preferences (GSP) for export to Japan, EU, USA, Canada and East European countries.

Government has also recognised 24 private Inspection Agencies and 10 Government Inspection Agencies to supplement the work of quality certificate under the act. Twenty-four agencies have also been recognised for fumigation of export cargo.

6.5.2 EIA on Quality Complaints

A standing committee on quality complaints has also been constituted to co-ordinate the quality complaints and to determine the measures to eliminate such complaints. A training centre to impart pre-service and in-service training has also been set-up at Chennai. Besides, the EIAs conduct seminars/ workshops in the context of ISO-9000 standards requirements. These seminars are arranged at different places to propagate the adoption of quality systems in the export units.

To collect and analyse quality complaints, a Data Bank has been set-up under the Export Inspection Council. In order to meet the increasing demand for prompt, efficient, accurate and comprehensive testing of engineering products, particularly from the Small Scale Sector, the EIC has set-up a Pilot Test House (PTH) at Mumbai. Apart from carrying out testing of samples drawn by EIAs from export consignments, PTH offers several technical support facilities to the industry, such as, assessment of the quality parameters of products, assistance in obtaining approval under the IPQC system, providing common facilities for testing,

R&D projects for quality upgradation and tailor-made training programmes for industry.

6.5.3 Grievances Committee in EIA

Grievance Committee has been set-up to deal with the problems/complaints of exporters such as delay in issuance of the GSP certificates, inspection certificates and other complaints with respect to working of EIA.

6.5.4 Notification for Extension of Term Period

As per the Notification No. S.O. 101(E), 28th January, 2005 the term of Export Inspection Council has been extended by three months w.e.f. 10th January 2005 or till the new council is reconstituted, whichever is earlier (www.eximin.net/govt-policy/notification-DGFT).

6.6 INDIAN INSTITUTE OF PACKAGING

The Indian Institute of Packaging was established in the year 1966 jointly by Ministry of Commerce, Government of India and the Packaging and Allied Industries with the object to improve the standard of packaging of the Indian export goods in the export market and to sustain appropriate improvements in the standards of packaging.

The Institute has nearly 1000 members on its roll comprising of industries having the common bond of interest in packaging.

6.6.1 Quality Policy

The Quality policy of Indian Institute of packaging, is to provide assured tests and measurements at all times conforming to the specification laid down in national, international or customer specific standards. The Institute believes in and strives for the involvement of every member of the institute in evolving and implementing an effective and efficient Quality Assurance Programme as laid down in ISO/IEC—17025 : 1999.

6.6.2 Objectives

The objectives of IIP are as follows :

(a) To stimulate consciousness of good packaging;
(b) To undertake and promote study, Research and Development in package design;
(c) To recommend standards for packages, packaging materials, and equipment;
(d) To test, evaluate and certify packages, packaging systems, packaging materials, equipment and processes;
(e) To provide consultancy services on packaging problems;
(f) To study packaging for export commodity-wise and country-wise and suggesting measures to authorities concerned for effecting improvements;
(g) To provide short-term and long-term training in packaging technology, personnel employed in industry, commerce and Government;
(h) To develop interest and new insight;
(i) To analyse the implication of a sound policy on packaging on domestic consumption and domestic prices;
(j) To study the packaging requirements with special reference to trade through water, rail and air;
(k) To study the impact of packaging on marketing;
(l) To undertake advertising, publicity and exhibition to promote packaging conciousness;
(m) To established relation and co-operate with any other agency of having similar objectives in India and abroad;
(n) To provide and disseminate information relating to packaging;
(o) To prepare, print and publish any paper or periodicals or report on package.
(p) To establish and maintain libraries and information services to facilitate the various goals which the society is established;
(q) To constitute regional institutes at convenient places in India and to promote the objects of the society.
(r) To invite representatives of Government, industry, trade and other organisations, Indians and foreigners to deliver lectures on related subject.

The IIP also organises a two year Post-graduate programme in packaging and conduct intensive campus/correspondence training programmes for improved technology in the field of packaging as discussed earlier. The IIP is one of the founder members of the Asian Packaging Federation established for exchange of all information on packaging and for chalking out common programmes for the development of packaging standards in the Asian region.

6.6.3 Research Findings Regarding Indian Institute of Packaging (IIP)

6.6.3.1 Rating of Working of IIP

55.71% of respondents rated IIP as fair, 42.86% as good and 1.43% as excellent (Graph 6.8).

GRAPH 6.8
Rating on Working of IIP

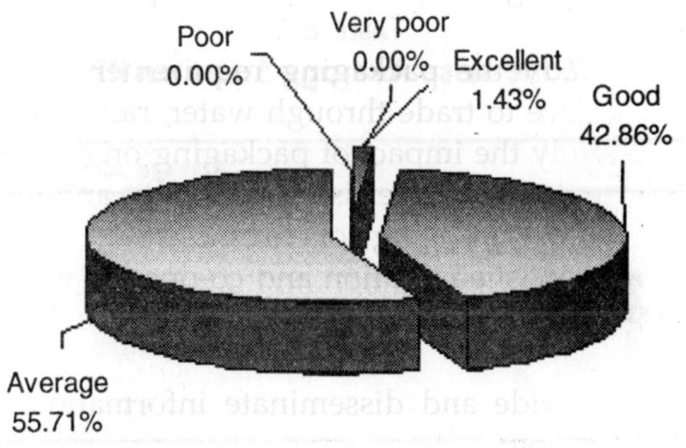

6.6.3.2 Average Score

(a) Average score on this attribute came out to be 3.46 which is greater than the overall average score 3.20. It can be said that the respondents are satisfied with the services of IIP.

(b) Average score and status of respondent and zonal classification.

(i) Super star trading house's average score was highest for IIP, i.e. 4 which is (close to) good on 5 point scale.

TABLE 6.4
Average Score on IIP with Respect to Status of Respondents

Export Status of Respondents	*Average score*
100% EOU	3.33
Export House	3.50
Trading House	3.00
Super Star Trading House	4.00
Any other	3.46

(ii) Similarly, zone-wise average score calculated are as follows on this attribute.

TABLE 6.5
Zone-wise Average Score on IIP

Zone	*Average score*
East	3.50
North	3.45
South	3.60
West	3.43

6.6.3.3 Chi Square Test

Ho4 = Status of Exporter and working of Indian Institute of packaging are independent attributes.

The χ^2 value calculated at 5% level of significance at 8 degrees of freedom came out to be 18.59. As the calculated χ^2 value (18.59) is greater than the tabulated value (@ 5% level of significance, df = 8) 15.5, hence the null hypothesis is rejected, i.e. status of exporter and working of IIP are not independent attributes.

6.7 INDIAN COUNCIL OF ARBITRATION

6.7.1 An Introduction

The Indian Council of Arbitration Established in 1965 is the apex arbitral organisation at the national level, the undisputed leader in dispute resolution services in India for over 40 years. The main objective of the council is to promote the amicable and quick settlement of industrial and trade disputes by arbitration.[20]

ICA Arbitration Clause

"Any dispute or indifferences whatsoever arising between the parties out of or relating to construction, meaning and operation or effect of this contract or the breach thereof shall be settled by Arbitration in accordance with the Rules of Arbitration of the Indian Council of Arbitration and the award made in pursuance thereof shall be binding on the parties".

The Government of India, the Federation of Indian Chambers of Commerce and Industry, the other important chambers of commerce and trade associations in India as well as export promotion councils, public sector undertakings companies and firms are in its membership.[21]

6.7.2 Services of ICA

The council's rules of Arbitration have recently been revised, based on Arbitration and Conciliation Act, 1996. It maintains a panel of arbitrators consisting of Retd. Judges, Advocates, Shipping Experts, CAs, Chartered Engineers, Businessmen, Foreign Nationals and Executives having specialization in more than 20 fields. The council has entered into arbitration service agreements with important foreign arbitral institutions in more than 30 countries to administer arbitrations under their rules if arbitration is held in India.

The council also provides arbitration services for settlement of maritime disputes arising out of charter party contracts and it has framed maritime arbitration rules for such disputes.[22]

The council also provides the provision of Fast Track Arbitration, under which the arbitrators have to decide the matter within the time frame on written submission without oral hearings.

The council has a special website on Internet called ICANET to provide information on arbitration and commercial laws.

ICA is a member of Federation of International Commercial Arbitral Institution and has mutual co-operation agreements with International chambers of Commerce, Institutional Court of Arbitration, London Court of Arbitration and apex arbitration bodies in many countries.

The council organises conferences/training programmes, publishes literature (viz. ICA Arbitration Quarterly) and provides advisory services to business organisation and arbitration practitioners on trade terms and arbitration clause.

6.7.3 Rules of Arbitration of ICA

The ICA has framed its rules of arbitration comparable to international standards for conduct of arbitration proceedings. The 1996 Act provides statutory recognition to conciliation as a distinct mode of dispute settlement and contains detailed procedure governing arbitration and conciliation proceedings.

Under the rules of arbitration of the ICA, either a sole arbitrator or three arbitrators may be appointed. Where the claim is below rupees one crore, a sole arbitrator is appointed, unless the two parties agree that three arbitrators should be appointed for the particular case. For claims above rupees one crore, three arbitrators are appointed, unless the parties agree that a sole arbitrator may be appointed. The sole arbitrator is appointed by consent of the parties and, failing such a consent, the Council appoints the sole arbitrator. Where three arbitrators have to be appointed, each of the parties appoints one arbitrator and the Council appoints the third arbitrator who acts as the Presiding Arbitrator of the arbitral tribunal.

Under institutional arbitration in India, the parties are free to choose their arbitrators from panel of arbitrators established by the institution. The panel of arbitrators maintained by the ICA includes about one thousand five hundred persons from various professions and businesses, lawyers, chartered accountants, engineers, etc. They are put on the list by the Arbitration Committee after the latter is satisfied about their competence, integrity and impartiality to act as arbitrators. The list also includes foreigners.

All in all the council is a non-profit service organization for promotion of the use of commercial arbitration and the smooth flow of trade.

NOTES AND REFERENCES

1. Banerji, A.C., T.D.A. : 'Pinpointing Export Promotion, International Trade Forum', Oct.-Dec., 1971.
2. Varshney, R.L., Bhattacharyya, B., 'International Marketing Management. An Indian Perspective', Sultan Chand and Sons, New Delhi, 15th Edition, 2002.
3. The Board of Trade is the highest forum for Government Industry Interface on Trade Policy Issues. It has its Members—Presidents of FICCI, ASSOCHAM, CII, FIEO, Chairman of SBI and EXIM Bank, DGFT and Representatives from Ministry of Finance, Industry and Textiles and PMO. The Board of Trade is Presided over by Commerce Minister.
4. Murlidhar, Geetha (GM, ECGC of India), 'Export Credit Insurance Coming of Age', *Chartered Financial Analyst*, Oct. 2005.
5. Goswami, Nandini, 'ECGC to log on to IRDA Accounting Norms this Year', *The Economic Times*, New Delhi, 25th Feb., 2004.
6. For example, Till March 2004 ECGC Guided by the Government Norms for Deploying its Investment Surplus. This Format will Change as the Nature of Investments and the Revenue Accounting will be on the Lines of a General Insurance Company.
7. 'ECGC to Recast Accounting and Solvency Norms', *Business Standard*, 30th Jan., 2004.
8. 'Equity Base of ECGC Raised', *Business Standard*, 29th Jan., 2004, New Delhi.
9. The Additional Capital would Provide Comfort under the Current IRDA Norms.
10. The DUNS Number, a nine digit identification sequence, is the global standard for keeping track of the world's business. It is recognised, recommended and or required by more than 50 global industry associations. Following are the advantages of the DUNS number :

    - Get noticed by international buyers for export products and services.
    - Exporters will be a part of Dun and Bradstreet's global database, which comprises more than 75 million businesses worldwide.
    - Exporters can obtain globally recognized unique identification for their company.

11. ECGC Annual Report, 2003-04.
12. *Ibid*.
13. In case of bancassurance, current regulations restrict the tie-ups to just one-to-one, which means that one bank is allowed to tie-up with just one insurance company. ECGC, however has the permission to tie

up with a bank which may already have an arrangement with another general insurer.
ECGC have Bancassurance agreement with 10 banks. Recently ECGC entered into a Bancassurance agreement with Allahabad Bank. (ECGC, Allahabad Bank tie up, *The Economic Times,* 18 Feb., 2004) and Overseas Bank.

14. ECGC Annual Report, 2003-04.
15. Exim Bank, 22nd Annual Report, 2003-04, www.eximbank.india.com.
16. Vikraman, Shafi and Ramakrishnan, Hema; 'Exim bank capital base set to be bolstered', *The Economic Times,* New Delhi, 3 Aug., 2003.
17. Vikraman, Shaji, Nayak, Gayatri, 'Exim Bank to get interest equalisation support from Government', *The Economic Times,* New Delhi, 15 March, 2004.
18. Narendranath, K.G., 'Exim to take tax sops to food processing', *The Economic Times,* New Delhi, 9 June, 2004.
19. 'Exim Bank get stable rating from Moody's', *The Economic Times,* New Delhi, 27 April, 2004.
20. ww.iipp.com.
21. Nabhi's Exporters' Manual and Documentation', Nabhi Publication, New Delhi, 2004.
22. Wtp.//www.ficci.com/icanet/ica.htm

ANNEXURE 6.1 (a)
Countries Transferred from Restricted Cover Category to Open Cover Category

Sr. No.	*Country*	*Rating*	*Sr. No.*	*Country*	*Rating*
1.	Bulgaria	C2	12.	Mozambique	D
2.	Burundi	C2	13.	Nigeria	C1
3.	Cambodia	C1	14.	Palestine	D
4.	Cote D'Ivoire	B2	15.	Russia	B1
5.	Democratic Republic of Congo	D	16.	Sudan	D
6.	Ethiopia	C2	17.	Uganda	C2
7.	Fiji	C1	18.	Yemen	C1
8.	Indonesia	B2	19.	Yogoslavia	D
9.	Iran	B2	20.	Zambia	C2
10.	Malawi	C2	21.	Zimbabwe	B2
11.	Mauritania	C2			

ANNEXURE 6.1 (b)
Countries in Restricted Cover where Specific Approval will be Given on Case-to-Case Basis on Merits

Sr. No.	*Country*	*Rating*	*Sr. No.*	*Country*	*Rating*
1.	Afghanistan	D	5.	Libya	C2
2.	Argentina	B1	6	Iraq	D
3.	Cuba	C2	7	North Korea	D
4.	East Timor	D	8	Somalia	D

ANNEXURE 6.2
Criteria for Seven-Fold Classification

A1(1/7) Politically stable, broad-based, strong and well developed economy with a diversified export portfolio, strong external payments position with no possibility of transfer delay whatsoever.

A2(2/7) Politically stable, relatively strong and well developed economy. Comparatively well diversified export portfolio, moderately strong external payments situation which is unlikely to lead to transfer delays.

B1(3/7) No pronounced political instability, relatively strong economy but either structurally imbalanced or with poor growth rates, comparatively not well diversified export portfolio, rather weak external payments position which is however unlikely to lead to transfer delays.

B2 (4/7) Political instability (either present or imminent) and/or structurally imbalanced or with poor growth rates, and not well diversified export portfolio which however is unlikely to lead to transfer delays. Should these occur they are resolved without refinancing or reschedulings.

C1 (5/7) Political instability and/or unstable economy characterised by severe structural imbalances and poor or negative growth rates and characterised by narrow export base and pronounced weak external payments position which is likely to lead to transfer delays. Payment problems, including refinancing or reschedulings are likely. Full recovery on all debts is likely over the long-term.

C2 (6/7) Pronounced political instability and/or unstable economy characterised by very severe structural imbalances, poor or negative growth rates and weak and narrow export base and pronounced weak external payments position. Serious payment problems, including reschedulings and/or prolonged arrears are likely. Losses on some debts are likely over the short and medium-term. Write-offs cannot be discounted.

D (7/7) Acute and severe political instability, chronically

unstable economy characterised by severe structural imbalances, very poor and/or negative growth rates, very weak and narrow export base, severe and chronical external payments problem including a record of repeated reschedulings and prolonged arrears are inevitable. Eventual forgiveness or effective repudiation likely. Severe losses on most debts are a possibility over the long-term.

Source : ECGC.

ANNEXURE 6.3
Institutional Linkages of Exim Bank

(*Exim India*)

Multilateral Agencies	*Trade and Invt. Promotion Agencies*	*Export Credit Agencies*
• World Bank	• Development Bank of Zambia	• Exim Bank of China
• Asian Development Bank	• Western African Development	• Croatian Bank for
• African Development Bank	• Bank (BOAD)	• Reconstruction and Development
• European Bank for Reconstruction and Development	• Board of Investment of Sri Lanka	• Czech Export Bank
• Multilateral Investment Guarantee Agency (MIGA)	• China National Technical Import and Export Corporation	• Hungarian Exim Bank Ltd.
• International Finance Corporation (IFC)	• Polish Agency for Foreign Investment (PAIZ)	• Uzbekinvest—National Export-Import Insurance Company
• UNIDO—Industrial Promotion Offices (China, Italy, Poland)	• Sharjah Chamber of Commerce and Industry, UAE	• Finnish Export Credit Ltd.
• Afriexim Bank	• Hungarian Investment and Trade Development Agency	• Exim Bank of Romania
• Eastern and Southern African Trade and Development Bank (PTA Bank)	• Board of Investment of Mauritius	• Export-Import Bank of the Russian Federation

ANNEXURE 6.4
Balance Sheet as at 31st March, 2004 of Exim Bank

General Fund

Assets	*Schedules*	*This year (As at 31.03.2004) (Rs.)*	*Previous year (As at 31.03.2003) (Rs.)*
1. Cash and Bank Balances	VI	25,765,892,040	12,704,535,257
2. Investments	VII	14,573,307,311	16,410,790,311
3. Loans and Advances	VIII	106,377,895,564	86,886,380,899
4. Bills purchased, Discounted, Rediscounted	IX	1,373,200,000	850,000,000
5. Fixed Assets	X	630,063,739	503,045,243
6. Other Assets	XI	6,471,174,899	5,834,282,808
7. Profit and Loss Account			
Total		155,191,533,553	123,189,034,518

Notes : 1. Cash and Bank Balance includes term deposits with banks.
2. Previous year figures have been regrouped wherever necessary.

(*Contd.*)

ANNEXURE 6.4 (Contd.)

Liabilities	*Schedules*	*This year (As at 31.03.2004) (Rs.)*	*Previous year (As at 31.03.2003) (Rs.)*
1. Capital	I	6,499,918,881	6,499,918,881
2. Reserves	II	14,933,014,180	13,170,904,893
3. Profit and Loss Account	III	470,000,000	450,000,000
4. Notes, Bonds and Debentures	IX	76,700,580,430	64,902,091,020
5. Bills payable		—	—
6. Deposits	IV	20,922,102,710	9,120,755,855
7. Borrowings	V	21,582,667,243	16,466,863,518
8. Current Liabilities and Provisions		13,397,276,241	11,830,612,186
9. Other Liabilities		685,973,868	747,888,165
Total		155,191,533,553	123,189,034,518

	Contingent Liabilities	*This year (As at 31.03.2004) (Rs.)*	*Previous year (As at 31.03.2003) (Rs.)*
(i)	Acceptances, Guarantees, endorsements and other obligations	15,768,884,000	16,132,906,000
(ii)	On outstanding forward exchange contracts	—	—
(iii)	On underwriting commitments	—	—
(iv)	Uncalled Liability on partly paid investments	13,115,250	14,245,500
(v)	Claims on the Bank not acknowledged as debts	3,318,800,000	3,318,800,000
(vi)	Bills for collection	—	—
(vii)	On participation certificates	—	—
(viii)	Bills Discounted/Rediscounted	—	—
(ix)	Other monies for which the Bank is contingently liable	628,113,000	313,540,000
	Total	19,728,912,250	19,728,912,250

Export Promotion Institutions

It is apparent that the requirement for export competitiveness in global market is universal. Export promotion as an artificial trade stimulant is widely used in the industrialized world.[1] This chapter throws light on export promotion programmes and working of other institutions, in general, a thorough understanding of export promotion organization and agencies so as to understand the need to tailor assistances offered by such institutions to the changing requirements of a firm over the exporting process.

7.1 EXPORT PROMOTION COUNCILS (EPCs)

7.1.1 Historical Perspective

The proposal for the formation of export promotion councils was first mooted in India at the meeting of the Export Advisory Council held on 29th November, 1953.

The then Minister for Commerce and Industry stressed at this meeting the need for the commercial and industrial interests setting up appropriate organisations like Export Promotion Councils to "conduct market research, promotion of standardisation and quality control and to undertake such other activities as might be necessary to persuade foreign buyers to buy the goods manufactured in India". At the suggestion of Government the Federation of Indian Chambers of Commerce and Industry took active interest in formulating proposals for the formation of the Export Promotion Councils for cotton textiles and engineering goods. At a meeting convened in Calcutta on 16th December, 1953 the concerned interests, including the two associations connected with engineering industries, agreed to form a Council under the aegis of the FICCI. Soon after a Consultative Meeting was held in Bombay under the Chairmanship of the Minister for Commerce and Industry for the formation of the Cotton Textiles Export Promotion Council. The Council was set-up in October 1954, largely with the assistance of funds provided by the Cotton Textiles Fund Committees. Action was initiated simultaneously for creation of export promotion councils for items such as silk and rayon textiles, plastics, cashew and engineering. Other councils followed in due course.

Exhaustive recommendations were given regarding the organization, role and working of export promotion councils by 'Review Committee on EPC' chaired by Mr. Prabhu V. Mehta[2] (May 1965) like :

(i) EPCs should continue to be registered under the Companies Act (Para 3.3 and 3.4).

(ii) It should be ensured that one person does not continue to be chairman for years together (Para 3.12).

(iii) To achieve a greater degree of commodity specialization, the panels of the councils should be given a great degree of autonomy in formulating recommendations and they should be provided with proper secretarial assistance (Para 3.14).

(iv) Every council should have a regular programme of—

  (a) advertisements and features articles in newspapers,
  (b) Radio talk,
  (c) Seminars, and
  (d) Participation (Para 4.4).

(v) Every council should regularly publish a home bulletin including information about the production, domestic consumption, exports, prices, quality, etc. (Paras 4.9 and 4.10).

(vi) Each proposal for export assistance should be carefully analysed in consultation with technical authorities before the council sends up its recommendations to Government.

Other than the above mentioned recommendation many other recommendations were given by the committee for the smooth working of EPCs.

7.1.2 Objectives and Functions of Export Promotion Councils

EPCs perform both advisory and executive functions. Generally EPCs assist the exporters in the following manner :

(1) Help the exporters in expanding overseas market of their products.

(2) Exchange the trade delegates between the foreign countries.

(3) Provide information on latest development in the field of export trade.

(4) Gather information relating to overseas imports, imports regulations and competitor's activities.

(5) Give information relating on Exim policy/Drawback/ Incentives available on various items falling within the purview of the council.

(6) Give information on the export performance of the various items falling within the purview of the respective councils.

(7) Augment all the important representation submitted to the Ministry relating to classification of items, review of import replenishment, request for release of Grants-in-aid, inclusion of various trade agreements being concluded with different countries, etc. to be actively followed up for speedy disposal.

(8) Recommend for release of foreign exchange and visa and arranges for certificate of origin.

7.1.3 List of Export Promotion Councils in India

At present there are twenty-two Export promotion councils in India. Earlier there were just 21 EPCs, one has been recently added to the list. The newly formed Pharmexcil has bagged the mandate to represent the entire range of drug and pharma businesses from chemexil, becoming the sole council of pharmaceuticals exports in the country pharmexil would also be responsible for promoting biotech and biological products, contract manufacturing, clinical trials, ayurvedic, unani and homeopathic medicines.[3]

The list of EPCs in India are as follows :[4a]

1. Apparel Export Promotion Council (AEPC).
2. Basic Chemicals, Cosmetics Export Promotion Council (CHEMEXCIL).
3. The Cashew Export Promotion Council of India [(CCEPC) IN PROMOTION].
4. Carpet Export Promotion Council (CARPCIL).
5. Chemicals and Allied Products Export Promotion Council (CAPEXIL).
6. The Cotton Textiles Export Promotion Council (TEXPROCIL).
7. Electronics and Computer Software Export Promotion Council.
8. Engineering Export Promotion Council (EEPC).
9. The Gem and Jewellery Export Promotion Council (GJEPC).
10. Export Promotion Council for Handicrafts (CRAFTCIL).
11. The Handloom Export Promotion Council (HEPC).
12. The Indian Silk Export Promotion Council (ISEPC).
13. Council for Leather Exports (LEXPROCIL).
14. Plastic Export Promotion Council (Plexcouncil).
15. Shellac Export Promotion Council.
16. The Sports Goods Export Promotion Council.
17. The Synthetic and Rayon Textiles Export Promotion Council.
18. Wool and Woollens Export Promotion Council.
19. The Powerloom Development and Export Promotion Council (PDEXCIL).

20. Overseas Construction Council of India.
21. Pharmaceutical Export Promotion Council (Pharmexcil).
22. Export Promotion Council for Export Oriented Units and SEZ Units (EPCES).

It will be difficult and rather would be impossible to explain all EPCs in detail, therefore the EPC will be explained by taking single case of CAPEXIL.[4b]

7.1.4 CAPEXIL

7.1.4.1 The Vision

The vision of CAPEXIL is to catalyze development and promotion of India's export of wide spectrum of chemical-based allied products including minerals and ores, and thereby stimulate the country's economic growth.

7.1.4.2 About CAPEXIL

CAPEXIL (Formerly Chemicals and Allied Products Export Promotion Council) an ISO 9001 : 2000 certified Export Promotion Council, has been serving the cause of exporters from late 1950s, when it was started as a Government-Industry initiative to develop the overseas market. From a mere 71 members in 1958, the community of Indian exporters of chemicals and allied products has grown to a current strength of about 4000[5] (Graphs 7.1, 7.2).[6]

CAPEXIL's member-exporters account for an estimated annual export of US $ 4.85 billion (Financial year 2003-04). This represents about 7.4 per cent of India's total exports.

Headquartered in Kolkata, CAPEXIL has regional offices at New Delhi, Mumbai, Kolkata and Chennai.

7.1.4.3 Product Spectrum

The products under the canopy of CAPEXIL are broadly Minerals and non-Mineral products which are as follows :

- Natural Stone, namely Granite, Marbels, etc.
- Ceramic and Refractories

GRAPH 7.1
Membership Trend of CAPEXIL

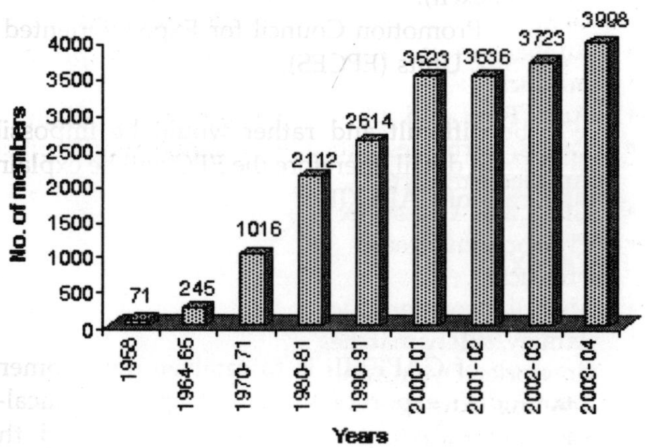

GRAPH 7.2
Region-wise Membership Strength

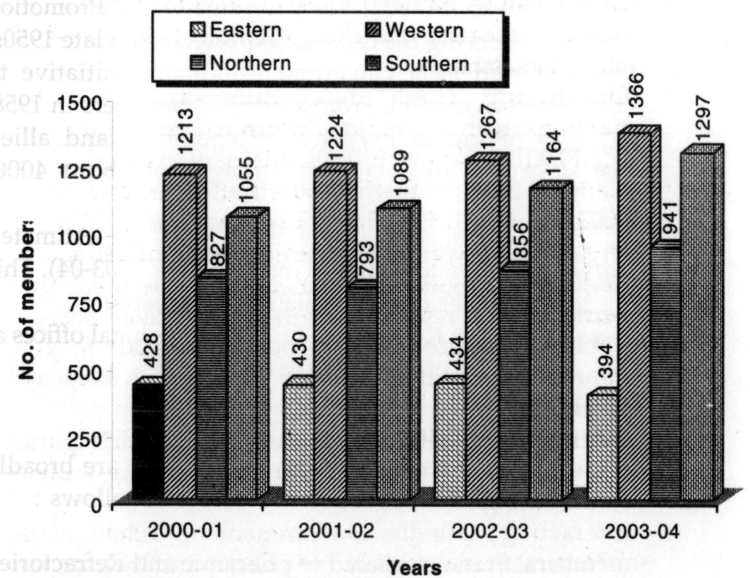

Source : CAPEXIL Annual Report, 2003-04.

- Processed Minerals
- Bulk minerals and Ores
- Rubber manufactured products
- Auto Tyres and tubes
- Paints, varnishes and Applied Products
- Glass and Glassware
- Plywood and wood products
- Miscellaneous products, namely, safety matches, fireworks, Dyeing and Tanning extracts, Activated Carbon, Fertilizers
- Cement, Clinker and asbestos cement products
- Paper, Paper Board and paper products
- Bones/Bones product
- Ossein and Gelatin
- Graphite and Explosives

7.1.4.4 CAPEXIL's Services to its Members

- Disseminating market/policy information, conducting market research, matching markets and updating importers database.
- Organizing trade delegations and ensuring participation in major international trade fair (CAPEXIL took part in India International Trade Fair, National Expo, Industrial India Trade Fair, Panel Expo 2003, the North East Trade Expo and Stone, 2004).
- Organizing Buyer-Seller meets in India and abroad.
- Conducting regular seminars, open house meets and workshops on regular basis in export-related areas.
- Publishing trade news, a journal devoted to give information on market trends, and foreign language brochures.
- Setting up web site www.Capexil.com and B2B portal www.Capexil trade.com and providing video-conferencing facilities.
- Interacting with the Government on behalf of its members on issues related to policies and their impact on exports.[7,8]

- Disbursing Government assistance under the MDA scheme.
- Conducting short term Executive Development Programmes on 'International Marketing' through its educational service division.

7.1.4.5 Export Performance

CAPEXIL adopted an overall export target of Rs. 211,325.00 million (US $ 4,378.00 million) for 2003-04. As against this, the estimated export for 2003-04 was to the tune of Rs. 218,160.00 million (US $ 4,848.00 million). In other words, the export performance outstripped the export target by 3.23 per cent in rupee terms and 10.74 per cent in dollar terms.

The overall financial performance can be judged by seeing the balance sheet of CAPEXIL as given in Annexure 7.1.

With export promotion support programs, CAPEXIL, hopes to contribute towards India's Export Mission of achieving 1.5 per cent of the world trade by 2009.

Also CAPEXIL has chalked out a series of innovative strategies like setting warehouses at international destinations for effective trade, organising buyer-seller meet in Kenya, Mauritius and South Africa and concentrating on the north-east of India (Council has office in shillong operational from March 2005 which is the only office among all other EPCs in the country) to reach its target export figure of $ 9.4 billion by 2008-09.[9]

7.1.5 Research Findings Regarding Export Promotion Councils (EPCs)

7.1.5.1 Process of Registration with EPCs

Fifty respondents were satisfied with the process of registration with EPCs and 20 respondents said they were not satisfied since it is time consuming. While asking them to fill the questionnaire many respondents also revealed the fact that since it is mandatory to be registered with EPC or FIEO most of times they have to do this forcefully (Graph 7.4).

7.1.5.2 Rating the Working of Export Promotion Councils in Discharging its Functions

Thirty-five respondents rated the working of EPC as good,

Graph 7.3
Export Value and Growth Trend : All Categories (Products Under CAPEXIL)

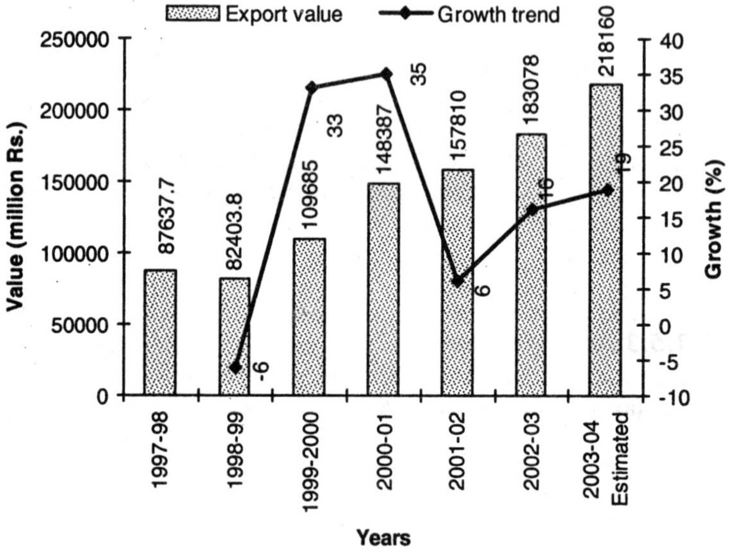

Graph 7.4
Unsatisfaction Associated with Process of Registration with EPC

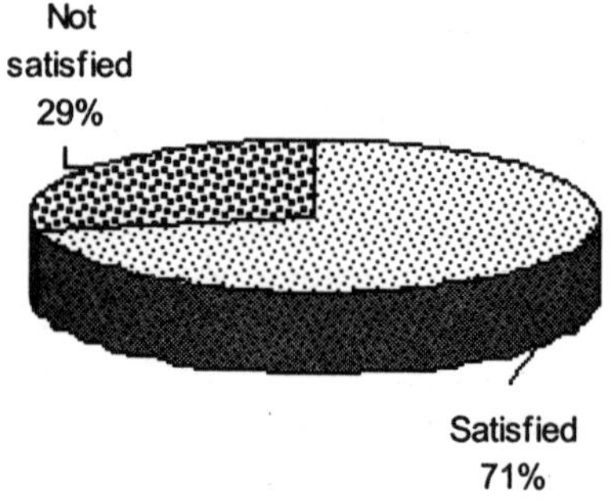

28 rated it as average and 7 respondent rated it as poor. No body rated excellent or very poor (Graph 7.5).

GRAPH 7.5

Rating on Working of EPC

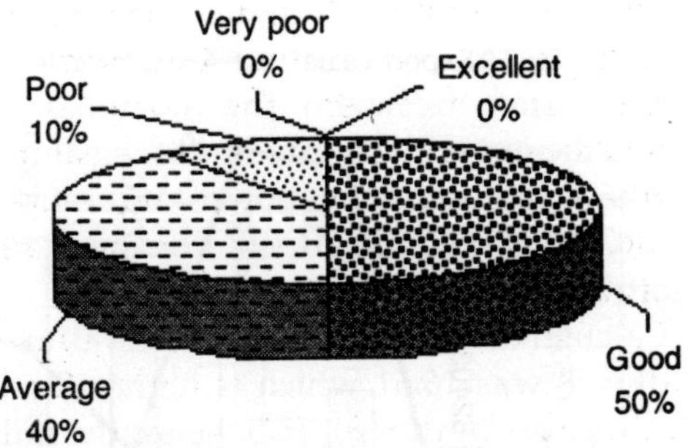

7.1.5.3 Average Score

(a) Average score on working of EPCs in discharging its functions properly was 3.40 which is high than overall average score 3.20 which means that in the eyes of respondents EPCs is discharging its functions properly.

(b) Average score on working of EPC and Export status :

TABLE 7.1

Status-wise Average Score Regarding the Working of EPC

Export status	*Average score*
100% EOU	3.83
Export House	3.83
Trading House	3.00
Super Star Trading House	4.00
Any Others	3.23

7.1.5.4 Chi-Square Test

(a) Ho5—There is no significant difference between the status of exporter and satisfaction with the process of registration with EPCs.

χ^2 calculated at 5% level of significance at 4 degree of freedom came out at 11.30. Since the calculated value 11.30 is higher than tabulated value (@ 5%, df = 4), 9.49, hence null hypothesis is rejected and alternative hypothesis is accepted, i.e. there is significant difference between the status of exporter and satisfaction with the process of registration with EPCs.

(b) Ho6—The status of exporters and rating of working of EPC in discharging their functions are independent attributes.

Calculated value of χ^2 at 5% level of significance at df = 8 was 16.51 which is higher than the tabulated value (@ 5%, df = 8), 15.5, hence the null hypothesis is rejected and alternative hypothesis is accepted, i.e. the two attributes are not independent attributes.

(c) Ho7—There is no significant difference between the (un)satisfaction level with process of registration with EPC and rating of working of EPC in discharging its functions.

Calculated χ^2 value at 5% level of significance for 2 degrees of freedom was 22.72. Since the calculated value is more than tabulated value (@ 5% and df = 2), 5.99, hence null hypothesis is rejected and alternative hypothesis is accepted, i.e. there is significant difference between process of registration with EPC and its working.

(d) Ho8—The zones and process of registration with EPC are independent attributes.

Calculated χ^2 value at 5% level of significance for 3 degrees of freedom was 3.25. As the calculated value is less than tabulated value (@ 5% and df = 3), 7.81, hence the null hypothesis is accepted.

7.2 COMMODITY BOARDS

Commodity Boards are statutory bodies and are responsible for production, development and export of their respective commodities. They also advise the Government of India on export matters such as fixing the quota for export, signing trade agreements with foreign countries, etc.

Commodity Boards assists the exporters in the same manner as the EPCs do. These are statutory boards for the following commoditie—Handicrafts and Handlooms, Silk, Powerloom, Coffee, Coir, Rubber, Tea, Tobacco and spices.

Spices Board will be discussed in detail under commodity board in this chapter to understand the functions and activities of commodity boards.

7.2.1 Spices Board

The Spices Board[10] (Ministry of Commerce, Government of India) established in 1987 is the apex organisation for the development and world-wide promotion of Indian spices. It plays an important role as a developmental, regulatory and promotional agency for Indian spices.

The Board is a link between the Indian exporters and the importers abroad. Its broad-based activities include formulation and implementation of quality improvement systems, R&D programmes, education and training of farmers, processors, packers and exporters on post-harvest handling and registration and licensing of traders and exporters.

Spices Board acts a data bank and communication channel for importers and exporters and promotes Indian Spices abroad. The board has close association with international agencies like International Trade Centre (ITC), Geneva, United Nations Development Programmes (UNDP), International Pepper Community (IPC), Jakarta, American Spice Trade Association (ASTA), European Spice Association (ESA), All Nippon Spice Association (ANSA), Japan, International Spice Group (ISG), Food and Agricultural Organization (FAO), Commonwealth Secretariat (COMSEC), London, International General Producers' Association (IGPA), United Nations Industrial Development Organisation (UNIDO).

As many as 52 spices and spice products like spice oils and oleoresins, curry powders, spice powders and spice mixtures come under the purview of the spices board.

The spices board has its focus on quality upgradation, improvement (like introduction of Indian spices logo, spice house certificate and brand name registration) and empowering rural communities to export spices as discussed below :

(i) *Empowerment of rural communities to export of organic spices* : The main programmes envisaged under the project are improvement and promotion of organic production of spices, certification and export of selected spices.[11]

(ii) *Spice House Certificate* : The certificate is issued to those processors/exporters who have a genuine commitment to quality, and whose long-term objective is sustained export growth. The Spice House Certificate seeks to identify quality assurance at all stages of processing—from raw-material selection to final shipping (including cleaning, grading, processing, packaging and warehousing). In total 57 exporters have received spice House certified.

(iii) *Indian Spices Logo* : The logo—a fresh green leaf inside an elliptical ring denoting freshness, growth and excellence—is predominantly displayed on all packs cleared and approved by the Spices board, so that the consumer can easily spot the pack that spells Indianness and quality. 19 Exporters have been awarded spices logo.

(iv) *Brand name Registration* : In order to asses the exporters in selection of consumer pack and brand names and to promote the export in branded consumer pack and protect the individual brands, Board has introduced a system to register their brand names with the spices board. Registration of brand is given to those packs which satisfy stipulated standards of packaging and labelling (seventy-one) 71 exporters are registered with spices board having brand name.

Export Promotion Schemes : The assistance and various promotion schemes are open to all registered exporters of spices and spice product, viz. scheme for technology transfer and process upgradation, for R & D efforts, for participation in informational food fairs, for adopting ISO 9000, for product promotion abroad and for printing of brochures abroad.

7.3 MPEDA AND APEDA

Along with EPCs and commodity Boards there is also Marine Products Export Development Authority (MPEDA) and Agricultural and Processed Development Authority both of which falls under the Ministry of Commerce for promotion of Marine products and agricultural and processed products respectively. MPEDA and APEDA will be discussed briefly.

7.3.1 Marine Products Export Development Authority (MPEDA)

It helps in the development of marine products meant for export with special reference to processing, packaging, storage and marketing, etc. As per section 9 of Marine Products Exports Development Authority (MPEDA) Act, 1972, following are the major functions of the authority:

(i) The development of the marine products industry with special reference to exports.
(ii) Developing and regulating off-shore and deep-sea fishing and undertaking measures, for the conservation and management of off-shore and deep-sea fisheries.
(iii) Registration of fishing vessels, processing plant, exporters and conveyances used.
(iv) Regulating the export of marine products.
(v) Improving the marketing of marine products outside India.
(vi) Collection of statistics relating to the marine products industry.
(vii) Training in various aspects of the marine products industry.

The schemes/programmes of MPEDA are covered under four major plan schemes which are as under :

(i) Export Promotion—Capture Fisheries
(ii) Export Promotion—Culture Fisheries.
(iii) Induction of New Technology and Modernisation of Seafood Industry.
(iv) Market Promotion.

To develop the industries relating to concerned products for export by way of providing financial assistance or otherwise for undertaking surveys and feasibility studies.

7.3.2 APEDA

The authority serves as the focal point for agricultural exports, particularly the marketing of processed food in value added form. The functions of APEDA are :

- Fixing of standards and specifications for the agricultural and processed food products for the purpose of export.
- Registration of persons as exporters of the product concerned.
- Carrying out inspection of meat and meat products in any slaughter house, processing plant and storage premises, etc.
- To improve the packaging of those products.
- To promote export-oriented production and development of these products.

7.4 NIRYAT BANDHU (NODAL OFFICERS)

Many times the problems that exporters face can be easily resolved at the State level. Most of their problems relate to the infrastructure, availability of power, other inputs, raw materials, Inter-state movement of raw material, remission in taxes by the State Governments, etc. Within the State, these issues are dealt with in separate Departments, and the exporter has no single nodal point to approach for getting his problem resolved. In this context, the State Governments were requested to nominate a Senior Officer at the level of the Commissioner of Industries/ Secretary Industries as Niryat Bandhu so that the exporters' problems could be resolved by a co-ordinated approach by various Departments of State Governments.

In response to the Commerce Ministry's request, all the State Governments have nominated nodal officers (Niryat Bandhus) for export promotion work. Exporters should refer their problems/suggestions, etc. to the Nodal Officers (Niryat Bandhus) of the concerned State Government for early redressal.

7.5 STATE LIAISON OFFICER

State Governments have appointed liaison officers (export promotion) with responsibility to develop export trade in goods produced in their States in consonance with the policies of the Central Government. Some of the States have separate Directorates of export promotion. The Directors of Industries in each State including small-scale industries also take keen interest in export promotion activities particularly in relation to industries registered with them.

7.5.1 Research Findings Regarding State Liaisoning Officer

Out of 70 respondents 45 said that they were satisfied with the working of state liaisoning officer. According to 18 respondents the role of state liaisoning officer was unsatisfactory. Seven respondents said that they can't say anything about the role of state liaisoning officer.

7.6 FEDERATION OF INDIAN EXPORT ORGANISATION (FIEO)

7.6.1 An Introduction

Federation of Indian Export Organization (FIEO) was established in 1965 by the Ministry of Commerce, Government of India and private trade and industry.

FIEO provides the content, direction and thrust to India's expanding international trade. It expresses all the dynamism and resurgence that are the hallmark of India's open, liberal and progressively market-friendly economic and trade regime, representing the Indian export promotion effort in its entirety. FIEO represents, directly or indirectly, over one lakh exporters across India. Its membership, largely comprising professional exporting firms with strong credentials, called Government recognised export Houses, Trading Houses, Star Trading Houses and Super Star Trading Houses and consultancy exporting firms, contribute a major share of India's total annual exports.

FIEO has forged strong links with counterpart organizations in several countries as well as international agencies. It has access to information/data originating from UN bodies and world agencies like IMF, ADB, ESCAP, World Bank, FAO, UNIDO, UNCTAD and others.[12]

7.6.2 Membership

Membership to FIEO is open to Indian firms and organisations engaged in export trade, or trade promotion. FIEO's members include EPCs, Commodity Boards, Chambers of Commerce, Super Star Trading/Star Trading/Trading/Export Houses, consultancy firms, 100 per cent EOU, units in EPZ and banking and financial institutions.

The federation has the following categories of membership:

(i) *Ordinary member* : EPCs, commodity Boards, chamber of commerce and other institutions engaged in trade promotion.

(ii) *Associate Member* : Companies/firms/organisations engaged in global trade.

(iii) *Honorary member* : Distinguished persons in public service, or eminent persons in export trade, or other interested in the aims and objectives of FIEO.

7.6.3 Organisation

- The Federation's affairs are overseen by a Managing Committee headed by a President.
- President is elected by the Managing Committee members from amongst themselves.
- The Managing Committee is composed of Government representatives, Chairmen of EPCs, Commodity Boards, EDAs (as *ex-officio* members) and elected members from super star trading/star trading/trading houses, Export houses and consultancy companies.
- The Federation also has regional committees and various sub-committees on specialised import and export subjects which study in detail regional and sectoral problems and issues and advise the Managing Committee on them.

7.6.4 Federation's Activities

- The Federation organises and participates in National and International seminars and workshops related to export-import trade in India and abroad.
- Helps and assists its members and Government departments and agencies related to exports and imports.
- FIEO sponsors business delegations to different parts of the world to open up markets for India.
- The Federation interacts closely with Banks, RBI, FIs, Foreign Exchange Dealers' Association of India as well as the ECGC in its endeavour to protect India's International trade interests.
- The Federation is the nodal agency nominated by the Government of India for promoting exports of consultancy and other services. The Federation is also the agency for processing applications and also disbursing grants given by Ministry of Commerce under Marketing Development Assistance.
- The Federation has a number of specialized divisions handling a broad spectrum of activities related to Exim Policy and Procedures, Customs and Excise; Market Research and Development Services; Banking and Direct Taxes; Market Development Schemes, Electronic data interchange and Electronic Commerce, besides publicity, publications and memberships.
- FIEO undertakes multimedia activities, including commissioning of short films, preparing special publications, and issuing supplements in leading news papers/magazines in India and abroad.
- FIEO brings out a fortnightly bulletin titled FIEO news to keep Indian trade and industry informed of the latest global economic and commercial development. FIEO provides single window access to buyers of Indian goods and services.
- FIEO website is being made more dynamic which is helpful for both buyers and sellers. For example, FIEO members can submit the Market Development

Assistance application forms to FIEO through the website.

7.7 FEDERATION OF INDIAN CHAMBERS OF COMMERCE AND INDUSTRY (FICCI)

The Federation of Indian chambers of Commerce and industry (FICCI) was established in 1927, on the advice of Mahatma Gandhi, to garner support for India's independence and to further the interests of the Indian business community. Starting with twenty-four members, the number rose to 103 by 1947. Today with a membership of over 500 Chambers of Commerce, Trade Associations and Industry bodies, it speaks directly and indirectly for over 2,50,000 business units-small, medium and large—employing around 20 million people.[13]

The chambers works as an interface between the industry and the Government. Because of its vast interaction base with different segments of the industry, its recommendations enjoy authenticity.

FICCI has been successful in establishing Joint Business Council (JBC) with over sixty counterpart chambers worldwide, to help India become a major international player. FICCI is the secretariat for the following crucial alliances :

- Indo-Israel Business Alliance.
- India-Brazil Commercial Council
- India-South Africa Commercial Alliance.

Also FICCI is the nodal point for the chapters of—Confederation of Asia Pacific Chamber of Commerce and Industry (CACCI), Indian Ocean Rim Business Forum (IORBF), International Chambers of Commerce (ICC), SAARC Chamber of Commerce, G-15 Federation of Chambers of Commerce and Industry and Services (G-15 FCCIS) and India-Lebanon Business Forum.

The Cyber Centre at FICCI-FICCI-BISNET (with its vast database and seven in-house portals) meets domestic and international information needs of industry with high quality value-added information to enable businessman to take decision with speed and precision.

7.7.1 Research Findings Regarding FIEO and Chambers of Commerce and Industry

7.7.1.1 Working of FIEO and Chambers of Commerce and Industry

22.86 per cent said it was good, 61.43 per cent rated its working as fair and no body rated it very poor (Graph 7.6).

GRAPH 7.6
Rating on Working of FIEO and Chambers of Commerce and Industry

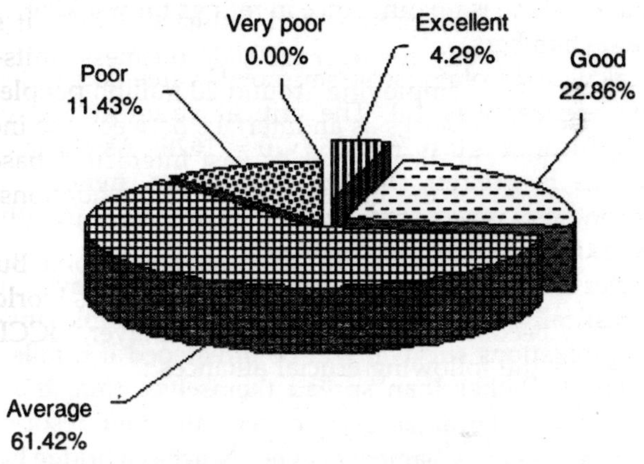

7.7.1.2 Average Score

(a) Average score on this attribute was 3.20 which is equal to the overall average score 3.20.
(b) Exporter's status and average score.

Super star trading houses' average score on this attribute is highest, i.e. 4.50, towards excellent and average score of 100% EOU and other not having status was low, i.e. 2.67 and 3.13 respectively.

7.7.1.3 Kolmogorov-Smirnov one-sample Test

Null hypothesis can be stated as :

TABLE 7.2
Exporters' Status and Average Score

Export status	*Average score*
100% EOU	2.67
Export House	3.50
Trading House	3.50
Super Star Trading House	4.50
Any others (not having status)	3.13

Ho9—There is no difference in ratings for working of FIEO and chambers.

Calculated Kolmogorov-Smirnov D value (largest absolute difference) was 1.0. The critical value at 5% level of significance is 0.1626 ($1.36/\sqrt{70} = .1626$). As the calculated value is greater than critical value, hence the null hypothesis is accepted, i.e. there is difference in ratings for working of FIEO and chambers.

After liberalization, the role of chambers have changed drastically. They have to indeed become think tanks. Any organizations survival will be threatened if it fails in this respect. Rather than spread themselves thin, they must identify niche areas and concentrate their resources on specific issues. Chambers generally act as a bridge between regulatory authorities and industry and can help to develop a conducive environment for industry.

7.8 INDIA TRADE PROMOTION ORGANISATION (ITPO)

7.8.1 About ITPO

ITPO is the premier trade promotion agency of India and provides broad spectrum of services to trade and industry so as to promote Indian exports. ITPO, during its existence of 26 years has played a proactive role in catalysing trade, investment and technology transfer process. ITPO was set-up under section 25 of the Companies Act, 1965 due to the merger of the erstwhile Trade Fair Authority of India and Trade Development Authority. With the Headquarters at Pragati Maidan in New Delhi and regional offices at Bangalore, Chennai, Kolkata and Mumbai, ITPO ensures representative participation of trade and industry from different regions of the country at its events in India and abroad.[14]

7.8.2 Fairs in India and Abroad

ITPO organised and is organising various trade fairs and exhibitions like annual India International Trade Fair (IITF) (which it has been organised from 1981), Tex Styles India Fair and India International Leather Fair, etc.[15]

ITPO also has leased its facilities in Pragati Maidan to organizers of trade events (In the F.Y. 2003-04 as many as 63 events were organized in Pragati Maidan by EPCs and Industry Associations, etc.).

During the year 2003-04, ITPO organized participation in 55 overseas trade fairs in West Asia/Africa region, Europe and in South-east Asia; out of which 38 were specialized events and 16 were general fairs and one exclusive exhibition named 'Incredible India'.

7.8.3 Trade Development Activities

- ITPO organised various buyer-seller meets, seminars, catalogue shows and other export development programmes.
- ITPO maintains a data of export worthy units which are enrolled as regular members of ITPO and provides them a package of services which include trade enquiries received from foreign offices, product development and details on importers, etc.
- ITPO has set-up the Business Information Centre (BIC) and trade portal, www.tradeportalofindia.com to provide trade information to Indian exporters and overseas buyers. The BIC has online access to KOMPASS (a database of 1.8 million companies in 80 countries, classified under mfg./importer/distributor and by country and products).
- ITPO has provided assistance to State Governments in setting up Regional Trade Promotion Centres (RTPCs) for creating export infrastructure in state capital.
- Techno Economic Feasibility Report (TEFR) on

revamping of the exhibition facilities in Pragati Maidan and Constructing an world-class convention centre has also been completed.

- Publishes 'Udyog Vyapar Patrika' and 'Darpan' (in house journals).

7.8.4 Financial Highlights

The working of the organisation for the year 2002-03 resulted in a surplus of Rs. 21.93 crore compared to Rs. 20.97 crores during 2001-02. The total income of the organisation for the year 2002-03 was Rs. 115.14 crore as against a total expenditure of Rs. 93.21 crore.

7.9 INDIAN INSTITUTE OF FOREIGN TRADE (IIFT)

The Indian Institute of Foreign Trade (IIFT)—was established in 1964 by the Government of India, with the objective to strengthen the country's external trade sector through Human Resource Development[16] (HRD). Since then, the institute has been the pioneer in imparting training in Foreign Trade Management in the country besides undertaking research and consultancy in various areas of international trade and has come a long way as a centre of excellence in the field of international business.

The institute was given the status of Deemed University in May 2002 by the Ministry of HRD enabling it to award degrees to start its own doctoral programme and also to get the acceptability and recognition in the internationally competitive academic milieu.

The institute enjoys close and enduring linkages with the Ministry of Commerce, Govt. of India and established ties with leading industrial and Trading Houses and Academic Institutions which made it the premier organisation in India.

Its principal activities and recent initiatives taken includes :

- The Centre for International Trade in Technology (CITT) has been set-up by the Indian Institute of Foreign Trade with financial and technical support from the Department of Scientific and Industrial Research, Government of India, with the primary objective of actualising India's potential in technology trade and addressing some of these institutional complexities.

- Conducting Research Studies in the areas of International Trade. Like CITT established by IIFT with the support of DSIR recently has taken following research project—

  (i) Valuation of Intangible,
  (ii) Implications of WTO -TBT Agreement on Exports.
  (iii) Global Marketing of R&D services.
  (iv) FDI and Technology Exports.
  (v) A study on Technology Intensive Exports from India : Based on Reports of Trade Delegations.
  (vi) A study on policies and Incentives for accelerating technology intensive exports : exporter's perspective.

Also Compendium on Technology Exports was prepared by DSIR and IIFT presenting data of 250 organizations.

- IIFT is a unique institution of its own type. The Institute offers a wide variety of executive development programmes to suit the needs of executive at different levels in export organisations. The institution offers full time courses like two year Masters Programme in International Business (MPIB), one year Executive Masters in International Trade (EMIT), PG Diploma in International Trade, Ph.Ds. etc.
- The Institute is involved in marketing, functional and policy research.
- IIFT has been identified as a partner in the implementation of a project EDECAD (Education and E-Commerce for Asia-EU Economic Development) supported by the European Commission, the main focus of which is to develop shared understanding while generating competitive advantage and enhancing capabilities for global business.

Also IIFT has been identified as one of the institutional stakeholders in the project titled 'Clustured Advantage : Project to Network Small and Medium Enterprises and Regional Stakeholders in UK and in India in Business clusters; implemented by British Council.

- The Institute has been organising seminars, conferences and meetings on various aspects of international trade.

7.10 MARKETING DEVELOPMENT ASSISTANCE (MDA) SCHEME

7.10.1 MDA : Its Objectives

To facilitate various measures undertaken to stimulate and diversify the country's export trade, the Marketing Development Assistance Scheme is being implemented by the Department of Commerce with following objectives :

(a) To assist individual exporters for export promotion activities abroad.

(b) To assist EPCs to undertake export promotion activities for their product(s) and commodities.

(c) To assist consortium marketing approach abroad.

(d) To assist improved organisations/trade bodies in undertaking limited exclusive non-recurring innovative activities connected with export promotion efforts of their members.

(e) To assist EPCs to contest countervailing duty/Anti-dumping cases initiated abroad.

(f) To assist Focus Area Export promotion programmes in specific regions abroad like focus Latin American Countries (LAC), Focus Africa and Focus Commonwealth of Independent States (CIS) programmes.

(g) To promote residual essential activities connected with marketing promotion efforts abroad.

Format of Application form and claim form is given in Annexure 7.2A and 7.2B.

7.10.2 Administration of the Scheme

- The utilization of the scheme is administered by the Export and Marketing Development Assistance Division (E & MDA) in the Department of Commerce, Government of India. Recognized EPCs, Commodity Boards and Export Development authorities are eligible for MDA assistance for development and promotional activities to promote exports of their products.
- MDA budget allocation to recognized EPCs are finalized in annual meetings with the respective EPCs, which are chaired by the Additional Secretary and Financial Advisor (AS and FA), Department of Commerce. Proposals for *adhoc* grants for exclusive innovative export promotional activities are examined by the E & MDA Division and decided with the approval of AS and FA.
- Proposals for reimbursement of MDA assistance to individual exporters for eligible export promotion activities abroad on receipt of specific recommendation from FIEO, EPCs, Commodity Boards and EDAs are considered at final stage and approved by the MDA committee under the chairmanship of Director (MDA), Department of Commerce with Director/Dy. Sec. (Finance), Director/Dy. Sec. from one commodity division on annual rotation basis as members and U. Sec. (MDA) as member Secretary.
- Proposals received from concerned EPCs for assistance to contest countervailing duty and Anti-dumping duty proceedings initiated abroad are considered by a specific committee constituted in this regard under the chairmanship of AS & FA.

7.10.3 Important Assistances under MDA

7.10.3.1 Assistance to Individual Exporters for Export Promotion Activities Abroad—Participation in EPC etc. Led Trade Delegations/BSMs/Trade Fairs/ Exhibitions[17]

(i) Exporting companies with an f.o.b. value of exports of upto Rs. 5 crore in the preceding year will be eligible for MDA assistance for participation in EPC etc. led trade delegations BSMs/Trade Fairs/Exhibitions abroad to explore new markets for export of their specific product(s) and commodities from India in the initial phase. This will be subject to the condition that the exporter is having complete 12 months' membership with concerned EPC, etc. and filing of returns with concerned EPC/organisation regularly.

(ii) Assistance would be permissible on travel expenses by air, in economy excursion class fair and/or charges of the built up furnished stall, @ 90% for exporters having valid SSI registration certification and @ 75% for others including merchant exporters. This would, however, be subject to an upper ceiling mentioned below in the table per tour.

TABLE 7.3
Assistance to Individual Exporters for Export Promotion Activities Abroad

S.No.	*Area/Sector*	*No. of visits eligible*	*Maximum Financial ceiling per event*		
			BSM/Trade fair/delegations/ exhibition, etc. abroad [Travel grant (A)]	*Trade Fair Exhibition abroad (Stall charges)*	*Total (in Rs.)*
(1)	*(2)*	*(3)*	*(4)*	*(5)*	*(6)*
1.	Focus LAC	1	Rs. 90000.00	Rs. 50000.00	140000.00
2.	Focus Africa WANA (including countries)	1	Rs. 60000.00	Rs. 50000.00	110000.00
3.	Focus CIS	1	Rs. 60000.00	Rs. 50000.00	110000.00
4.	Focus ASEAN	1	Rs. 60000.00	Rs. 50000.00	110000.00
5.	General Areas	1	Nil	Rs. 50000.00	50000.00
	Total	5			

The participation of individual companies in the above activities shall be subject to the following conditions:

(1) For EPC etc. led Trade Delegations/BSMs only air-fare by Economy Excursion class shall be permissible. For

participation in Trade Fairs/Exhibitions shall charges in addition to travel expenditure shall also be permissible subject to ceilings mentioned in the column 6 in the above table.

(2) Maximum number of permissible participations shall be five in a financial year as indicated in above table (No travel grant is permissible for one visit to General Areas).

(3) Assistance shall be permissible to one regular employee/director/partner/proprietor of the company. Assistance would not be available to exporter of foreign nationality or holding foreign passport.

(4) Intimation application must be received in the concerned EPC etc. with a minimum of 14 days' clear advance notice excluding the date of receipt of application in the office of the concerned organization and the date of departure from the country.

(5) The company shall not be under investigation/ charged/prosecuted/debarred/black listed under EXIM Policy of India or any other law relating to export and import business.

(6) Maximum MDA assistance shall be inclusive of MDA assistance received from all Governments bodies/ FIEO/EPCs/Commodity Boards/Export Development Authorities/ITPO, etc.

(7) A maximum of three participations in a particular trade fair/exhibition would be eligible for MDA assistance and exporting companies after availing assistance three times including past cases for a particular fair/exhibition, have to participate in that fair, if any, on self-financing basis.

7.10.3.2 Publicity through Printed Material

Cost of production of publicity material like product catalogue, brochure, information handout, etc. for use abroad during sale-*cum*-study, trade fairs, etc. would be permissible @ 25% of the total approved cost subject to an upper ceiling of Rs. 15,000. This would be subject to meeting the following conditions :

(1) Assistance would be provided once in a financial year.
(2) A copy of the publicity material is to be submitted along with the claim.
(3) Quotations from a minimum of three printers is to be obtained and submitted alongwith the claim. Assistance will, however, be allowed on the lowest quotation subject to the upper ceiling as mentioned above.
(4) Rules 4, 5, 6 same as discussed earlier in section 7.10.3.1—4, 5, 6 and 7.

7.10.3.3 Sales-cum-Study Tour

Assistance would be permissible on travel expenses by air, euro-rail, etc. in economy excursion class fair @ 90% for exporters having valid SSI registration certificate and @ 75% for other merchant exporters. This would, however, be subject to an upper ceiling of Rs. 60,000 per tour (Rs. 90,000 for LAC region). This would also be subject to meeting the conditions of para 3 and as under :

(1) Exporting companies with f.o.b. value exports upto Rs. 4 crore during the preceding financial year would only be eligible for individual sale-*cum*-study tour(s) with MDA assistance and others, having achieved exports more than Rs. 4 crore during the preceding financial year have to do on self-supporting basis.
(2) A maximum of two sale-*cum*-study tours to a particular country would be eligible for MDA assistance and exporting companies after availing MDA assistance two times including past cases to a particular country, have to visit that country, if any, on self-financing basis.
(3) The tour to single country or a group of countries shall be with a minimum of four-nights stay abroad excluding journey period.

Rules 4, 5, 6 and 7 are same as discussed earlier in section 7.10.3.1 (S. No. 4, 5, 6 and 7).

7.10.4 Reimbursement of Assistance to Exporters

- Intimation application duly completed and signed in

the prescribed format shall be submitted by the exporter to the concerned FIEO/EPC/Commodity Board/APEDA/MPEDA giving clear 14 days' advance notice.

- Concerned organization (FIEO, EPC, etc.) on receipt of application form in the prescribed format.
- Claim along with the declaration duly completed shall be submitted by the exporter to the concerned organization (FIEO, EPC) in the prescribed format along with necessary documents immediately on return to India/production of publicity material.

7.10.5 Consortium Marketing Approach Abroad

Three to five SSI manufacturer exporters and/or merchant exporters with f.o.b. value of average exports less than Rs. 2 crore per annum per member during the preceding three financial years, can participate in trade fairs and exhibitions abroad through a consortium marketing approach (subject to necessary conditions). The consortium should have a Memorandum of Understanding (MOU) and should have an action plan for export promotion, skill upgradation and technology upgradation, etc. and register it with the concerned EPC. Also all members should be exporting similar type of products or their products should reach the users through the same outlets so that the consortium could offer large capacities or range of products to foreign importers/users.

7.10.6 Assistance to EPCs, other institutions and SSIs

EPCs are required to send their detailed annual action plan to E&MDA Division six months in advance. The activities approved in the annual meetings with each EPC well before the start of the financial year shall only be financed from MDA funds. EPCs shall have to utilise the MDA funds in a financial year for purposes for which these are sanctioned. EPCs shall have to furnish detailed accounts activity-wise for each approved code activity certified by a CA and the utilization certificate for the funds released in a financial year by 30th September of the succeeding financial year positively. MDA assistance to IIFT, IIP, ICA for specific development activities directed towards export growth of Indian products and commodities would be considered by the Government for part financing. Allocation for ITPO from MDA would be kept to the minimum and confined to the special fairs to meet deficit as approved by the Exhibition Advisory Committee in the Department of Commerce.

Financial assistance will be given to SSI's for adoption of international numbering standards used in Bar-coding/E-commerce application. Reimbursement of 75 per cent of the registration fee will be paid to EAN India (under Ministry of Commerce, Govt. of India) by SSI units. The MDA scheme also offers funding for individual overseas study tours, individual assistance for participation in overseas fairs/exhibitions and production of publicity material for overseas publicity.

7.10.7 MDA 2004-05

The budget for MDA has been curtailed and new norms are being introduced for availing grants through export promotion window. The rules for MDA, under which nearly Rs. 25 crore per annum would be spent from 2004-05 onwards, have been tightened. Meant for small exporters with a turnover of up to Rs. 5 crore per annum, this scheme would now fund only promotion efforts aimed at Latin American, African, CIS and Asean Markets.[18]

7.11 MARKET ACCESS INITIATIVE (MAI)

7.11.1 Objectives of MAI

Financial assistance shall be available under the scheme to the EPCs, industry and trade associations and other eligible entities, (as may be notified from time to time) on the basis of the competitive merits of proposals received in this regard for the following purposes which *inter-alia* includes :

(i) Marketing studies on country product focus approach basis.

(ii) Setting up of common showrooms under one proof and warehousing facility in the identified centres on the basis of marketing studies abroad.

(iii) Participation in sales promotion campaigns through international departmental stores.

(iv) Publicity campaign for launching identified products in selected markets.
(v) Participation in international trade fairs, seminars, buyers-sellers meet.
(vi) Promotion of selected brands, i.e. brand promotion.
(vii) Transport subsidies for select agriculture products.
(viii) Registration charges for product registration abroad for pharmaceuticals, bio-technology and agro-chemicals and testing charges for engineering products.
(ix) Research and Project Development.
(x) Setting up of "business centre" in Indian Mission abroad for visiting Indian exporters.
(xi) Export potential surveys of states to identify product groups.

7.11.2 MAI—2004-05

Indian exporters will get assistance for establishing warehouses and showrooms in select markets through the revised MAI with the outlay for the year 2004-05 being increased to Rs. 40 crore, the budget for MAI is now estimated at nearly Rs. 450 crore for four years. The MAI and MDA schemes will support the ASIDE scheme for development of export infrastructure and the brand equity fund which is now being managed by CII exclusively to promote Indian brands in overseas market.[19]

The revamped MAI scheme would focus on sustained export promotion efforts rather than one time projects like participation in an overseas trade fair. Moreover, funds would be spent only on 'focus markets' and 'focus products' identified by commerce department. Assistance from the MAI scheme would be routed through Government organisations, EPCs, commodity boards and recognised industry chambers. Individual exporters can access the scheme for registration of Pharmaceuticals, bio-tech products or ago-chemicals in selected markets.

7.12 RESEARCH FINDINGS WITH RESPECT OF MARKETING DEVELOPMENT ASSISTANCE (MDA) AND MARKETING ACCESS INITIATIVE (MAI)

7.12.1 Ratings of the Various Assistances Offered by MDA and MAI

5.71 per cent respondents have rated the MDA for

participation in trade fair, exhibition as excellent. On other parameters like publication, R&D, opening of foreign office or warehouse none have rated excellent (Table 7.4).

TABLE 7.4
Rating of the (Overall) Various Assistances Provided by MDA and MAI

	*Assistances**		*Excellent*	*Good*	*Fair*	*Poor*	*Very poor*	*No response*
A.	Participation in Trade fair, Exhibition	No.	4	28	34	1	0	3
		%	5.71	40.00	48.57	10.43	0.0	4.29
B.	Bringing out publication for use abroad and advt. in foreign media	No.	0	18	40	9	0	3
		%	0.0	25.71	57.14	12.86	0.0	4.29
C.	Research and Product Devt.	No.	0	5	18	43	1	3
		%	0.0	7.14	25.71	61.43	1.43	4.29
D.	Opening of foreign office	No.	0	3	13	45	6	3
		%	0.0	4.29	18.57	64.29	8.57	4.29
E.	Opening of ware house	No.	0	4	16	37	10	3
		%	0.0	5.71	22.86	52.86	14.29	4.29

* Assistances mentioned (a, b, c, d, e) will be hereafter referred as overall assistances.

7.12.2 Availing any of the above mentioned assistances provided by MDA

Thirty-five respondents, i.e. 50 percent said that they have availed MDA and 50 per cent respondents said that they have yet not availed MDA.

7.12.3 Release of approved MDA grant

44.20 per cent of respondents said that they are satisfied by it and 20 per cent of respondents said that they are not satisfied with the release of approved MDA grant (Graph 7.7).

7.12.4 Average Score

(a) Average score for particiption in trade fair and exhibition came out to be 3.37 which is greater than

Graph 7.7
Release of Approved MDA Grant

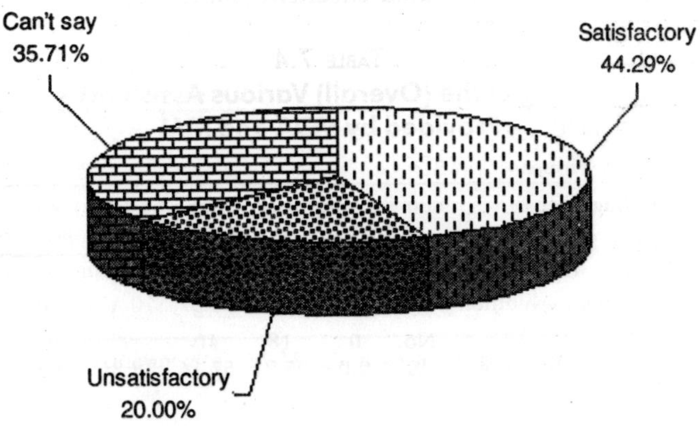

overall average score for overall MDA assistance (calculated by adding average score of each MDA assistance a, b, c, d and e and then taking average) 2.64 so on 5 point scale it can be considered satisfactory. Average score for bringing out publication abroad and advertisement in foreign media was 3.00, which is also greater than overall average score for MDA, i.e. 2.64. Average score for R & D , opening of foreign office and warehouse was 2.30, 2.10 and 2.11 respectively, all of which were less than overall average score for MDA (2.64).

(b) *Average score and status of exporter* : The relationship can be explained through the following Table 7.5.

It is very clear from the average score table that the average score for (e), i.e. opening of warehouse is even low for super-star trading house which in all other cases (a, b, c and d) is having high average score as compared to other firms.

7.12.5 Chi-square Test

Ho10—There is no significant difference between availing any assistance provided by MDA and the process of release of approved MDA grant.

TABLE 7.5
Average Score for MDA and Status of Exporter

Exporter status	Av. score (a)	Av. score (b)	Av. score (c)	Av. score (d)	Av. score (e)
(i) 100% EOU	4	3	2.5	2.67	2.50
(ii) Export House	3.3	3.14	2.42	2.25	2.25
(iii) Trading House	3.00	4.00	3.50	2.50	2.50
(iv) Super Star Trading House	5.00	4.00	3.50	3.00	1.98
(v) Any Others	3.25	2.88	2.15	1.94	3.00

* a, b, c, d, e refers assistances under MDA as mentioned earlier in the Table 7.4.

χ^2 value at 5 per cent level of significance with 2 degrees of freedom was 58.57, which is greater than the tabulated value (@ 5%, df = 2) 5.99, hence null hypothesis is rejected, i.e. availing any assistance provided by MDA and process of release of approved MDA grant are not independent attributes.

Ho11—There is no significant difference between availing any assistance provided by MDA and the process of release of approved MDA grant (excluding 'can't say option)—If the Chi-square value is calculated without the option 'Can't say' at a = 5% level of significance and df = 1, it comes out to be 28.47 which is also greater than tabulated value (@ 5%, df = 1) 3.84, hence in this case also null hypothesis is rejected.

7.12.6 'F' Test

(a) 'F' test can be applied to test the null hypothesis.
Ho12—There is no difference among the status of exporters with respect to overall assistances provided under MDA.
The table value of F at 5% for $V_1 = 4$ and $V_2 = 65$ (degrees of freedom) is 2.5187.
Since the calculated value (8.502) is more than tabulated value, hence null hypothesis is rejected and alternative hypothesis is accepted, i.e. there is

TABLE 7.6
Analysis of Variance

Source of variation	*Sum of squares*	*Degrees of freedom*	*Mean square*	*F ratio*
Between Sample	393.76	4	98.44	8.502
Within Sample	752.56	65	11.58	

difference among the status of exporters with respect to overall assistances provided under MDA.

(b) Ho13—Zone-wise rating for overall assistances provided under MDA, do not differ.

TABLE 7.7
Analysis of Variance

Source of variation	*Sum of squares*	*Degrees of freedom*	*Mean square*	*F ratio*
Between Sample	58.79	3	19.60	1.512
Within Sample	855.32	66	12.96	

The table value of F at 5% of $V_1 = 3$ and $V_2 = 66$ (degrees of freedom is 2.7503). Since the calculated value is 1.512 which is less than table value, hence the null hypothesis is accepted that there is no difference among the zones with respect to overall assistances provided under MDA.

7.13 FINDINGS ON SUPPORT OF LOCAL AUTHORITIES AND PROMOTIONAL AGENCIES

In the earlier section of this chapter and previous chapter, major institutions and organizations for export promotion were discussed that how they are functioning and providing integrated package of assistance to the enterprise for export development. At the same time it can't be ignored that for an export development. At the same time it can't be ignored that for an export orientation to emerge in developing countries, management at the enterprise level require motivation and a pro-export attitude. Export promotion efforts of Government cannot be carried out effectively without support and cooperation from local level. If at local level, there are too many obstacles, then it can demotivate the business community, hence local support is must. It may include many aspects like from project financing, site selection to getting the clearances from various departments and offices. Also the role of local promotional agencies become altogether important how local chambers or such agencies respond to the problems faced by exporters.

Research findings regarding the support of local authorities and promotional agencies are as follows:

TABLE 7.8
Rating of Respondents Regarding Support of Local Authorities

Ratings	*No. of Respondents*	*Percentage*
Excellent	3	4.29
Good	21	30.00
Fair	35	50
Poor	10	14.29
Very Poor	1	1.43

7.13.1 Support of Local Authorities

Fifty per cent rated good on this attribute. 14.29 per cent of respondents rated it poor (Table 7.8).

7.13.1.1 Average Score

- The average score on this attribute was 3.21 which was almost equal to the overall average score 3.20.

(a) Average score with respect to export status : Average score for super star trading house came out to be 4.50 and that of trading house 2.50.

It is clear from the table that average score of super-star

TABLE 7.9

Average Score on the Attribute (Support of Local Authorities) with Respect to Export Status

Status	*Average score*
100% EOU	3.50
Export House	3.17
Trading House	2.50
Super Star Trading House	4.50
Any Others (not having status)	3.17

trading house is highest, i.e. their overall rating on this attribute is close to excellent. It can also be interpreted from the same that big houses get the local support easily as compared to small and traditional exporters.

7.13.1.2 Kolmogorov Smirnov one sample Test

Null hypothesis can be stated as—

Ho16—There is no difference in ratings for the support of local authorities.

Calculated Kolmogorov-Smirnov D value (largest absolute difference) is 0.243. The critical value at 5% level of significance is .1626 ($1.36/\sqrt{70}$ = .1626). Since the calculated value is greater than critical value, hence the null hypothesis is rejected and alternative hypothesis is accepted, i.e. there is difference in ratings for the support of local authorities.

7.13.2 Findings on Support of Local Promotional Agencies

70 per cent rated it fair, 20% as good and 10% as poor, nobody rated it excellent or very poor.

7.13.2.1 Average Score

(a) Average score on this attribute was 3.10, less than the overall average score 3.20.

(b) Average score on this attribute and status of exporter

Table 7.10
Average Score on this Attribute and Status of Exporter

Status	*Average score*
100% Export Oriented Unit	3.33
Export House	3.25
Trading House	3.50
Super Star Trading House	4.00
Any Others (not having status)	2.98

Local promotional agencies was rated by Super-star trading house and lowest by those not enjoying any export status (2.98).

Thus in this chapter important export promotion institutions like EPCs, Development Authorities, Commodity Boards, ITPO, FIEO, IIFT and MDA and MAI were discussed. In the next chapter EOUs, SEZs, institutions for small exporters and infrastructural suport will be discussed.

Notes and References

1. 'Export Stimulation programs in the major industrial countries'. The US and eight major competitors, congressional research service : 95th congress, 2nd session, Washington DC, 6 October 1978, pp. 228-42.
2. From 'Report of Review Committee on Export Promotion Council' chaired by Shri Prabhu V. Mehta, New Delhi, 1965.
3. Chemexil has about 6500 members, 2000 of which are from Pharma industry, which will join pharmexcil soon. Pharmexil at present (Sept. 2004), is backed by 600 odd active pharma members. In July 2004, Pharmexcil bagged the authority to issue registration-*cum*-membership certificates.
   From Anand, M.S., 'Pharmexcil is lord of drugs, chemical has to make way', *The Economic Times*, New Delhi, 12 September, 2004.

4(a) Varshney, R.L.; Bhattacharyya, B. 'International Marketing Management—In Indian Perspective', Sultan Chand and Sons, New Delhi, 2002, pp. 142-59.

4(b) Important Characteristics of the Following :

(i) EPCH-Export Promotion Council for Handicraft established in the year 1986 to promote Indian Handicrafts worldwide.

Members = 7000 manufacturer-exporters.
Growth = From Rs. 3870 million exports in 1986 to Rs. 10465 million in the year 2003-04 exports growing at the rate of 15% every year.
Activities = Reviving Languishing crafts like Chikanbuti, Cane and Bamboo handicrafts, Publishing in house journal CRAFTCIL.

(ii) EEPC (1955)—ISO 9001 certified, 2500 member firms having ISO 9001. In 2000-01 total export were US$ 5.96 Billion.

(iii) Texprocil (1954)—Autonomous, non-profit organization Exports in 2003-04—95.62 million US$.

(iv) Plexconcil (1955) Membership—More than 2000. Export Trade in Millenium US$ 1 Billion.

5. CAPEXIL 2003-04—46th Annual Report.
6. *Ibid.*, 5.
7. According to CAPEXIL President MGS Ashokan Government should take more steps to helps exporters as India faces stiff competition from Chinese exporters and so Indian policy-makers need to take up on war footing the issues on tax reforms and building infrastructural facilities besides ensuring banking and finance and world class transportation and communication.
8. 'Capexil asks for more export promotion steps', *The Economic Times*, New Delhi, 25 Nov., 2004.
9. Mallick, Arnab, "Capexil to set-up warehouse overseas', Feb. 19, 2005, from Website. http://in biz.yahoo.com.
10. www.Indianspices.com.
11. The world Bank has approved a proposal called "Empowerment of Rural communities to export organic spices' which was jointly presented by Spices Board and ITC Geneva under World Bank Competition titled 'Development Market Place'. For this program websites have been launched for the NGOs associated with this project, viz. www.samanwita.com., www.pdsorganicspice.com, www.wsssindia.com, www.hopeinnilgiris.com.
12. www.fieo.com
13. www.ficci.com
14. 'Institutional Trade facilitation' from website http://commerce.nic.in/annual 2003-04.
15. The 23rd International Trade was organised from 14 Nov. to 27 Nov. 2003. The theme of this trade fair was 'Promoting Exports by Small and Medium Enterprises' and 'Tourism', 77 delegations from different countries visited the fair, in addition to 2,40,000 business visitors.
16. www.IIFT.ac.in.
17. Marketing Development Assistance Scheme, Revised Guidelines w.e.f. 01/04/2004. The Ministry of Commerce and Industry, Department of Commerce, Udyog Bhawan, New Delhi.
18. Subramaniam, Ganpathy, G., 'Government to pump in Rs. 450 crore for export marketing', *The Economic Times*, New Delhi, 14 March, 2004.
19. *Ibid.*

ANNEXURE 7.1

CAPEXIL

(Formerly CHEMICALS and ALLIED PRODUCTS EXPORT PROMOTION COUNCIL)
(Limited by Guarantee)

BALANCE SHEET AS AT 31st March 2004

	Particulars	*Sch. No.*	*31.03.2004 (Rs.)*	*31.03.2003 (Rs.)*
I.	SOURCES OF FUNDS			
A.	Shareholder's funds			
	Reserves and Surplus	1	3,59,32,088.49	5,42,07,217.25
	Sub-Total (A)		**3,59,32,088.49**	**5,42,07,217.25**
B.	Loan Funds			
	Secured Loan	2	15,58,540.51	10,86,869.72
	Sub-Total (B)		**15,58,540.51**	**10,86,869.72**
	Total Funds (A) + (B)		**3,74,90,629.00**	**5,52,94,086.97**
II.	APPLICATION OF FUNDS			
A.	Fixed Assets			
	Gross Block		3,73,28,883.93	3,23,89,785.31
	Less : Depreciation		1,43,86,976.91	1,25,32,178.49
	Net Block (A)	3	2,29,41,907.02	1,98,57,606.82
B.	Investment			
	Investment	4	250.00	250.00
	Sub-Total (B)		**250.00**	**250.00**
C.	Current Assets, Loans and Advances			
	Sundry Debtors	5	1,13,65,125.00	1,64,51,446.00
	Cash and Bank Balance	6	2,81,64,559.56	3,81,92,429.42
	Interest Accrued	7	23,03,962.07	39,41,620.33
	Loans and Advances	8	26,90,598.37	36,53,288.39
	Total Current Assets (C)		**4,45,24,245.00**	**6,22,38,784.14**

D.	Less : Current Liabilities and Provisions			
	Current Liabilities	9	2,98,85,545.33	2,67,12,326.30
	Provisions	10	90,227.69	90,227.69
	Total Current Liabilities (D)		**2,99,75,773.02**	**2,68,02,553.99**
E.	Net Current Assets (C—D)		1,45,48,471.98	3,54,36,230.15
	Total Funds (A+B+E)		**3,74,90,629.00**	**5,52,94,086.97**

Source : CAPEXIL Annual Report, 2003-04.

ANNEXURE 7.2

Application Form for Marketing Development Assistance for Sale-cum-study-tour Abroad

Ref. No. .... Date ....

1.	Name of the firm with full address	IBC No. ....
2.	EH/TH Certificate	No. and Date .... Valid upto ....
3.	FOB value of exports during last three financial years, year-wise	(Rs. in Crores)
4.	Name of the countries to be visited	Countries From To
5.	Particulars of tour	Date of departure from India Date of arrival in India
6.	Details of proposal(s) already submitted in the same financial year	1. Sales tour to .... (countries) During .... (month/year) 2. Participation in .... (fair/exhibition) During .... (month/year) 3. ....
7.	Details of sale tour to same country/countries earlier conducted with MDA assistance	
8.	Name and designation of the person going abroad	

Place: ....

Date : Signature

Appendix 7.2(A)

Application Form for Marketing Development Assistance for Participation in Trade Fair/Exhibition Abroad

Ref. No. .... Date ....

1.	Name of the firm with full address	IEC No. ....
2.	EH/TH Certificate	No. and Date .... Valid upto ....
3.	FOB value of exports during last three financial years, year-wise	(Rs. in Crores)
4.	Particulars of fair/exhibition	Name of fair : Place: Country: From .... To ....
5.	Particulars of visit	Date of departure from India Date of arrival in India ....
6.	Details of proposal(s) already submitted in the same financial year	1. Sales tour to .... (countries) During .... (month/year) 2. Participation in .... (fair/exhibition) during .... (month/year) 3. ....
7.	Details of earlier participation in the same fair with MDA assistance	
8.	Whether national participation organized by ITPO/EPC, etc.	Yes/No
9.	Whether participating through ITPO, EPC, etc.	Yes/No
10.	Whether waiver certificate taken from ITPO, EPC, etc.	Yes/No/N.A.
11.	Name and designation of the person going abroad.	

Place: ....

Date : Signature

APPENDIX 7.2(B)

Claim Form for Marketing Development Assistance for Sales-*cum*-Study Tour Abroad

Ref. No. .... Date ....

1.	Name of the firm with full address	IEC No. ....
2.	Approval letter No. and date	....
3.	EH/TH Certificate	No. and Date .... Valid upto .... (Please attach self-certified copy of the certificate issued by DGFT).
4.	Whether SSI?	Yes/No. (If yes, attach a self-certified copy of SSI Registration Certificate)
5.	FOB value of exports during last three financial years.	(Rs. in Crores)
6.	Name of the countries visited with duration of stay in each country	Country From To
7.	Date of actual departure from India	------------------------------ (Please attach self-certified photocopy of passport duly highlighting date of departure)
8.	Date of actual arrival in	.... India after completing (Please attach self-certified photocopy of passport duly highlighting date of arrival)
9.	Name and Designation of person gone on tour abroad	
10.	Details of tours undertaken in the past with MDA assistance to same country/countries.	
11.	Whether assistance received from other Government bodies/EPC/Commodity Board/APEDA/MPEDA/ITPO, etc. for the activity under reference.	Yes/No. (If yes, please give full details)

12.	No. of proposals already submitted in same financial year.	1. Sales tour to .... (countries)
		During .... (month/year)
		2. Participation in .... (fair/exhibition)
		during .... (month/year)
		3. ....
13.	Actual expenditure on return airfare by economy excursion class	Rs. .... (Please attach original air ticket/ jacket used during the journey).......
14.	Amount claimed	Rs. ....

Declaration

I solemnly declare that the particulars given in the above statement are correct. I bound myself and the company accountable and responsible for any incorrect information given in the above statement and shall immediately refund amount received on the basis of wrong information provided in the above statement.

Place : Signature ....

Date : Name ....

Designation ....

Office Seal

Supporting Institutions

8.1 INTRODUCTION

To achieve the target of 1 percent share in world merchandise trade by 2007 (Exim Policy, 2002-07, Government of India), to enhance foreign exchange earnings by promoting exports and to promote hassle free export activity the government of India has been eyeing upon the emerging concepts viz. Export-oriented units, Electronic Hardware Technology Park (EHTP), Software Technology Parks (STPs), Export Processing Zones (EPZs) and more specifically on Special Economic Zones (SEZs). The dazzling achievements of Singapore, the Shenzen of China and Nantez of Taiwan, which have been a lure for Indian industry and planners for decades is now materialising as the Industry wants the same success story to be repeated in India like China. The first part of Chapter discusses all this.

Also when thinking of achieving the export targets India can't ignore to think about small and medium scale exporters. The institutional support for small exporters is discussed in next part of this chapter and so this chapter tries to hold the right pulse of India's international trade. Final section of this chapter deals with the infrastructural support—roads, ports, railway as infrastructure bottlenecks are posing a major challenge to India's ambitious export plan.

8.2 EXPORT ORIENTED UNITS (EOUs), UNITS IN EXPORT PROCESSING ZONES (EPZs), ELECTRONICS HARDWARE TECHNOLOGY PARKS (EHTPs) AND SOFTWARE TECHNOLOGY PARKS (STPs)

8.2.1 Eligibility, Export and Import

Units undertaking to export their entire production of goods and services may be set up under the Export Oriented Unit (EOU) Scheme,[1] EPZ Scheme, EHTP[2] or STP Scheme.[3] Such units may be engaged in manufacturing, providing services, repair, remaking, reconditioning, re-engineering including making of gold/silver/platinum and articles thereof, agriculture, including agro-processing, aquaculture, bio-technology, horticulture, viticulture, sericulture, pisciculture, poultry and granites and may export all products except restricted items of exports in ITC (HS). Units for generation/distribution of power may also set-up in EPZs; however, no trading unit shall be permitted.[4]

An EOU/EPZ/EHTP/STP unit may export goods and services (including by products, rejects, waste scrap) and may import without payment of duty on all types of goods (including capital goods and second hand capital goods).[5]

8.2.2 Net Foreign Exchange Earning as a Percentage of Exports, Letter of Intent and Legal Undertaking

The minimum Net Foreign Exchange earning as a percentage of Exports (NFEP) and the minimum Export Performance (EP) shall be as specified in Annexure 8.1. Items of manufacture for export specified in the Letter of Permission (LOP)/Letter of Intent (LOI) alone shall be taken into account for calculation of NFEP and EP.

On approval, a Letter of Permission (LOP)/Letter of Intent (LOI) shall be issued by the Development Commissioner to EOU/EPZ/EHTP/STP unit. The LOP/LOI shall have an initial validity of 3 years. Its validity may be extended by another 3 years, beyond initial validity, by the competent authority. However, proposals approved prior to 01.04.2002 shall be considered on case to case basis by the Board of Approval (BOA).

LOP/LOI issued to EOU/EPZ/EHTP/STP units by the concerned authority would be constructed as a licence for all purposes, including for procurement of raw-materials and consumables either directly or through designated State Trading Enterprise.

The unit shall execute a legal undertaking with the Development Commissioner concerned and in the event of failure to fulfil the performance, it would be liable to penalty in terms of the legal undertaking or under any other law for the time being in force.

8.2.3 Application and Approvals

Only project having an investment of not less than Rs. 50 lakhs and above in building, plant and machinery shall be considered for establishment under EOU scheme. (This shall, however, not apply to existing units and units in EPZ/EHTP/STP/agriculture/floriculture/aquaculture/animal husbandry/information technology, handicrafts, services and such other sectors as may be decided by the BOA). Applications for setting up of EOU/EPZ/EHTP/STP units, satisfying the conditions mentioned in paragraph 6.7 of the Handbook (Vol. I) may be approved by the concerned Development Commissioner within 15 days.

In other cases, approval may be granted by the Board of Approval (BOA) set-up for this purpose.

Proposals requiring industrial license may be considered by the Board of Approval on a case to case basis.

8.2.4 Entitlements

- An EOU/EPZ/EHTP/STP unit may export goods manufactured by it through a merchant exporter/status holder recognized under the Exim policy or any other EOU/EPZ/EHTP/STP/SEZ.
- Supplies from the (Domestic Tariff Area) DTA to EOU/EPZ/EHTP/STP units will be regarded as "deemed exports" and the DTA supplier shall be eligible for the relevant entitlements (under paragraph 8.3 of Exim policy, 2002-07).

- The EOU/EPZ/EHTP/STP units shall be entitled for the following :

    (i) Reimbursement of central sales tax.
    (ii) Exemption from payment of Central Excise Duty on all goods as per entitlement.
    (iii) Reimbursement of Central Excise duty paid on bulk tea procured from licensed auction centres by Development Commissioner of concerned zone so long as levy on bulk tea in this regard is in force.
    (iv) Reimbursement of duty paid on fuels procured from domestic oil companies, by the Development Commissioner of the concerned zone as per the rate of drawback notified by the DGFT from time to time.
    (v) EOU/EPZ, gem and jewellery units shall be entitled for—participation in exhibitions abroad with the permission of Development Commissioner, export of branded jewellery (For display/sale in the permitted shops abroad and export through showrooms abroad and duty free shops).

- No licences are required for import/domestic procurement.
- Such units can repatriate their profits freely without any dividend balancing requirement.
- Such units has freedom to sub-contract part of the production and production process in the domestic area.
- EOU/EPZ/EHTP/STP units can clear goods upto 50 per cent of the value of exports in the domestic area on the concessional duty. Also such units are exempted from industrial licensing for manufacture of items reserved for small scale industry sector.
- Supplier of cut and polished diamonds, precious and semi-precious stones, synthetic stones and processed pearls from DTA to EOU/EPZ units shall be eligible for grant of Replenishment licences at rates and for the items mentioned in Handbook (Vol. 1).

- Rejects (Waste) may be sold in the DTA on payment of duties as applicable. Sale of rejects upto 5% of FOB value of exports shall not be subject to achievement of NFEP.

8.2.5 Bonding and Debonding

The initial bonding period for units under the EOU/EHTP/STP schemes shall be 5 years, which may be extended by the Development Commission concerned for a period of 5 years at a time.

Subject to the approval of the Development Commissioner, EOU/EPZ/EHTP/STP units may be debonded such debonding shall be subject to payment of duties of customs and excise and the industrial policy in force at the time of debonding.

8.3 CONFEDERATION OF 100 PER CENT EXPORT UNITS (CEU) AND EPCES

8.3.1 CEU

Confederation of 100 per cent Export units (CEU), a non-profit registered society, was established in 1982 specifically to service the promotional needs of 100% EOU. CEU is the apex industry organisation with exclusive focus on export production. Its chief activities include :

(i) Convening meetings, conferences, seminars, workshops and round table conference to promote export production and to serve business interests.
(ii) Maintaining overseas liaison with international and UN Agencies like ITC, GATT, UNCTAD, ESCAP, UNIDO, IMF, World Bank, ADB and ILO and establishing rapport with overseas chamber of commerce, trade associations, etc.
(iii) Sponsoring special projects related to the promotion of 100 per cent EOU and EPZ units.

8.3.2 EPCES

The newly set-up export promotion council for 100% EOUs and SEZs (EPCES) has grown into a proper council. The body now has a corpus of nearly Rs. 1 crore built from the contribution of 1,500 top exporters drawn from all the major export groups. EPCES is the commerce ministry instrument to promote the 23 SEZs (Special Economic Zones) in various stages of implementation[7] (Hardware and Software technology parks are not the part of council even as they are based on the pattern of EOU and SEZ scheme).

8.4 SPECIAL ECONOMIC ZONES

8.4.1 An Introduction

The Desi fervour of fancying the new and piling on en bloc is now happening to Special Economic Zones (SEZs) which in any case has been a concept long in coming to give strong fillip to the industrialization efforts of the country. How far the dreams of India could materialise depends very much on the success of emerging zones and institution.[8]

The International confederation of Free Trade Unions (ICFTU) defines EPZs/SEZs as: "a clearly demarcated industrial zone, which constitutes a free trade enclave outside a country's normal customs and trading sysem where foreign enterprises produce principally for export benefit from certain tax and financial-incentives."[9]

India's Exim Policy Defines SEZ as :

> "Special Economic Zone is a specifically delineated duty free enclave and shall be deemed to be foreign territory for the purpose of trade operations and duties and tariffs".

Goods going into the SEZ area from DTA shall be treated as deemed exports and goods comings from the SEZ area into DTA shall be treated as if the goods are being imported. SEZ units may be set-up for manufacture of goods and rendering of services, production, processing, assembling, trading, repair, remaking, reconditioning, re-engineering including making of gold/silver/ platinum jewellery and articles thereof or in connection therewith.

8.4.1.1 Origin

The dawn of the new millennium saw the birth of SEZs

which take on from all the previous concepts for industrial development through encouragement to high tech. industry and foreign investment. The then Union Commerce and Industry Minister Mr. Murosali Maran while announcing the New Exim Policy on 31st March, 2000 came up with a new concept of establishment of special Economic zone by merging the concept of Free Trade Zones and Export Processing Zones. Thus in 2000, with a view to provide an internationally competitive and hassle free environment for export production SEZ Scheme was introduced.

The Exim Policy provides for setting up of SEZs in the public, private, joint sector or by State Governments. It was also envisaged that some of the existing EPZs would be converted into SEZ. Accordingly, the EPZs at Kandla and Surat (Gujarat), Santa Cruz (Maharashtra) and Cochin (Kerala) were converted into SEZs.

SEZs is under the administrative control of the Development Commissioner.

8.4.1.2 Objectives

- To enhance foreign exchange earnings by promoting exports.
- To attract Foreign Direct Investment and induce technology transfers.
- To generate employment opportunities and assist in income generation.
- To develop and foster internationally competitive and hassle free environment for exports.
- To attract investment in export production and to boost exports.

8.4.2 Functional and Approved SEZs So Far

At present 8 Special Economic Zones are operational in India of which four were EPZs, which were converted to SEZ as per the Exim Policy. They are :

(i) Kandla SEZ, in Gandhidham, Gujarat (Multi-product SEZ, spread over 700 acres of land area).

(ii) SEEPZ SEZ, in Mumbai, Maharashtra (for Electronics

and gems and jewellery spread over 93 acres of land area).

(iii) Cochin SEZ, in Cochin, Kerala (Multi-product SEZ covering 103 acres).

(iv) Surat SEZ is a private sector developed multi-product SEZ covering 103 acres of land area and other four are :

Madras SEZs, Vishakapatnam SEZ, Falta SEZ and Noida SEZ.

The Government has also approved 27 other SEZs. Some of green field SEZs approved by Government includes—Positra SEZ (Gujarat), Nanguneri SEZ (Tamil Nadu), Bhadohi SEZ (UP), Dronagiri SEZ (Maharashtra), Kakinado SEZ (Hyderabad), Paradeep and Gopalpur, SEZ (Orissa), Kulpi SEZ (Kolkata) and Indore SEZ (MP).

The new SEZs are integrated townships comprising of a SEZ developer, who is usually a finance rich multinational infrastructure development company. As per the notification which came into effect from 15 August, 2003, the SEZ is divided into a processing area for exports by the approved SEZ unit, and a non-processing area under the developer who provides utility services to the processing area.[10] The SEZ units as well as the developer enjoy the privileges of duty free and control free export and import. The key decision like division of the Zone into processing and non-processing areas lies with the customs commissioner.

8.4.3 SEZs : International Experiences

To understand the success stories of SEZs, it is important to discuss the features of SEZs in some of the selected countries viz. :

China

Armed with preferential policies to attract foreign capital, boost-export-oriented production and market driven activity, the first Chinese SEZ was set-up in Shenzen in 1980. It has achieved a phenomenal 38 per cent compounded annual growth in its output from inception to 2003.[11] At present, China have five SEZs, including one spanning the entire province of Hainan (34,000 sq.

km) and three of the SEZs are in Guangdong province. Guangdong accounts for over 35% of China's total FDI inflows. Hongkong is the main gateway connecting Guangdong enterprises with the international market.

It is well established belief that if foreign investors are to be lured to set-up export-oriented units in the SEZs, they need to be given incentives for domestic market access as well. China recognised this fact long ago and framed the policy accordingly. India needs to learn from the Chinese experience.

The incentive offered by the SEZ are far more than what Indian SEZs give. Chinese labour laws are loose and foreign investors are free to hire or fire them. Also the infrastructural development is commendable. For Ex. Shenzen possess 8 harbours and 12 Cargo docks and is home to the Hungtian International Airport, which is the fourth largest airport in China. Additionally both the Beijing-Canton Railway and the Beijing-Kowloon Railway Converge in Shenzen.

Features of SEZs of other countries are summarized below in brief manner :

Philippines

- Year of Commencement—1995 (Philippines Economic Zones Act of 1995).
- Number of Zones—142 (till 2001).
- Total Area—23,940 Hectares (till 2001).
- Total investment—17.96 billion US$ (from 1995 till 2000).
- About 82.7 per cent of the investments in the zones are by foreign firm.
- Employment generated 0.7 million (till 2001).

Example : Clark Special Economic Zone, South of Manila Philippines (1995), area—33,653 acres, Principal exports—Electronics, Semi-conductor devices, etc.) furniture and fashion accessories.

Thailand

Year of Establishment— Early 60s (Board of Investment)

Total Number of zones — 27
Total size of the zone — 6208 Hectares
Total Investment — US$ 20 Billion
Employment — 400,000 (till 2001)

Indonesia

Year of Commencement — 1978 (Board of Investment Promoted Bonded Economic Zones)
No. of Zones — 26
Total area — 77,265 Hectares
Total Investment — US$ 7 Billion
Employment — 1,41,0000

Bangladesh

- Exports from EPZs contribute around 20% of total exports.
- 200 units in operation.
- 139,000 Employees (around 40% are women).
- Mainly manufacturing Units of textile and clothing and Leather Items.[12]

Mexico

- The concept of an EPZ is reflected in the Maquiladora programme.
- Employment—1 million in around 3000 maquiladoras.
- Exports account for over 40% of total export.
- Thrust areas—vehicles, electrical goods, textile and furniture.
- Gains from North American Free Trade Area (NAFTA).[13]

Mauritius

- Contribution of SEZs to the export basket of Mauritius is one of the highest in the world at 62%.
- Over 500 enterprises employing around 80 thousand workers.

- Primarily manufacturing : Textiles and clothing.
- Various incentive to offshore Banking units, viz. Exemption from compliance with exchange control act, from credit and interest rate, free repatriation of profits and low income tax, etc.

8.4.4 Important Incentives for SEZ Units

- The Government of India has exempted SEZ units from import duties and income-tax to promote exports.[14] Units in SEZs are eligible for an income tax break on export profits for 20 years, with deduction equivalent to 100% of export profits for the first five years.[15] SEZ units are also entitled to custom duty and excise concessions on the inputs source by them.[16]
- No license required for imports.
- All activities on self-certification basis.
- Offshore Banking units (OBUs) allowed in SEZs.
- An 100% EOU or any other unit with an export turnover of Rs. 50 crore will be allowed to function as virtual SEZ. A virtual SEZ unit will be outside the physical boundaries of SEZ, but all the fiscal benefits for SEZ will be extended to virtual SEZs.[17, 18]
- 100 per cent Foreign Direct Investment in manufacturing sector allowed through automatic route barring a few sectors.
- Facility to realize and repatriate export proceeds within 12 months.
- Full freedom for sub-contracting including sub-contracting abroad.
- In house custom clearance.
- No routine examination required for customs and Exim policy.
- No fixed wastage norms.
- SEZ shall be positive net foreign exchange earner. Net Foreign Exchange Earning (NFE) shall be calculated cumulatively for a period of five years from the commencement of commercial production[19] (as per the rules).

- SEZ unit shall be entitled for reimbursement of Central Sales Tax.
- Inter-unit transfer of goods, including partly processed/semi-finished goods from one SEZ unit to another unit will be allowed.
- Single window regulatory clearances.

8.4.5 Key Reforms Needed to Change Indian SEZs' Face; Generating New Success Stories

The success of SEZ is revealed by the success stories in international trade of many prominent countries implementing the dazzling concept of SEZ. The Govt. of India is also conscious of the fact that SEZ can do miracles for India's exports. The operating SEZs in India logged an average export growth of 46 per cent in dollar terms and 39 per cent in rupee terms in 2003-04, as against the overall export growth of 17 per cent and 11 per cent in the year. Exports from SEZs in 2003-04 stood at $3038 million (Rs. 14,004 crore) in 2003-04 as against $ 2079 million (Rs. 10,057 crore) in the year before. Yet, the share of SEZs in the overall exports are quite low at just over 3 per cent. In comparison, 23 per cent of UAE's total exports are from SEZs and 62 per cent of Mauritius's total exports are from SEZs.

Out of the 27 approved SEZs many have not yet started. Many SEZs were bogged down due to delays in land acquisition.

Key Areas of Reform

To develop success stories, these reforms and steps should be taken by the Government with respect of SEZs :

(a) Legal and Bureaucratic Changes

- Business friendly labour laws should be enforced just like China.
- A new Labour law incorporating a work ethic, removing contract labour restrictions, freedom for multiple and night shifts for workers of both sexes and designation of development commissions as labour commissioner is needed.
- Elimination of Price control and distribution control (on power) is needed.

- Also needed are removal of capital account restrictions/controls/prior permission for businesses operating within the SEZ.
- Unified industrial regulator, i.e. only one inspector for all continuing industrial regulations including pollution and labour safety, is needed.
- Reduction of red tape and bureaucratic procedures is strictly needed.
- There is a need of stable, efficient and transparent policy.

(b) *Focus on Incentives*

- SEZs should be exempted from MAT and Dividend tax.
- No excise/CST/ST/Octroi should be charged for sales from DTA to SEZs.
- There should be free entry and exit of telecom service providers into the SEZ without any service charges, subject only to the condition that the spectrum would be auctioned if and only if it ceases to be "free good" within the SEZ.
- Interconnectivity with other countries (ICD) should be free and unrestricted (subject to; that this cannot be used as a conduit for provision of unregulated telecom services into the DTA).
- Granting incentives in a streamlined manner.

(c) *Developing Sector Specific Economic Zones*

Sector specific economic zones should be developed to harness locational advantages, local skills and infrastructure (For example, SEEPZ which focuses on Electronics and gems and jewellery).

(d) *Developing Linkages between SEZ and Domestic industry*

- By sourcing raw materials from domestic sources.
- By developing local partnership through shared technology and investment in human resource.

(e) Developing Nodal Agency to Act as a Facilitator and Catalyst to

- Aid in improving quality, productivity, R and D and cater to training requirement.
- Act as a one stop service to provide assistance in identification of investment opportunities, site location and obtaining clearances. Examples of nodal agencies which are already operating in other countries includes :
  - Mauritius Export Processing Zones Development Authority (MEPZDA).
  - Bangladesh Export Processing Zones Authority (BEPZA).

(f) Involvement of Public Private Parties

- Law should be passed by the states under which 100% privately owned townships can be set and run by private developers as private municipalities. Private SEZs should be designated as private municipalities under this, and road, electricity and other links should be provided by Government
- Government should also undertake feasibility studies before the commencement of any SEZ. The role of Government should be clearly defined.
- Size of SEZ should be considered necessarily as large size generate economies of scale.

Thus, by following all these steps, definitely Indian SEZs can emerge as benchmark for others and can therefore change the whole picture of India's exports,

8.5 INSTITUTIONS SUPPORTING SMALL EXPORTERS

8.5.1 Good Things in Life begin Small

The export potential of small and medium sized firms has been a growing subject of interest. Now one clear question emerges—why should today's export promotion strategies focus on SMEs, rather than on large or micro-enterprises?

Lets try to find the answer :

- *Strong growth potential*—The current trend, points strongly towards a sustained growth in this shore, supported by expanding output and employment.[20]
- *New legal framework*—The WTO agreement has created a framework for more open global trading system, which has implications for smaller firms. By reducing tariff and non-tariff barriers and ensuring non-discriminatory treatment in foreign markets, the small exporters have been offered the same market access that was earlier available to large firms.
- *Lower transport and communications cost*—Technological developments in communications and reduced international transport costs make it easier for smaller firms to enter international markets. An export promotion strategy could facilitate market entry by assisting smaller firms to acquire technical know-how and familiarize themselves with new cost-saving innovations.
- *Dependency on institutions*—SMEs are almost entirely dependent on outside trade service providers. The impact of easily accessible and efficient services is crucial at the stage of initial market development efforts when SMEs need to commit scarce financial resources in advance without any guarantee of returns.

An export promotion strategy needs to define how best to help smaller firms exploit these opportunities and to overcome some of their constraints. Focus should be therefore on—(i) Developing export infrastructure, (ii) Improving financing conditions, and (iii) Strengthening marketing channels and Joint marketing consortia.[21]

8.5.2 Institutional Framework

8.5.2.1 Small Scale Industries Board

The board is the apex advisory body. It gives advice to the Government on all issues relevant to the small sector. It facilitates co-ordination and inter-institutional linkages.

8.5.2.2 National Small Scale Industries Corporation (NSIC)

NSIC is an ISO 9000 certified company. Since its establishment in 1955, it has been working to fulfil its mission of promoting, aiding and fostering the growth of small scale industries and industry-related with small scale industries in the country.[22]

For meeting the challenges of growth and competition, NSIC repositioned its strategies for managing globalization effectively. The strategic imperatives of NSIC's directions are thus aimed at :

(i) A Focused Sectoral Approach

Focus on specific sectors like—agro and food processing, auto components, glass and ceramics, biotechnology, IT, leather products, pharmaceuticals and chemicals, light engineering and knit wears and garments.

(ii) Technology

Technology is the key to enhancing a company's competitive advantage in today's dynamic information age. It undertakes—technology audits and benchmarking, technology sourcing, upgradation of product design, energy and environment services at selected centres.

(iii) Software Technology Parks (STPs)

NSIC established the first STP at Okhla in 1995 and second in Chennai in 2001 to activate software exports of small scale industries and to develop technology business incubators.

(iv) Marketing

NSIC acts as a facilitator to promote small exporters through many innovative programmes, some of which includes—market information and trade leads, suppliers' rating acereditation procurement for the UN systems, consortia marketing, brand building, trade fairs, organising techmart and buyer—seller meets, arranging global tender programme providing vital information.

(v) Credit Support and Export Financing

Finance is the lifeline of SSI units, and NSIC supports them by several credit and finance facilities. Pre and Post-shipment finance is provided to EOUs to meet their emerging requirements.

(vi) Exports of Products and Projects

NSIC is a recognized export house. It is involved in exporting products and projects of SSI of India to other countries. NSIC provides a complete package of export assistance including testing facilities, pre-shipment credit facility, and assistance is also rendered in preparing export worthy publicity material.

8.5.2.3 Office of the Development Commissioner for SSIs and the Small Industries Development Organisations (SIDO)

SIDO is the nodal agency for the promotion of exports from SSIs. It organizes specialized training programmes in export promotion, arranges for participation of SSIs in international exhibitions and assist them in international marketing. SIDO has liaison with EPCs, FIEO, CII, ITPO and similar bodies in the collection of statistics and represents the interests of SSIs in meetings of these organizations.

It processes various applications for grants of advance licenses and it also works for set-up unit as 100 percent EOUs and units within EPZs.

8.5.2.4 Small Industries Development Bank

There is a longheld belief that lack of financing is one of the principal obstacles to small firm exporting. Therefore, Small Industries Development Bank of India (SIDBI) serves as the principal financial institution for promotion, financing and development of industry in the small sector and to co-ordinate the functions of the institutions engaged in promoting financing in the small scale sector.

In a bid to improve credit flow to the small-scale industry (SSI) sector, the Credit Guarantee Fund Trust for Small Industries (CGTSI), promoted jointly by the Government and the Small Industries Development Bank of India, has taken a couple of initiaties.

Firstly, it has extended its role to act as a catalyst between industry associations and SSI entrepreneurs who are willing to take loans from banks. Next for starters, CGTSI has been experimenting with its new role to provide services to those SSI entrepreneurs who are already in the business of IT or software Development. CGTSI has launched another scheme on pilot basis, which is billed as mutual credit-guarantee scheme (MCGS), under which CGTSI will extend its guarantee coverage through industry associations which want to help their members to get bank finance.[23]

Assistance Schemes of SIDBI

SIDBI assist small and medium sized exporters in export financing through following schemes :

(a) Loans to obtain ISO 9000 certification (loan limit need based; Debt-equity ratio not more than 2:1 for the borrowing concern).

(b) Foreign currency Term Loans to SSI units for setting up new projects as well as for expansion, diversification, technology, etc. and for working capital purposes.

(c) Pre-shipment credit in Foreign Currency loans to small scale industries to enable SSI to raise finance at internationally competitive rates as per Reserve Bank of India guidelines to fulfil their export commitments.

(d) Export Bills Financing to provide post-shipment credit in foreign currency at internationally competitive rates of interest by discounting of usance export bills/ purchase of sight/demand export bills and negotiation of bills under licence.

(e) Technology Development and Modernization Fund scheme.

(f) Opening of foreign letters of credits (FLCs).

(g) Scheme of refinance assistance.

SIDBI has established a SME growth fund (in the year 2005) with a corpus of Rs. 500 crore. Small and medium units in knowledge-based industries such as pharma, biotech and IT will be provided equity support through this fund.

8.5.2.5 Small Industries Service Institutes (SISIs)

These institutes, which are established in different parts of the country serve as technical consultancy organizations for SSIs.

They identify products worthy of export and maintain contacts with export promotion agencies to enable exporters to benefit from the latest export policies and market trends. They undertake training programmes to familiarize participants with export procedures.

8.5.2.6 Other Institutions for Small Exporter's Assistance

Industry specific associations represent small and medium sized enterprises and help their members to increase their exports.

With a view of providing prompt, accurate and comprehensive testing facilities for engineering products, particularly from the small scale sector, the Export Inspection Council (EIC) has set-up Pilot Test House at Mumbai. Pilot Test House provides technical support facilities, R&D and organises training programmes for SSI on quality control and technology upgraded.

Then there are other institutes like IIP, EPCs, ITPO, State Export Corporation which also helps small scale exporters.

8.5.3 Credit Institutions and Small Exporters : An International Experience

In several countries (e.g. Denmark, Greece, Luxembourg), most exporters are small firms and they receive the greatest share of export-related services.

In the U.K., the 2000 Mission and Status Review of the Export Credit Guarantee Department (ECGD) recommend that the agency seek to attract more SME customers and to raise awareness of export insurance and finance among smaller exporters. UK prefers to assist SME exporters directly, rather than through a "trickle down effect" where large companies sub-contract business underwritten by ECGD[24] to smaller companies. UK has introduced a fast track system for processing applications for support from exporters. Also U.K. has developed a special website page providing 'help for smaller exporters'.

The Korea Export Insurance Corporation (KEIC) has a special interest in encouraging SME export activities through an article of special treatment for small firms contained in the Korean Export Insurance Act. The Export-Import Bank of Korea (K-Exim) established the SME Export Credit Group in 2002 from what was previously the Small Business Export Credit Department. K-Exim introduced generous provision for export related loans for smaller firms.[25]

Canadian EDC (Export Development Corporation) has committed itself to encourage smaller exporters.[26] EDC of Canada has established two teams to support small firms: (i) The Emerging Exporters Team (delivers short-term insurance services), (ii) The Small Business Financial Solutions Team which delivers medium and long-term product and services. Canada sends out 800,000 direct mails throughout the year and its SME representatives stationed in major centres make presentations and participate in seminars and trade shows, etc.

Canada EDC issues an SME score card on its progress in meeting SME targets, which include the number of SME customers served, number of new emerging exporters and average time for turnaround for SME credit approval requests. Canada offers 2 programmes to enhance working capital availability for SME exporters—Master Accounts Receivables Guarantee (MARG) and the Pre-Shipment Working Capital Programme.

The Japan Bank for International Co-operation (JBC) has set-up an Advisory and consulting office for SMEs which offers advisory and consulting services and organises lectures, seminars and study meeting to support small firms. Nippon Export and Investment Insurance (NEXI) of Japan provides information on export credits to small firms in the context of international investment seminars targeted to smaller companies.[27]

Similarly, other institutions of prominent nations works on related lines, the list of which is given in Annexure-8.2.

8.5.4 Challenges of a Global Market

SMEs are becoming increasingly aware of the growing competition at home and abroad.

- The challenges are :
- Lack of trade information, commercial intelligence and information analysis skills. SME must work upon it.
- Inability to differentiate a product, creating a brand

image. SMEs need to undertake product development, re-design or adaptation.

- SMEs must consider how to upgrade product quality and packaging to internationally acceptable standards.
- SMEs must work on improving productivity and reducing cost and on proper inventory planning.
- Knowledge, skills and experience soon become obsolete unless continuously upgraded, while opportunities for academic qualifications proliferate, SMEs in developing countries have little access to practical training which they really need.[28]

All the challenges should be met by the SMEs (institutions should help them in this respect) in order to be successful.

8.6 INFRASTRUCTURAL SUPPORT : A COMPREHENSIVE NOTE

8.6.1 Introduction

Dr. Amartya Sen, argues in his book, 'Development as Freedom' that development is a process of expanding the real freedoms that people enjoy. Growth of GNP or of individual incomes can of course, be very important as means to expanding the freedom enjoyed by the members of the society. But freedom depends also on other determinants, such as social and economic arrangements including infrastructure as well as political and civil rights.

Impressive infrastructurre acts as catalyst for social and economic development of a country. Infrastructural facilities are the best guarantee of their own future viability.

In this section emphasis will be made on the infrastructural bottlenecks, investment made in this sector and future plans of India to develop world class infrastructure.

How infrastructure play an important role can be made clear by taking the example of China. The exports of India in 2004 (Oct.) was $ 69.7 bn. whereas that of China was $ 112.8 bn. Shanghai, China's commercial capital has starking difference as compared to any major city of India. The city's metro, its elevated roads, the inner ring road, the pedestrian tunnel under the Wuangpu river and the new international airport all speaks about its success story. Shanghai also has the world's fastest train, the 'maglev' (which runs with the speed of 430 kmph).[29]

During the last two decades increased globalisation and intensified competition in world trade have resulted not only from the liberalisation of trade policies but also from significant advances in transport, communication, storage and power facilities. In India, some worthy but unheeded works have started to come out which deal explicitly with non-price factors as the most important barriers to India's success in foreign trade (Peters, 1990; Marjit and Roychoudhary, 1993; Exim Bank, 1998). Thus, the required transport and communication services essential for modern logistics management will increasingly determine their ability to compete for export market and direct foreign investments. On one hand Mexico's maquiladora operations, Chile's exports of fruits, Columbia's cut flowers and Kenya's horticultural products are examples where countries have been able to meet logistic requirements of their overseas customers and on the other hand, there are many examples of countries which are losing the competitive edge because of shortcomings in both key infrastructure as well as in institutional and procedural delays, especially relating to custom processing and transport services.[30]

8.6.2 Infrastructure Bottlenecks

Infrastructure bottlenecks in India poses major challenge to its ambitious plan to increase its share of global exports to 1.5 per cent in the next five years.

The difficulties faced by exporters include slow movement of cargo, red tape which delays government clearances, unreliable power supply, inflexible labour laws and inability to speed up banking transactions.

Bottlenecks at one point of the export infrastructure chain leads to consequential delays in other segments too and the net effect is failure of the exporter to deliver goods in time. The additional costs on account of the delays also blunt export margins and make Indian goods uncompetitive.[31]

The Indian ship-building industry is in the doldrums—with limited capacities, excessive manpower and lack of mechanisation. However, the new maritime policy (2004) can be breakthrough for shipping industry because of the various incentives being anounced (viz. all exemption from service tax, sales tax, import duty, 20-30 year subsidy support plan)[32] but still there are so many problem which it is facing.

In India, another problem is the freight rate and transit time. The freight rate of container traffic and transit times through ports exceed those of her Asian competitors by large margins. More than 70 per cent of India's international trade takes place through ports.[33] So it become altogether important to give emphasis on ports. Exporters end up paying more sea freight since large ships avoid Indian ports due to delays in loading and unloading cargo. Therefore, exporters are forced to go in for trans-shipment at ports like Colombo, Dubai or Singapore and this results in higher costs and longer time to deliver export good.

A backlog of over 10,000 import containers at Jawahar Lal Nehru Port Trust (JNPT) over the past few months (2004) forcing restriction on imports from 13.09.2004 for north bound Inland container Depots[34] is another issue. If import containers are not cleared within a stipulated time, rules should be worked out promptly to prevent them from blocking other cargo.

The annual throughput of Rotterdam port is in excess of 325 million tonne of good, that of Singapore is near to 300 million tonnes.[35] Traffic at the major ports of India is near to 230 million tonnes. In April-Nov. 2003 traffic at the major port of India grew by 7.34 per cent from 203.18 million to 218.1 million tonnes[36] [(which in 1970-71 was 56.154 MT (Total port cargo)]. It may appear to be a high rate of growth but in any international comparison our port intensity is representative of our trivial trade orientation. (China's port traffic was 5 times that of India even in 1996-97).

Next obstacle is power shortage which hampers production activities.

8.6.3 Steps to Overcome Obstacles

- There is an urgent need to plan our infrastructure to meet future requirements for exports and imports. While efforts are on to strengthen the country's road network, the Government needs to take immediate steps to enhance the handling capacity of railways as well as Indian ports.

- Instead of going in for numerous small ports, the Government should develop at least two large facilities each in west coast and east coast, supplemented by additional capacities in the southern region, so as to develop world class port similar to port of Rotterdam.
- Railway connectivity needs to beefed up (35% of the country's cargo is handled by railways).
- The Government should take step to liberalise rules so that banking transactions, customs and excise clearances are expedited.
- Monopoly agencies like container corporation of India (concor), should be abolished so that more investment flows into railways. Concor, a 63 per cent of Indian railways is so far the only provider of containerised goods transport by rail in India with an over 31% share of Exim Cargo (Shipping lines and port operators have been bargaining with concor for improved service and reduced rates for carrying containers from the north to southern ports, but have founded the going tough. To drive rates down, competition is the only way).
- Private sector should get a larger role in the development of railways, roads, power and telecommunication to overcome the current difficulties.
- Huge investments are required for infrastructural development.

In 1993-94, India invested 5.4 per cent of its GDP in infrastructure. This had fallen to 3.5 per cent of GDP by 2002-03. It was projected by the Government that there should be increment in infrastructure spending from 5.5% of GDP in 1995-96 to 7% by 2000-01 and 8% by 2005-06 and the share of private sector investment should rise from 1% of GDP in 1995-96 to 2.5% by 2000-01 and 3.5% by 2005-06, but these targets have not been met yet.[37]

India needs to spend about 7% of its GDP to build world-class infrastructure but again that should be done carefully.

Total expenditure on Infrastructure is described in the Table 8.1.

TABLE 8.1

Total Expenditure on Infrastructure (March, 2005)

Roads	33,000 Rs. crore
Power	40,000 Rs. crore
Petroleum	38,000 Rs. crore
Ports/Airport shipping	9,000 Rs. crore
Telecom	32,000 Rs. crore
Railways	66,000 Rs. crore

Source : 10th Plan, IES, Merrill Lynch, Economic Times Intelligence Group.

The cost of infrastructure according to World Bank estimates is as follows :

		Unit cost ($)
Electricity	→	1900 per kw of generation capacity
Roads	→	410,000 per km. of 2-lane paved road
Railway	→	900,000 per km. of rail
Sanitation	→	700 per connected household
Mainlines	→	400 per line
Mobiles	→	580 per subscriber

8.6.4 Research Findings Regarding Infrastructure

(a) Rating on Roads

2.86 per cent of respondents rated roads as excellent, 54.29 per cent of respondents rated it as good. Only 1.43 per cent rated road infrastructure as very poor (Graph 8.1).

(b) Rating on Ports (Infrastructure, Traffic Handling, Time Taken, etc.)

Seven respondents rated Indian ports excellent and 4 rated it very poor. Maximum respondent, i.e. 31 rated ports as good. 22 respondents rated it fair (Graph 8.2).

(c) Rating on Electricity/Power Supply

Twenty-five respondents rated power supply as good, 23 rated it as fair and 19 respondents rated it poor. One respondent

GRAPH 8.1
Rating on Support of Infrastructure—Roads

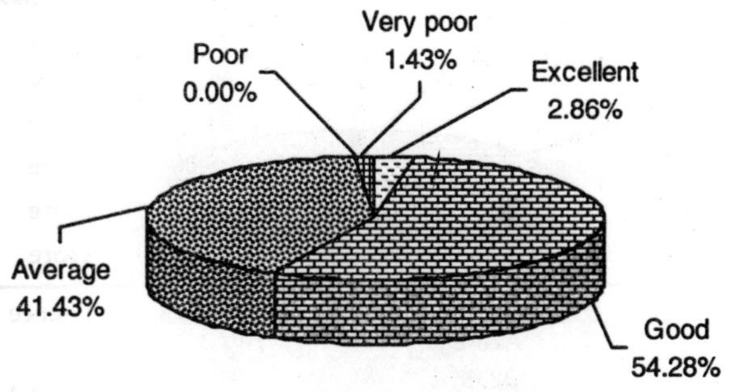

GRAPH 8.2
Rating on Support of Infrastructure—Ports

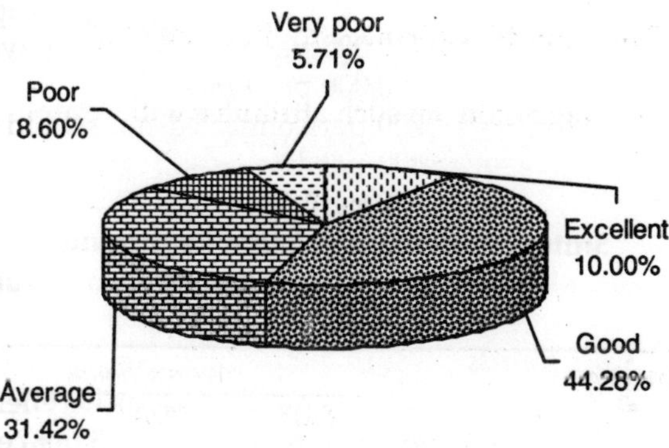

rated it excellent and 2 respondents rated it as very poor (Graph 8.3).

8.6.4.1 Average Score

(i) Average score on the 'road infrastructure' was 3.57, on ports it was 3.40 and on power supply it was calculated as 3.06, of which average score on roads and ports were high as compared to overall average score of institutional support and that of electricity was less than it.

GRAPH 8.3
Rating on Support of Infrastructure—Power Supply

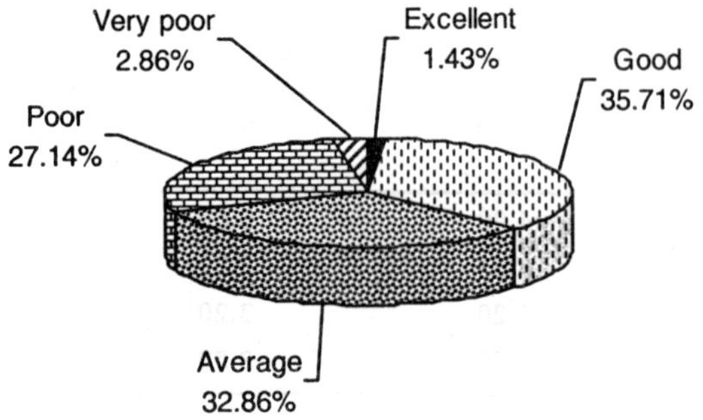

(ii) Average score on such attributes with respect to Status of Exporters.

This can be explained by this Table 8.2.

(iii) Average score on such attributes with respect to zones.

TABLE 8.2
Status-wise Average Score Regarding Infrastructural Support

Status of Exporter	*Average Scores*		
	Road	*Ports*	*Electricity/ Power Supply*
100% Export-oriented unit	3.67	3.67	3.50
Export House	3.67	3.33	3.17
Trading House	3.50	4.50	3.50
Super Star Trading House	4.00	4.50	4.00
Others	3.52	3.29	2.92

8.6.5 What Lies Ahead .... ?

In the speech of P. Chidambaram, Finance Minister, Govt. of India, while presenting the budget for the year 2005-06

TABLE 8.3
Zone-wise Average Score Regarding Infrastructural Support

Zones	*Average Scores*		
	Road	*Ports*	*Electricity/ Power Supply*
East	4.00	5.00	4.00
North	3.53	3.33	2.94
South	3.20	3.20	3.40
West	3.79	3.50	3.21

announced some important provisions for infrastructure development which are as follows :

- *Rural India*—'Bharat Nirman' has been conceived as a business plan, to be implemented over a period of four years, for building infrastructure especially in rural India. The important goals are to connect all villages that have a population of 1000 with a road, to construct 60 lakh additional houses for poor, to give telephone connectivity to the remaining 66,822 villages and to offer electricity connection to 2.3 crore households and covering 1.25 lakh villages.
- *Telecommunication*—By the end of January 2005, India had achieved a tele density of 8.75 per cent. A provision of Rs. 1200 crore has been made for 2005-06. 1687 sub-divisions will support under the universal service obligation (USO) fund.
- *National Highway Development Project*—It has made steady progress, and 5,172 kms of National Highways have been four-laned till Jan. 2005 under NHDP I and II. Union budget have proposed Rs. 1,400 crore for this (golden quadrilateral) purpose in 2005-06 to four-lane 4000 km.
- *Special Purpose Vehicle (SPV)*—The most glaring deficit in India is the infrastructure deficit. Infrastructure projects (roads, ports, air ports) which are financially

viable but, in the current situation, face difficulties in raising resources may be funded through SPV. Rs. 10,000 crore has been fixed as borrowing limit for 2005-06. Also a provision of Rs. 1500 crore has been made for 'viability gap'.

- *PURA Clusters*—PURA or Provision of Urban Amenities in Rural Areas is an idea that contains within itself possible solutions to a number of problems that affect rural India such as unemployment, isolation from markets, lack of connectivity and migration to cities. The objective is to expand production and employment in the unorganised enterprises around existing clusters of industrial activities.
- Government also believes that investments in institutiuons of higher education, R & D organisation, banking as they are equally important as physical infrastructure.

Still many measures have to be taken by Government which are found missing as earlier discussed.

From this discussion, it is clear that the success of economic reform, which is essentially a sort of export-led growth strategy, crucially hinges on the level, development and utilisation of transport, communication and power and other infrastructural facilities.

Notes and References

1. The EOU Scheme was introduced in the year 1980 vide Ministry of Commerce resolution dated 31st December, 1980. The purpose of the scheme was basically to boost exports by creating additional production capacity. It was introduced as a complementary scheme to the Free Trade Zones/EPZ scheme introduced in the sixties which had not attracted many units due to locational restrictions.
2. An EHTP may be an individual unit by itself or a Unit located in an area designated as EHTP complex. Under EHTP scheme, a unit can be set for the purpose of manufacture and development of electronic hardware, or electronic hardware and software in an integrated manner for exports.
3. Under STP scheme, a software development unit can be set up for the purpose of development of software, data entry and conversion, data processing, data analysis, control data management or call

services for exports. The STP and EHTP are administered by Ministry of Information Technology and the Provisions for them are same as that of EOU.

4. Export-Import Policy, 2002-07, Government of India, (Para 6.1).
5. *Ibid.*, Same page, (Para 6.2, 6.3, 6.4).
6. Nabhi's Exporters, Manual and documentation, A Nabhi Publication, New Delhi, 2004, pp. 428-33.
7. Goyal, Arun, 'Higher Global Oil, Steel Prices make commodities dearer : Export Import Notes, Academy of Business Studies, *The Economic Times*, New Delhi, 15 April, 2004.
8. An enclave or fenced zone is monitored by an around the clock customs presence. Fenced zones are typical of Latin America and the Caribbean. Non-fenced zones, which allow the enterprises to bypass the normal customs and duty free import procedures, rely primarily on the firms' self-declaration of input inflows and output outflows. This self-declaration system is used, for example, in Mauritius.
9. Diwan, Parag: Thothathri Raman, A. 'SEZS, Issues, Laws and Procedures', Bharat Publishing House, New Delhi, 2002. p. 6.
10. Goyal, Arun, 'New rules for SEZ units notified', Academy of Business Studies, *The Economic Times*, New Delhi, 4 August, 2003.
11. Kurane, Supriya. 'The first private, greenfield special economic zone. . . .', *Business World*, 12 July, 2004, pp. 40-41.

12,13. Paper presented by Mr. Shankarnarayan Rao, Chief General Manager, Export-import bank of India on 'Success Factors in Special Economic Zones', Exim Bank's Perspectives', Feb. 3, 2005 in WFTZ EXPO 2005, Mumbai, World Free Trade Zone Expo.

14. Subramaniam, Ganapathy G., 'SEZs and EOUs may be spared education Cess', *The Economic Times*, New Delhi, 1 August, 2004.
15. Ramakrishnan, Hema and Narendranath, K.G., 'Rs. 50 Crore turnover EOU may function as virtual SEZ', *The Economic Times*, New Delhi, 6 August, 2004.
16. Subramaniam, Ganapathy G., 'Opt for SEZs and Enjoy Incentives, *The Economic Times*, New Delhi, 23 August, 2004.
17. *Ibid.*
18. Narendranath, K.G. 'Now its going to be virtual SEZs', *The Economic Times*, New Delhi, 15 July, 2004.
19. Exim Policy, 2002-07, Govt. of India, Para 7.5.
20. Francais Espanol, 'Export Strategies for small firms, New Challenges for trade promotion', International Trade Forum, The quarterly magazine of the International Trade Centre, Issue 1/1999, p. 9.
21. The points has been excerpted from an ITC technical paper on trade prromotion strategies in developing countries. The study was directed by Monwarul Islam, ITC's Chief of Functional Advisory Services, Paul Cook of the Institute for Development Policy and Management, University of Manchester, UK, with other ITC staff.
22. www.nsiciddia.com.
23. Ganguli, Ratna, 'SSIs to get credit on big bodies' guarantee', *The Economic Times*, New Delhi, 25 March, 2004.

24. OECD, Enhancing SME competitiveness, The OECD Bologna Ministerial Conference, OECD, Paris (2001a).
25. OECD, OECD Small and Medium Enterprise outlook, 2002, OECD, Paris (2002).
26. OECD, Export Credit Financing Systems : in OECD member countries and Non-member economics, OECD, Paris (2001b).
27. Sakai, Kentaro, Global Industrial Restructuring Implications for small firms, STI working paper PSTI/DOC, OECD, Paris, 2002.
28. *Source* : Speech extract, "Meeting the challenges of the Global Market", delivered at the first Asian Pacific Conference on SMEs, Ghangzhou, China, Oct. 1998, by M. Islam, International Trade Centre.
29. Raghuraman, Shankar, 'Shanghai Surprise: Big apple of the world'. *Sunday Times of India,* New Delhi. Oct. 24, 2004, p. 8.
30. De Prabir and Buddhadeb Ghosh, 'Indian ports and Globalisation—Grounding Economics in Geography'. *Economic and Political Weekly.* August 25, 2001, pp. 3271-83.
31. Subramaniam, Ganapathy G., 'Here come the traffic stoppers', *The Economic Times,* New Delhi, 8 Oct., 2004, p. 5.
32. Nagaraj, Sudha, 'New Policy to get Shipping out of dock', *The Economic Times,* New Delhi, 21 Sept. 2004, p. 5.
33. Mukherjee, Writankar, 'Ports Ahoy', Government Vows all Support, *The Economic Times,* New Delhi, 27th Feb., 2004.
34. Singh, Shalini, 'It's a logistic loggano', *The Economic Times,* New Delhi, 8 Oct., 2004. p. 5.
35. Edwin, Tina, Rotterdam Route, *The Economic Times,* New Delhi, 8 Oct. 2004, p. 5.
36. Zadoo, Vishaka, 'Port Traffic misses Target, *Business Standard,* New Delhi, 4 Dec., 2003.
37. The Infrastructure Survey, *Business World,* 31 January, 2005, pp. 36-39.

ANNEXURE 8.1
Minimum NFEP and EP Requirement Under the EOU/EPZ/EHTP/STP Scheme (Paragraph 6.5 of the Policy)

Name of the Sector	*Minimum NFEP*	*Minimum EP for five years*
(1)	*(2)*	*(3)*
MANUFACTURING/PROCESSING SECTOR		
• Units with actual investment in plant and machinery, both imported and indigenous of Rs. 5 crore and above	Positive	US $ 3.5 Million or 3 times the CIF value of imported capital goods whichever is higher.
• Electronics Hardware value of imported capital goods whichever is higher	Positive	US $ 1.00 Million or 3 times the CIF
• Agriculture, aquaculture, animal husbandry, horticulture, pisciculture, viticulture, poultry and sericulture	Positive	-do-
• EOU in Agriculture Export Zones, Floriculture, Food Processing	Positive	US $ 0.25 Million or 3 times the CIF value of imported capital goods, whichever is higher.

(*Contd.*)

ANNEXURE 8.1 (Contd.)

(1)	(2)	(3)
• Biotechnology and Toys all kind	Positive	US $ 0.50 Million or 3 times the CIF value of imported capital goods, whichever is higher.
• Computer software and IT enabled Services	10%	US $ 0.25 Million or 3 times the CIF value of imported capital goods, whichever is higher.
GEM AND JEWELLERY		
Gold/Platinum/Silver		
• Gold/platinum/silver unstudded chains and bangles or combination thereof manufactured by fully mechanised process and coins, medallions, findings mouldings	3%	US $ 1 Million or 3 times the CIF value of imported capital goods, whichever is higher.
• Plain gold/platinum/silver jewellery and articles or combination thereof and ornaments like Mangalsutra containing gold and black beads, imitation stones, cubic zirconia, etc. only but excluding diamonds, precious and semi-precious stones.	7%	US $ 1 Million or 3 times the CIF value of imported capital goods, whichever is higher.

• Repair/remake of plain gold/platinum/ silver jewellery	7%	US $ 1 Million or 3 times the CIF value of imported capital goods, whichever is higher.
• Studded gold/platinum/silver jewellery and articles thereof or combination thereof	10% on gold/ silver/platinum content plus 5% over the value of studdings.	US $ 1 Million or 3 times the CIF value of imported capital goods, whichever is higher.
• Repair/remake of gold/platinum/silver studded jewellery.	10%	US $ 1 Million or 3 times the CIF value of imported capital goods, whichever is higher.
DIAMOND		
• Cut and polished diamonds (with per carat realization of more than US$ 575 FOB	7%	US $ 1 Million or 3 times the CIF value of imported capital goods, whichever is higher.
• Cut and polished diamonds (with per carat realization of more than US $ 400 and upto US $ 575 FOB).	15%	US $ 1 Million or 3 times the CIF value of imported capital goods, whichever is higher.

(Contd.)

ANNEXURE 8.1 (*Contd.*)

(1)	*(2)*	*(3)*
• Cut and polished diamonds (with per carat realization of more than US $ 260 FOB and upto US $ 400 FOB).	20%	US $ 1 Million or 3 times the CIF value of imported capital goods, whichever is higher.
• Cut and polished diamonds (with per carat realization of more than US $ 125 upto US $ 260 FOB)	25%	US $ 1 Million or 3 times the CIF value of imported capital goods, whichever is higher.
SERVICES		
(Other than IT enable services)	10%	US $ 0.50 Million or 3 times the CIF value of imported capital goods, whichever is higher.
All others	10%	US $ 1 Million or 3 times the CIF value of imported capital goods, whichever is higher.

ANNEXURE 8.2
Export Credit Agencies of Various Countries and their Definition of Small Exporters

Country	*Export Credit Agency*	*Definition*
Australia	Export Finance and Insurance Corporation (EFIC)	Business turnover not exceeding AUD 10 million (subject to change in the next 12 months)
Belgium	Ducroire/Delcredere	Annual turnover not exceeding EUR 5 million and overseas exports not exceeding EUR 0.62 million.
Canada	Export Development Canada (EDC)	Medium-sized exporters: total annual sales between CAD 5 million to 25 million; small sized exporters: total annual sales less than CAD 5 million; emerging exporters: total annual export sales less than CAD 1 million.
Denmark	Eksport Kredit Fonden (EKF)	No specific definition for SME exporters
France	COFACE	No specific definition for SME exporters
Germany	Hermes Kreditversicherungs-Aktiengesellschaft (HERMES)	Maximum 500 employees.
Japan	Nippon Export and Investment Insurance (NEXI)	No specific definition for SME exporters

(*Contd.*)

ANNEXURE 8.2 (*Contd.*)

(1)	*(2)*	*(3)*
Korea	Korea Export Insurance Corporation (KEIC)	Maximum 300 employees and net assets not exceeding 8 billion Korean Won (USD 6.1 million) for manufacturing firms.
Netherlands	Nederlandsche Credietverzekering Maatschappij (NCM)	Maximum 99 employees.
Norway	Garanti-Instituttet for Eksportkreditt (GIEK)	Maximum 250 employees, annual turnover less than NOK 300 million or total assets less than NOK 200 million
Portugal	Companhia de Seguro de Creditos, S.A. (COSEC)	No specific definition for SME exports
Spain	Compania Espanola de Seguros de Credito a la Exportacion, S.A. (CESCE)	No specific definition for SME exports
United Kingdom	Export Credits Guarantee Department (ECGD)	Common European Union definition
United States	Export-Import Bank of the United States (Exim bank)	Maximum 500 employees or net gross revenues which differ depending on industry sector and sub-sector

9

Conclusions and Suggestions

Export promotion institutions are the key to helping a critical mass of firms succeed, not just the individual companies that make it despite the odds. The institutions and export strategies must focus on more than trade promotion and embrace development if countries are to increase exports. Developing higher value-added export performance must be directly supported through forward and backward linkages. As suggested by William J. Miller[1] also, to build comparative advantage four elements must be considered:

- The region being considered,
- The economic clusters in the region,
- The infrastructure needed to support growth of the economic clusters, and
- The institutions and processes for implementing policy.

When communities pay attention to these elements, they can successfully create comparative advantage.

This research study aims to assess the role of institutional support in India's export promotion measures. In the earlier chapters all major institutions like ECGC, Exim Bank, EPC,

Commodity Boards, IIP, ICA, FIEO, FICCI, Development Authorities, EIC, BIS, Institutions for small exporters, infrastructural support and many others were covered. There are some institutions like banks and investment institutions, communications technology entities, women entrepreneurs group, environmental industry groups and educational institutions, etc. which did not find place in this research work (due to the scope of the research work) but are equally important seeing the broader perspective. Here it must be made clear that export promotion institutions are not solely responsible for country's exports; there are other factors also which influence exports (like strategies, incentives, currency fluctuations, global economic environment and other political, legal factors) but at the same time their importance cannot be ignored. Transforming such institutions into a broader trade support network helps countries use export development as a stepping-stone to economic growth. The changing trade environment demands a second look at the prevailing trade promotion strategies and institutions.

This chapter is focused on the results, conclusions, suggestions and future research studies which can be carried out.

9.1 RESULTS

To test the overall satisfaction level of respondent with the institutions and supporting agencies F-test can be conducted.

9.1.1 F-Test

To study whether the Export status of respondents and the rating of various components are different or not, F-test can be conducted.

The various components taken are :

- Support of local authorities,
- Support of local promotional agencies,
- Support of Infrastructure (Roads, Ports and Railways),
- Export documentation,
- Role of FIEO and chambers, and
- Role of IIP.

All of which hereafter will be referred as aggregate supporting agencies and infrastructural support.

(a) Null hypothesis can be tested :

Ho17—There is no difference among the status of exporters with respect to working of aggregate supporting agencies and infrastructural support.

TABLE 9.1
Analysis of Variance

Source of Variation	*Sum of squares*	*Degrees of freedom*	*Mean square*	*F-ratio*
Between sample	388.84	4	97.21	11.42
Within sample	553.25	65	8.51	

The table value of F at 5% level of significance for $V_1 = 4$, and $V_2 = 65$ is 2.5187.

Since the calculated value, 11.42 is more than the tabulated value, hence null hypothesis is rejected and alternative hypothesis is accepted, i.e. there is difference among the status of exporters with respect to working of aggregate supporting agencies and infrastructural support.

(b) Ho18—Zone-wise rating for aggregate supporting agencies and infrastructural support do not differ.

TABLE 9.2
Analysis of Variance

Source of Variation	*Sum of squares*	*Degrees of freedom*	*Mean square*	*F-ratio*
Between sample	222.89	3	74.30	7.765
Within sample	631.54	66	9.57	

The table value of F at 5 per cent level of significance for $V_1 = 3$ and $V_2 = 66$ is 2.75031.

Since the calculated value 7.765 is greater than table value 2.75031, hence the null hypothesis is rejected and alternative hypothesis is accepted, i.e. zone-wise rating for aggregate supporting agencies and infrastructural support differ.

9.1.2 F-test

(a) To study whether the rating by different status of exporter on various institutions differ or not, F test can be applied.

Here the various institutions taken are :

- Export Credit Guarantee Corporation.

(ECGC)—its policies and payment of claims.

- Exim bank in terms of financial and other assistances.
- Working of Export promotion councils.
- Aggregate supporting agencies and infrastructural support (described earlier). All the parameters hereafter will be referred as overall institutional support.

(a) Null hypothesis can be stated as :

Ho19—There is no difference among the status of exporters with respect to role of overall institutional support.

TABLE 9.3
Analysis of Variance

Source of Variation	*Sum of squares*	*Degrees of freedom*	*Mean square*	*F-ratio*
Between sample	3164.36	4	791.09	
				19.777
Within sample	2599.98	65	40.00	

The table value of F at 5 per cent level of significance for $V_1 = 4$ and $V_2 = 65$ is 2.5187.

Since the calculated value 19.77 is more than the table value, hence null hypothesis is rejected and alternative hypothesis is accepted, i.e. there is difference among the Export status with respect to role of overall institutional support.

(b) Null hypothesis :

Ho20— Zone-wise rating for overall institutional support do not differ.

TABLE 9.4
Analysis of Variance

Source of Variation	*Sum of squares*	*Degrees of freedom*	*Mean square*	*F-ratio*
Between sample	1100.48	3	366.83	7.204
Within sample	3360.83	66	50.92	

The table value of F at 5 per cent level of significance for $V_1 = 3$ and $V_2 = 66$ is 2.75031.

Since the calculated value (7.204) is greater than table value hence the null hypothesis is rejected and alternative hypothesis is accepted, i.e. zone-wise rating for overall institutional support differ.

9.1.3 Average Scores

Role of overall institutional support on the basis of status of respondents.

The overall results on average score can be plotted on graph with respect to status of exporters (different categories) (Graph 9.1).

9.2 SUMMARY OF FINDINGS

Total 70 exporters were surveyed. They belong to 20 different commodity groups. Following is the summary of findings:

GRAPH 9.1
Role of Overall Institutional Support with Respect to Status of Exporters—Overall Results on Average Scores

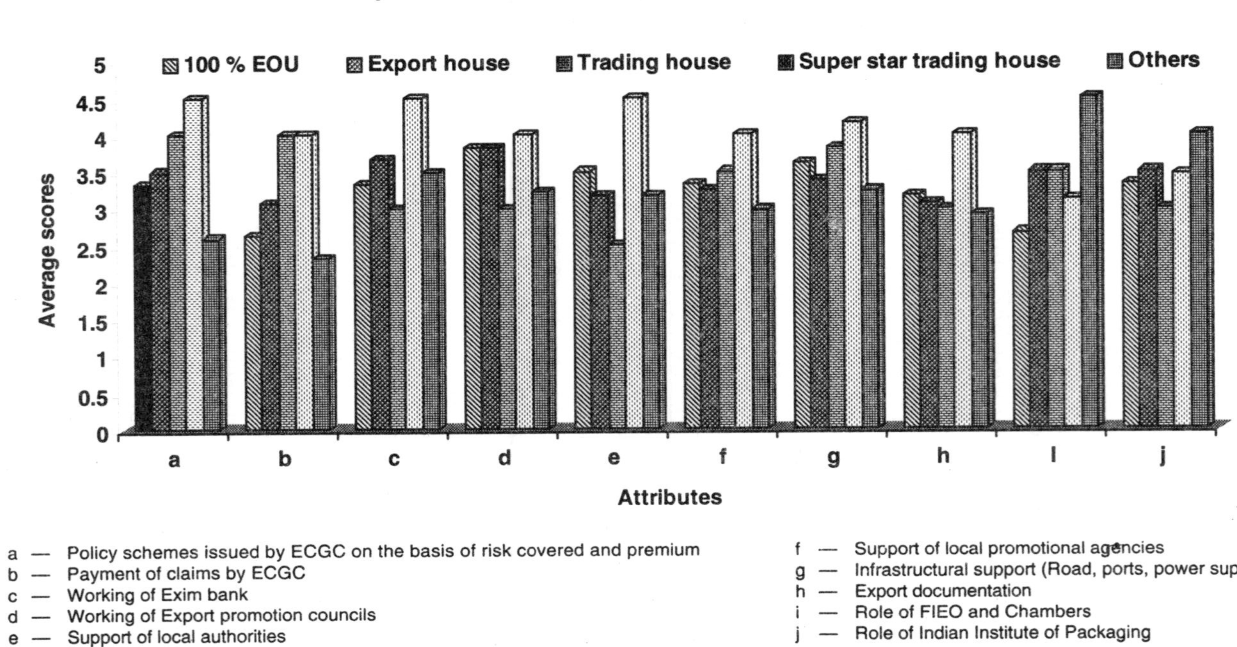

a — Policy schemes issued by ECGC on the basis of risk covered and premium
b — Payment of claims by ECGC
c — Working of Exim bank
d — Working of Export promotion councils
e — Support of local authorities
f — Support of local promotional agencies
g — Infrastructural support (Road, ports, power supply)
h — Export documentation
i — Role of FIEO and Chambers
j — Role of Indian Institute of Packaging

1. Majority of respondents, i.e. 68.57 per cent of respondents were not having any status. 2.86 per cent of respondents were having status of super star trading house, 8.56 per cent were 100 per cent EOU and 17.14 per cent were Export houses, and 2.86 per cent were trading houses.
2. 91.4 per cent did not belong to any unit. 4.92 per cent were EHTP unit, 1.43 per cent were STP unit and 2.86 per cent were SEZ units.
3. Majority of respondents, i.e. 94.29 per cent were merchandise exporter.
4. Fifty-five firms were not having any certification like ISO 9000, 14000, etc.
5. Fifty per cent were in favour of Green card facility taken by Government and 50 per cent not. 74.29 per cent of respondents were satisfied with the conditions, quantity and other terms of export and import of free trade sample.
6. 64.29 per cent of respondents said that the Export obligation to be fulfilled for EPCG should be 8 years.
7. Those having Advance licence (42.86%) and DEPB (47.14%), 89.47 per cent were satisfied with it.
8. 78.57 per cent of respondents were aware of ECGC polices. 62.96 per cent rated the policy schemes of ECGC as good. 58.18 per cent rated the payment of claims and settling of claims as average. 85.45 per cent were not interested in suggesting any risk cover not covered by ECGC.
9. 48.57 per cent of respondents rated the services of Exim bank as average and 47.83 per cent as good.
10. 57.14 per cent of respondents were unable to say anything regarding access to Exim bank finance. 31.43 per cent said it is difficult.
11. 48.57 per cent of respondents rated the participation in trade fairs and exhibitions as fair and 40 per cent as good under MDA. Regarding publications for use abroad and advertisement in foreign media 57.14% of respondents rated it is average. For research and product development 61.43 per cent rated it poor and for opening of foreign offices 64.29 per cent of

respondents rated it as poor. Regarding opening of warehouses also 52.86 per cent rated it as poor.

50 per cent of respondents have availed MDA assistances. 44.29 per cent were satisfied with release of approved MDA grant and 20 per cent were not.

12. Regarding working of Export promotion councils, 50 per cent rated it as good, 40 per cent as average and 10 per cent as poor. 71.43 per cent were satisfied with process of registration with EPCs.
13. 52.85 per cent of respondents were satisfied with the process of obtaining letter of permission and 58.57 per cent of respondents were satisfied with its validity period.
14. 64.29 per cent of respondents rated the role of state liaison officer as satisfactory.
15. 50 per cent rated the support of local authorities as fair and 70 per cent rated the support of local promotional agencies as fair.
16. 54.29 per cent respondents rated roads of the country as good and 41.43 per cent said it is average.

    44.29 per cent rated the ports (infrastructure, traffic handling, etc.) as good, 31.43 per cent as fair, 35.71 per cent rated the power supply as good, 32.86 per cent as fair and 27.14 per cent as poor.
17. Regarding the export documentation with respect to other developed countries 52.86 per cent of respondents rated as fair, 24.29 per cent as good and 21.43 per cent as poor.
18. 61.43 per cent rated the role of Federation of Indian export organization and FICCI as fair and 22.86 per cent as good.
19. 55.71 per cent rated the working of Indian Institute of Packaging as fair and 42.8 per cent as good.

9.3 CONCLUSIONS

The conclusion of this research work is divided into 2 sections.

Section 9.3.1 deals with conclusion on hypotheses and section 9.3.2 deals with general conclusions.

Conclusion on Hypothesis can be explained by the help of Table 9.5.

Hypothesis in this part will be referred by number, the statements are given in Chapter 5.

9.3.1 General Conclusion

The general conclusion drawn from the research work are as follows :

- It can be concluded from the research findings and literature review that export promotion institutions can't be called excellent as compared to such institutions in developed world, thus there is tremendous scope for the institutions for improvement, the process of which have already been started.
- The urgent requirement and strictly necessary measure is removal of red tapism and corruption from the system which was felt all the time by the researcher during her interaction with exporters, academicians and key people in the field. Unshackling of controls and creating an atmosphere of trust and transparency is very important.
- Simplifying procedures and bringing down transaction costs are crucial subject which again needs urgent hearing.
- The general weakness of trade promotion and export development in developing nation is a pervasive concern that demands attention. Institutions that design export promotion strategies face a critical choice : Whether to adopt an all embracing approach or given resource limitations, to focus on particular sectors. With few exceptions, National Export Promotion Organizations, have chosen to adopt a broad approach in the past. With their resources spread too thinly, this approach has reduced the effectiveness of many export promotion programmes.
- Average growth rate of exports of India over the last ten years (1993-03) is (10.1%) is well above Singapore, Indonesia, Hongkong, South Korea and Malaysia.

TABLE 9.5
Conclusion Drawn from the Hypotheses

S. No	*Hypotheses*	*Calculated value @ 5%*	*Table value/ critical value*	*Conclusion drawn*
(1)	(2)	(3)	(4)	(5)
1.	Ho1	c^2 = 8.75 (df=4)	c^2 = 9.49 (df=4)	Ho1 accepted, i.e. there is no difference between the status of exports and awareness regarding ECGC policies.
2.	Ho2	c^2 = .058 (df=3)	c^2 = 7.81 (df=3)	Ho2 accepted, i.e. no significant difference between zones and awareness regarding ECGC policies.
3.	Ho3	Kolmogorov Smirnov D-value = 1	Critical value = 0.1626	Ho3 Rejected. There is difference in the ratings for working of exim bank.
4.	Ho4	c^2 = 18.549 (df=4)	c^2 = 15.5	Ho4 = Rejected. Exporter's status and working of IIP are not independent attributes.
5.	Ho5	c^2 = 11.30 (df=4)	c^2 = 9.491	Ho5 = Rejected. Exporter's status and satisfaction with process of registration with EPC are not independent attributes.
6.	Ho6	c^2 = 16.51 (df=8)	c^2 = 15.5	Ho6 = Rejected. Exporter's status and rating of EPC are not independent attributes.
7.	Ho7	c^2 = 22.72 (df=24)	c^2 = 5.99	Ho7 = Rejected. There is significant difference between the process of registration with EPC and its working.

8.	Ho8	$c^2 = 3.25$ (df=3)	$c^2 = 7.81$	Ho8 = Accepted, i.e. Zones and process of registration with EPC are independent attributes.
9.	Ho9	Kolmogorov Smirnov D-value = 1	Critical value 0.1625	Ho9 = Rejected. There is difference in rating for working of FIEO and chambers.
10.	Ho10	$c^2 = 58.57$ (df=2)	5.99	Ho10 = Rejected. Availing any assistance under MDA and release of grant by it are not independent attribute.
11.	Ho11	$c^2 = 28.47$ (df=1)	$c^2 = 3.84$	Ho11 = Rejected. Availing any assistance under MDA and release of grant by it are not independent, attribute, excluding the 'can't say' option.
12.	Ho12	F = 8.502 (V_1=4, V_2=65)	F = 2.5187	Ho12 = Rejected. There is difference among the Exporter's status with respect to overall assistances provided under MDA.
13.	Ho13	F = 1.512 (V_1=3, V_2=66)	F = 2.75031	Ho13 = accepted. There is no difference among the zones with respect to overall assistances provided under MDA.
14.	Ho14	$c^2 = 3.53$ (df=4)	$c^2 = 9.49$	Ho14 = Accepted, i.e. there is no significant difference between the Exporter's status and satisfaction derived from DEPB and advance licence.
15	Ho15a including can't say option)	$c^2 = 34.47$ (df=2)	$c^2 = 5.99$	Ho15a = Rejected, i.e. there is difference between the satisfaction associated with obtaining LOP and its validity period.

(*Contd.*)

TABLE 9.5 (Contd.)

(1)	(2)	(3)	(4)	(5)
	Ho15b (excluding can't say option)	c^2 = 0.67 (df=1)	c^2 = 3.84 (df = 1)	Ho15b. = Accepted.
16.	Ho16	D = value = 0.243	Critical value 0.1626	Ho16 = Rejected, i.e. there is difference in rating for the support of local authorities.
17.	Ho17	F-Ratio = 11.42	F = value = 2.5187	Ho17 = Rejected, i.e. there is difference among the Exporter's status with respect to working of aggregate supporting agencies and infrastructural support.
18.	Ho18	F = ratio 7.765 (V_1=3, V_2=66)	F = 2.75031	Ho18 = Rejected, i.e. Zone-wise rating for aggregated supporting agencies and infrastructural support differ.
19.	Ho19	F = 19.77 (V_1=4, V_2=65)	F = 2.5187	Ho19 = Rejected, i.e. there is difference among the Exporter's status with respect to role of overall institutional support.
20.	Ho20	F = 7.204 (V_1=3, V_2=66)	F = 2.75031	Ho20 = Rejected, i.e. Zone-wise rating for overall institutional support differ.

- India's major trade partners are countries of European Union which accounts for 22 per cent of the country's exports (Sept.-Oct. 2004) and the US—17.4%. Though India has started programmes like Focus LAC (Latin American Countries) and African Nation, new destinations must be explored to push up export growth. To achieve the target of exports of worth $ 150 bn. by 2009-10, there is need to diversify the export basket, improving the attractiveness of locational advantage and strengthening high quality network.
- Issues like electronic fund transfer, digital signatures, relaxed import noms and focus on services were the areas which found due consideration in the Exim policy 2003-04 and Mini Exim policy (2004).
- Next the duty foregone on various export promotion scheme was at over Rs. 39,000 crore (2003-04). From the research finding it was found that DEPB was popular with exporters (but prone to rampant misuse). The DEPB scheme could well be scrapped by 2005 as it is WTO incompatible but seeing its benefits the term for DEPB should be extended. Merchandise exports, that account for 80 per cent of Indian exports would be given fillip by creation of export clusters and townships of export excellence.
- Sound policy implementation is important to tap India's export potential.
- Despite reduction in interest rates, Indian exporters pay more interest than their counterparts in other countries.
- Exporters pay various levies like sales tax, Octroi, entry tax without being able to get refunds. This results in export of taxes, making Indian goods less competitive. Indian exports face high cost disability factor ranging between 19% and 21%, covering un-neutralized taxes and duties, high cost of credit, power and transaction costs. India faces stiff competition from Chinese exporters and so Indian policy-makers need to take up on war footing scale the issues on tax reforms and building infrastructural facilities.

- Process of setting up more SEZs is quite slow and they constitute less than 4 per cent of the country's exports.
- Infrastructural support should be restrengthened and cost should be reduced. World bank report (2000) has pointed out that the total costs of moving a container through a terminal in India are over 70% to 80% higher than those in Japan and USA. Productivity at container terminals in the JNPT, Mumbai is less than half that of Colombo. It is more important factor to clear congestion at ports. Teledensity in India is also low. It is only 7% (Financial year 2004), though it has increased from 5.1 per cent (Financial year 2003) to 7.0 (Financial year 2004). Therefore, good infrastructure is the need of time.
- Co-ordination is deficient between business and government; and between various levels of Government.

It can be concluded that :

- A pro-exporting attitude and commitment to exporting are essential.
- There is a need to motivate firms into export action, to maintain, or increase their export commitment.
- Tax incentives for innovation and exports are required.
- A model should be used by export promotion organization to design the export promotion programme and to evaluate the same. The following model is proposed which can be used by EPOs in designing and evaluating the programmes.

9.4 SUGGESTIONS

Following suggestions can be made, concerned with the present research work :

- States should play active role in promoting exports. State Government should co-ordinate with central Government on all such issues related to foreign trade. Also there must be real and effective partnership between public and private sectors.

FIG. 9.2
Model Designing and Evaluating Export Promotion Programmes by Export Promotion Institution

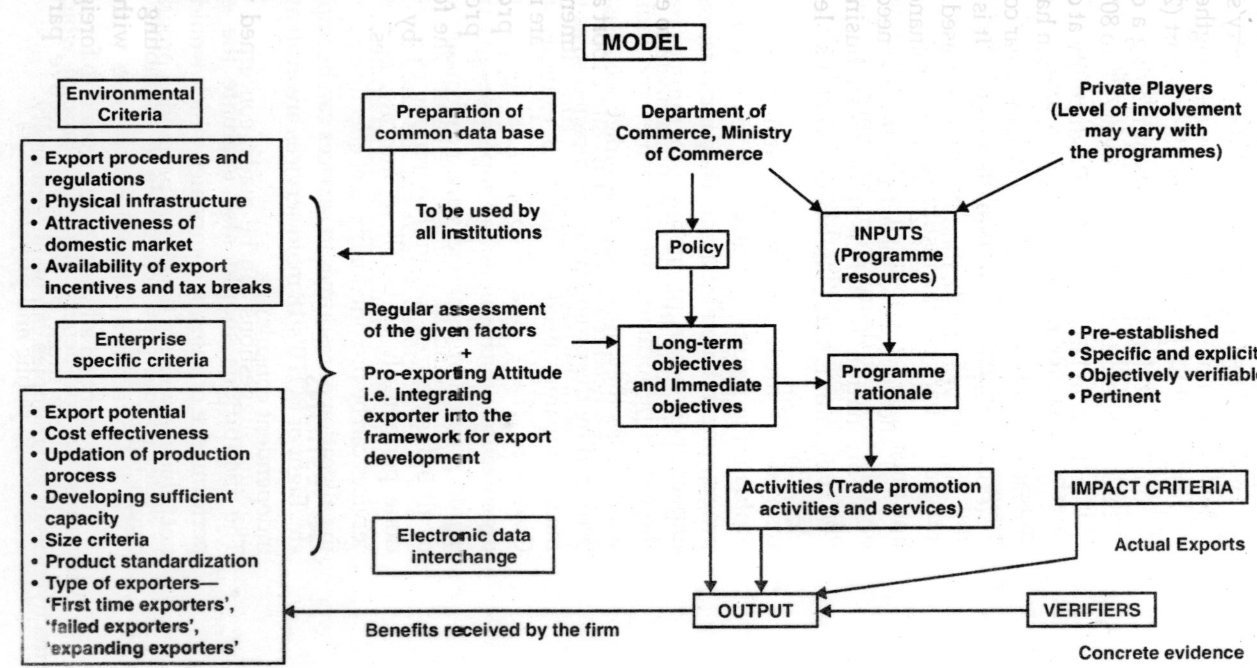

- Government should activate Embassies as key players in export strategy for real time trade intelligence and enquiry dissemination.
- Attempts should be made to unshackle exports from redundant procedural controls in a bid to reduce the transaction cost. The community of status-holding exporters should be broadened by lowering the threshold for being a status holder (may be upto 3 crores).
- Integration between the institution is quite necessary and so must be fostered. Not only there must be integration between the institution within the country but must also be associated with apex international organisations to learn from the success stories of others. Also this provides a platform for professional exchanges.
- Institutions must periodically and systematically evaluate the results and effects of export promotion programme initiated by them. They must assess what impact, their export promotion programmes have on the export performance of companies and India as a whole. Also they must assess whether the assistances provided by the programme are directed so as to best meet companies needs or not. For example, British Overseas Trade Board (BOTB) is the umbrella organization which guides and supervises government export promotion. Its services are most comprehensive of all industrialized nation. Programme evaluation is done periodically at BOTB to indicate, how export services can be provided more cost effectively and how the allocation of resources to services can be improved etc. Eight of BOTB's 18 main services are evaluated by independent consultants.
- The institutions should also evaluate the export performance or sales of companies which would have not achieved without the export promotion programme conducted by them.

They must do cost-benefit analysis, through which the effectiveness of programmes can be judged easily.

- Export promotion programmes should focus on the type of users, whether the users are 'first time exporters' or 'expanding exporters' or 'continuing exporters', 'failed exporters'. Since many a times 'first time exporters' strongly need more assistances as compared to the existing exporters, so the programme must be directed accordingly. To facilitate this, institutions should maintain data-base which can be shared between different export promotion institutions.
- Tax incentives should be provided for innovation and exports.
- Export support programmes should place greater emphasis on the needs of smaller firms as many such firms are unaware of programmes run by the institutions.
- The National Export goal must be explicitly stated and a permanent National Export Council should be established.
- Co-operation among the exporters must be fostered so as to check unethical practices and to reduce the risk of insolvency. For example, if healthy cooperation exists between exporters than the information about the fraud buyer can be communicated easily to all and this will say the other exporters from becoming the victim of same.
- Training Programmes should be prepared for exports. Training on various dimension of exports and on international trade should be imparted to entrepreneurs. Special training programmes should be prepared for traditional exporters and small exporters as the awareness about the export practices is very low among them and hence it is actually needed.
- Institution should strengthen its network, wherever required it should establish its offices and should recruit agents or representatives for providing the services efficiently.
- Institutions should encourage and help the exporters to acquire quality certification (ISO 9000) and other common certifications (like ISO 14000, ISO 18000, etc.).

- Buyer-Seller Meet must be organised for small exporters.
- The process of release of MDA grant takes almost 6-8 months. This time should be reduced. Equal benefits should be provided to both merchant and manufacturer exporter.
- Local authorities and local promotional agencies should improve their work processes to help exporters and to avoid unnecessary delays.
- Institution should learn from success stories of institutions abroad.

The best example which can be taken to explain this point is that of Korea Trade Investment Promotion Agency (KOTRA) which received two awards, "Best Trade Promotion Organization from Developing Country" and also "Best of the Best" trade promotion organization (TPOs) at 5th world conference of TPOs in Malta by International Trade Centre.

KOTRA was founded in 1962 and is based in Seoul with 12 decentralized offices in Korea; and 98 overseas centres in 72 countries, KOTRA began organizational reform in 1997 to meet the challenges of the changing environment. The main vision of KOTRA is to raise customer satisfaction to 75 per cent, to secure 50% or more of domestic exporting companies as KOTRA customers and raise the level of financial independence from 15 per cent to 20 per cent.

KOTRA has oriented its entire administration towards the "CUSTOMER". KOTRA has in-house internet system, a central knowledge management system to share and create the knowledge, experience and information among the staff, a Customer Relationship Management System (CRM) to respond to customers more quickly and a Management Information System (MIS), which is an internal control centre for budget and projects. KOTRA also aims to establish 'virtual KOTRA', enabling on-line meetings between Korean exporters and overseas buyers.

Thus, just from the glimpse of operation of KOTRA, the gap between institutional set-up of India and that of International Standard is evident.

India should also work on the concerned dimensions and export promotion institutions should treat exporters as their 'customers' and should strive for continuous improvement. Indian EPOs can learn from KOTRA, Australian Trade Commission (AUSTRADE), Uganda Export Promotion Board (UEPB), Jamaica Promotions Corporation (JAMPRO) and Bulgaria's Trade Promotion Agency (BTPA), etc. which have transformed the economy as such by adopting reform process and 'staying relevant' with time.

- Computerised Aligned Pre-shipment Export Documentation System (CADS), a software to facilitate the use of new export document by the exporter should be popularised. Through a masking technique 18 documents can be reproduced through 2 Master documents. Many small exporters have no idea about it. Institution should spread awareness regarding such softwares to exporters.
- The 'N' form procedure that allows cargo to go through to the customs stations and the submission of evidence to show that the cargo has been exported is sufficiently messy and corruption ridden and leads to unnecessary costs. Therefore, necessary steps must be taken in this direction to simplify the process and to reduce unnecessary costs.
- The institutions like Export Promotion Councils should adopt 'innovative strategies'. They can think of new 'tools' for promoting exports for example they can set-up 'information kiosk' centre at the international airports of the country. They should conduct short duration course and with it facilitating exchange process of students between the countries to have international exposure, information and to develop links beforehand.
- New Export Promotion Councils can be established to promote tourism, hotel industry and consultancy service as there is tremendous scope in all these sectors.
- DEPB clearance can be speeded up if the customs department honours the credit issued by DGFT, through electronic verification. It takes 2 days the DGFT to issue the licence and 5-6 days for the customs

department to verify it . To stop misuse of DEPB, it must be issued in dematerialized form.

- The software and hardware technology parks which are under the Ministry of Information and Technology should be brought under the purview of Export Promotion Council for 100 per cent EOUs and SEZs (EPCES).

Smooth infrastructure both virtual and physical, reduction of red tape; reforms in bureaucracy, labour laws, rules and procedure; revitalising the Export Promotion Organisations and developing framework of international standard is urgently required to strategically respond to the changing trade environment and to develop 'overall competitiveness' to contribute to nation's economic growth.

This research work with all its flaws inherent in the research of this magnitude can act as a good base for future research studies. Research studies which can be taken in future are as follows :

- This research can act as vital input for least developed countries (LDC). It is quite pathetic that over the last 40 years (1964-2004) LDC's share of world trade declined from 1.96 to 0.6 per cent. While developed world has forged ahead, most developing countries have not. As stated the situation is most dramatic for the world's 50 poorest nations. Thus, future research studies can be taken not only in strengthening institutional support to promote exports but on drafting overall strategy on export promotion measure for such countries.
- Since the scope of this research study was not broader, hence the same study with large sample size and broader scope including all the export promotion measures taken in India can be done.
- Experimental research work and casual study of selected nations before institutional reforms and after reforms can also be taken.
- Comparative study between the export promotion institutions of developed and developing countries can

be taken, or comparative study on the basis of regional bloc like SAARC, ASIAN, etc. can also be done.

- Research projects can also be conducted, taking visionary approach, projecting the future (till 2010), how reform process for selected institution can be drafted to achieve overall competitiveness during that period.

Thus in this chapter, summary of findings, conclusions and suggestions for further researches have been discussed.

Reference

Miller, William F., Building Comparative Advantage, *Foreign Trade Review*, IIFT, New Delhi, Vol. XXVII, No. 4, Jan., Mar. 1993.

Bibliography

Adams, F.G. and L.R. Klein (eds.): Industrial Policies for Growth and Competitiveness, Lexington, Mass : D.C. Health and Co., 1983.

Asheghian, Parviz and Ebrahimi, Bahman, International Business, Harper Collins, 1993.

Banerji, A.C., T.D.A. : Pinpointing Export Promotion, International Trade Forum, Oct.-Dec., 1971.

Baron, D.P. : "Fluctuating Exchange Rates and the Pricing of Exports", *Economic Inquiry*, 14 (1976).

Beri, G.C., Marketing Research, Tata McGraw-Hill, New Delhi, Third Edition, 2000.

Berstein Committee Report, Review Committee for Balance of Payments Statistics, Washington, DC. U.S. Govt. Printing Office, 1964.

Bhagwati, Jagdish : International Trade : Cambridge, 1981.

Blomstrom, Magnus, Transnational Corporations and Manufacturing Exports from Developing Countries, UNCTC, New York, 1990.

Buckley, Peter, J. and Mark Casson: The Future of the Multinational Enterprise, London : Macmillan, 1976.

Bunn, D.W. and Mustafaoglu : "Forecasting Political Risk", *Management Science*, 24 (1978).

C.P. Kindleberger: Terms of Trade; An European Case Study, New York, 1956.

Cases in International Marketing, IIFT, New Delhi, 1979.

Cateora, Philip R. and Graham, John L., International Marketing, McGraw-Hill, 1999.

Chakravarty, Subrata, N. : "Economic Darwinism", Forbes, Oct. 1986.

Czinkota, Michael R., Ronkainen Ikka A. and Moffett, Michael, H., International Business, The Dryden Press, 1994.

Czinkota, Michael, R., Export Development Strategies : US Promotion Policy, Praeger, New York, 1982.

Daniels, John D. and Radebaugh, Lee, H., International Business, Addison Wesley.

Destler, I.M., Making Foreign Policy, Washington DC : Brookings Institution, 1980.

Dos, Vves and Prahalad, C.K., The Multinational Mission : Balancing Local Demand and Global Vision, The Free Press, New York, 1987.

Douglas, Susan P. and C. Samuel Craig, International Marketing Research. Englewood Cliffs, Prentice-Hall, New Jersey, 1983.

Elvey, Lisa A., "Export Promotion and Assistance : A Comparative Analysis", in 'International Perspectives on Trade Promotion and Assistance, (S.T. Cavusgil and M.R. Czinkota, editors), Quorum, New York, 1990.

Export Incentives in Developed and Developing Countries, International Trade Forum, International Trade Centre, Nov. 1967.

Export Promotion by Governments in nine Counties, National Swedish Industrial Board, Stockholm, Liber Tryck, A.B., 1985.

Export Research and Policy, Conference Report, EVD Netherlands, Export Promotion and Information Service, The Hague, 1986.

Frazier, Michael, Implementing State Government Export Programs, Praeger, New York, 1992.

Giersch, Herbert, Services in World Economic Growth, Westview Press, Boulder, Colo, 1989.

Gordon, D., Export-oriented Financial Institution. A Vital Element for Trade Promotion, International Trade Forum, Jan.-March, 1985.

'Greater Export Opportunities for Small and Medium Size Firms' Amsterdam—Rotterdam Bank Report, January, 1983.

Green, Paul E. and Dull, Donald S., Research for Marketing Decisions, Englewood Prentice Hall, Inc., Englewood Cliffs, New Jersey, 1970.

Guide to the Evaluation of Trade Promotion Programmes, Geneva, Switzerland; International Trade Centre, UNCTAD/GATT, 1987.

Gupta, S.P., Statistical Methods, Sultan Chand and Sons, New Delhi, 2000.

Gupta, S.P., 'Statistical Methods, Sultan Chand and Sons, New Delhi, Twenty-eighth Edition, 2000.

Haberler, Gottfried : "Survey of International Trade Theory". In *Special papers in International Economics,* No. 1, Princeton, 1961.

Haner, F.T. : "Rating Investment Risks Abroad", *Business Horizons,* 22 April, 1979.

Harrison, Andrew, International Business, Oxford, 2000.

Hawkins, R., and Prasad, A.J., Research in International Business and Finance, Vol. 2, Greenwich, CT : JAI Press, 1981.

Hill, Charles W.L., International Business, McGraw-Hill, 2000.

Husted, Steven and Melvin Michael, International Economics, Harper and Row, New York, 1990.

Hymer, S.H. : The International Operations of National Firms. A study of Direct Foreign Investment, Cambridge, 1976.

"International Patterns of Comparative Advantage", Industry in the 1980s. : Structural Change and Interdependence, New York : United Nations, 1985.

Jackson, John H., The World Trading System, Mass: MIT Press, Cambridge, 1989.

Johansson, Johny K., Global Marketing, McGraw-Hill, 2000.

Kerlinger, Fred N., Foundations of Behavioural Research, Surjeet Publications, New Delhi, 1983.

Khanna, S.R., Export Marketing of India's New Manufactures, University of Delhi, 1985.

Kish, Leslie, Survey Sampling, John Wiley, New York, 1965.

Korth, C.M., International Business—Environment and Management, Englewood Cliffs, Prentice Hall, New Jersey, 2nd Edition, 1985.

Luck, David J., Rubin Ronald S.; Marketing Research, Prentice Hall of India, New Delhi, 7th Edition, 2002.

Luostarinen, Reijo, and Lawrence Welch, International Business Operations, Kyuri Oy, Helsinki, Finland, 1990.

Luthans, Pred and Hodgetts M. Richard, International Business, McGraw-Hill, 1995.

Machlup, F., Economic Integration, Worldwide, Regional, Sectoral, McMillan, London, 1978.

Mahoney, Darrell, *et. al.*: International Business—A Management Perspective, Longman, 1997.

McKibbin, Warwick J. and Jeffrey D. Sachs, Gobal Linkages, Macro-economic Interdependence and Cooperation in the World Economy, Brooklings Institution, Washington, D.C., 1991.

Ministry of Commerce (Govt. of India), Annual Reports.

Murray, T., Trade Preferences for Developing Countries, McMillan, London, 1977.

Ohlin, Bertil, Interregional and International Trade, Harvard University Press, Boston, 1933.

Ohmae, Kenichi, Triad Power : The Coming Shape of Global Competition, The Free Press, New York, 1985.

Olson, H.C., Studies in Export Promotion, Acta Universitatis Upsaliensis, Alquist and Wiksell International, Stockholm, 1975.

Porter, Michae E., The Competitive Advantage of Nations, The Free Press, New York, 1990.

Pucik, Vladimir, Noel M. Tichy and Carole K. Barnnett, Globalizing Management : Creating and leading the competitive organization, John Wiley, New York, 1992.

Raipuria, K.M., Export-led Growth : India's Strategy and Policy Options, *Foreign Trade Review*, April-June, 1980.

Reich, Robert B., The work of Nations : Preparing ourselves for 21st Century Capitalism, Random House, New York, 1992.

Robinson, Richard, International Business Management. Hindsale, IL : The Dryden Press, 1978.

Robock, Stefan H. and Simmonds, Kenneth, International Business and Multinational Enterprises, Irwin, 1989.

Root, F., International Trade and Investment, Cincinnati, 1989.

Root, Franklin R. International Trade and Investment, South Western Publishing, Sixth edition, 1990.

Root, Franklin, Entry Strategies for International Markets, Mass : Lexington Books, Lexington, 1987.

Schitzer, M.C., Liebrenz, M.L., Kubin, K.W., Interational Business, Cincinnati, Ohio, South-Western Publishing, 1985.

Singh, M., India's Export Trends, Oxford, 1966.

Sundaram, A.K. and J.S. Black, "The Environment and Internal Organization of Multinational Enterprises", *Academy of Management Review,* (October, 1992).

Sundaram, Anant K. *et. al.* : The International Business Environment, Prentice Hall of India, 1999.

Swoboda, A.K., Credit Creation in the Euromarket : Alternative Theories and Implication for Control, New York : Group of Thirty, 1980.

Tagqart, Jumes H. and Mcdormott, Michael C., The Essence of International Business, Prentice Hall of India, 2000.

Terpstra, Vern, International Marketing, New York, 1972.

Thunberg, Hartland P. and M.H. Crawford, Government Support for Exports—A Second Best Alternative, Lexington Books, Lexington, 1982.

UNCTAD, Economic Cooperation and Integration among Developing Countries, Vols. I and II, Genewa : United Nations, 1976.

UNCTAD, The Role of Commodities in Least Developed Countries, (UNCTAD/DITC/CON/32), 2001.

United Nations, Handbook of International Trade and Development Statistics, New York, 1989.

Venkataraman, C., Trade Policy and Export Promotion, *Foreign Trade Review*, IIFT, New Delhi, April-June, 1981.

Vernon, R. and L.T. Wells, Jr. : The Manager in the International Economy, Prentice Hall, 1968.

Vittal, N., Free Trade Zones and Export Strategy, *Foreign Trade Review*, IIFT, New Delhi, Oct. Dec., 1977.

Waldmann, Raymond J., Managed Trade : The Competition between Nations, Mass : Ballinger, Cambridge, 1986.

Walter, I. and Areskoug, K., International Economics, 3rd Edition, Wiley, New York, 1981.

Wilkins, M., The Emergence of the Multinational Enterprise, Harvard University, 1970.

Williamson, O.E. : The Economic Institutions of Capitalism, New York, 1985.

Wolf, Charles, Jr., Linking Economic Policy and Foreign Policy, New Brunswick, New Jersey, Transaction Publishers, U.S., 1991.

Periodicals

IMF Survey, Fortnightly, The Economist, Weekly; Financial Express Daily.

Business World, Fortnightly; International Trade Forum, Quarterly, ITC, Geneva.

Foreign Trade Review, IIFT, Quarterly.
Business India, Fortnightly, The Economic and Political Weekly.

News Papers

The Economic Times, New Delhi.
Business Standard and The Times of India.

WEBLIOGRAPHY

- www.oecd.org
- www.unido.org
- www.texprocil.com
- www.exportghana.org.
- www.leatherindia.org
- http://gjepc.org.
- www.businessonline india.com
- www.buyusa.gov
- www.aepc.com
- www.ciionline.org.
- www.ecgcindia.com
- www.ieport.com
- www.rbi.org.in
- www.cbec.gov.in
- www.apeda.com
- www.aepcindia.com
- www.indiancarpets.com
- www.cashewindia.org
- www.unctad.org
- www.capexil.com
- www.india.coffee.org
- www.eepc.gov.in
- www.indiansources.com
- www.mpeda.com
- www.projectexports.com
- www.plexconcil.org.
- www.indianspices.com
- www.fieo.com
- www.ficci.com
- www.fedai.org.in
- www.dnb.co.in
- www.iift.edu.
- www.eouindia.com
- www.sezindia.com
- www.sportsgoodsindia.org.
- www.tradeforum.org.
- www.indiamart.com
- www.intracen.org.
- http:/indiabudget.nic.in
- www.infodrive.india.com
- www.kotra.or.kr.
- http://commerce.nic.in
- www.Google.com

Index

Advance Licence, 89
Agarwal, S.P., 110
Agri Export Zones, 85
Allied and Agricultural Products, 42
Allied Products and Chemicals, 55

Balance of Payments, 29
Battiwala, C.J., 108
Banerjee, Subrata, 112
Bonding and Debanding, 238
Brand Name Registration, 200
Bureau of Indian Standard, 169
  Organisation, 170
  Functions, 170
Business Environment Ranking, 26
Buyer Underwriting, 151

Central Assistance to States, 83
CFTRI (Central Food Technological Research Institute), 166
Commodity Boards, 198
Commodity Consumption, 42
Cottage and Handicraft Sector, 84
Country Underwriting, 151
Credit and Export Financing, 249
Crude Products and Petroleum, 55

Debroy, Bibek, 107
Deemed Exports, 5, 93
Desai, H.B., 113
DFAC (Duty Free Replenishment Certificate), 89, 96
Duty Entitlement Passbook Scheme, 90
Duty Exemption/Remission Scheme, 88

East Asian Countries:
  Exports, 25
ECGC (Export Credit Guarantee Corporation), 96, 146
EIA :
  Grievances Committee, 173
EIA on Quality Complaints, 172
EIC (Export Inspection Council), 171
Electronic Data Interchange, 88
Engineering Goods, 54
EOUs (Export Oriented Units), 235
Exim Bank Finance :
  Access, 168
Exim Bank :
  Institutional Linkages, 184
Exim Bank's Operation, 162
Exim Policy, 2002-07, 79, 94, 99
  Introduction, 79
  Features, 80
Export Contracts :
  Denomination, 83
Export Credits :
  For Indian Companies, 162
  For Commercial Banks, 164

Export of :
Services, 61
Spares, 83
Gifts, 82
Samples, 82
Export Performance Level, 86
Export Promotion Institutions, 104, 144, 188
Research Methods, 120
Importance, 120
Export :
Promotion Schemes, 200
Classification, 4
Excellence, 84
Insurance, 148
Import Bank of India, 161
Benefits, 6
As an Engine of Growth, 2
Import Intensity, 64
Road Map, 72
Export-Import Intensity, 69

Fairs in India, 209
FDI :
Foreign Direct Investment, 16
in India, 17
and Exports, 16
Trends, 19
Policy, 17
FICCI (Federation of Indian Chambers of Commerce and Industry), 206
FIEO (Federation of Indian Export Organisation), 203
Finance Programme, 164
Financial Guarantee to Bank, 150
Foreign Trade, 36

Global Market :
Challenges, 253
Green Land Facility, 137

ICA :
Rules of Arbitration, 178
IIFT (Indian Institute of Foreign Trade), 210
India :
Foreign Trade, 10
Indian Council of Arbitration, 177
Indian Economy and Exports, 7
Indian Exports by Region, 64
Indian Institute of Packaging, 173
Indian Spices Logo, 200
India's Exports and Imports :
Comparative Growth, 11
India's Trading Partners, 68
Industry :
Exports Expectations, 63
Institutions Supporting Small Exporters, 247
ITC (International Trade Centre), 199
ITPO (India Trade Promotion Organisation), 208

Jewellery and Gems, 53

Kathi, Vijaya, 110
Kwan, Young-Chul, 113

Letter of Permission/Letter of Intent:
Validity Period, 138
Licence/Certificate Permission :
Terms and Conditions, 82

MAI (Market Access Initiative), 84, 218
Objectives, 218
Market Access Initiative, 84
Mathur, B.P., 105
MDA (Market Development Assistance), 212
Merchandise Exports, 4
Mini Exim Policy, 2004, 95
MPEDA (Marine Products Export Development Authority), 201
Narayana, M.R., 109
Nayyar, Deepak, 104
New Foreign Trade Policy, 2004-09, 97
Niryat Bandhu, 202

NSIC (National Small Scale Industries Corporation), 249

Olsan, H.C., 106
Ontario, Rolf Sevinghaus, 106

Panchmukhi, V.R., 108
Pandey, R.K., 112
Principal Commodities :
  Exports and Imports, 13
Project Exports, 5, 56
Pursell, Garry, 104

Quality Complaints, 86
Quality Policy, 173

Rao, V.L., 108
Reddy, K.C., 108
Registration-*cum*-Membership Certificate, 83
Restricted Goods, 81

Sachs, Goldman, 26
Service Exports, 60, 88
SEZ (Special Economic Zone), 93
Sharma, O.P., 109
SISIs (Small Industries Service Institutes), 251
Small Industries Development Bank, 250
Small Scale Industries Board, 248
Software and Services:
  Exports, 62
Software Exports, 62
Software Project Policy, 150
Spices Board, 199
Spice House Certificate, 200
State Liaison Officer, 203
Status Holders :
  Special Strategic Package, 87
State Trading, 82
Steering Committee on Foreign Direct Investment, 31
STPs (Software Technology Parks), 249
Supporting Institutions, 234

Terms of Trade, 36
Test Houses, 85
Thomas, Philip, 108

Underwriting Policy, 151
UNDP (United Nations Development Programmes), 199

What is Exports, 4